FLOREN(
& TUSC.

FLORENCE
e) TUSCANY

Laura Raison

A & C Black · London

© Laura Raison 1994

Photographs by Joe Cornish
Maps and plans by John Flower

A & C Black (Publishers) Limited,
35 Bedford Row, London WC1R 4JH

ISBN 0-7136-3821-4

A CIP catalogue record for this book is
available from the British Library

Photoset in 9 on 11pt Linotron Optima
by Rowland Phototypesetting Ltd,
Bury St Edmunds, Suffolk
Printed in Singapore by Imago

CONTENTS

FOREWORD
by John Julius Norwich

For many people, the concept of Italy automatically conjures up a vision of
Tuscany. The mountains of Savoy and Piedmont strike one as vaguely Alpine
rather than specifically Italian; the waveless plain of Lombardy is nondescript
and distinctly lacking in charm, while the low-lying marshes of the Veneto
and the delta of the Po inspire little enthusiasm, except as a prelude to the
excitements of Venice and Ravenna. As for the south, for the vast majority of
non-Italians – and Italians, for that matter – it remains, comparatively speak-
ing, *terra incognita*. Tuscany, by contrast, is immediately identifiable, even
by those who have never been there, thanks to the countless painters of the
Renaissance for whom it provided the perfect background to their portraits.
How well we all know those rolling green hills, crowned more often than not
with little towns and villages; those meandering rivers and streams, crossed
by little hump-backed bridges; and those cypresses, surely the most Italian of
all trees – sometimes half a dozen together, apparently in earnest consultation,
sometimes marching along some tawny ridge in Indian file, sometimes standing unforgettably alone, erect and solitary outlines, pencil-slim against the
cloud-streaked sky.

But there are other Tuscanies too. If you drive twenty or thirty miles or so
south of Siena you will find yourself in a barren, almost lunar landscape of
rocky, ash-coloured earth – not for nothing is it known as the *cenere* (ash) –
pock-marked with caves and frequently split into a network of ravines as if it
had been splintered by some gigantic hatchet. This is the world not of the
Leonardos or the Gozzolis or even of the Piero della Francescas, but of Duccio
and Simone Martini and those other Sienese painters of the *trecento* – a world
that I always used to dismiss as nothing more than a stylised backdrop until
I saw it for myself. You may of course find it too stark for your taste, but do
not despair: a short drive will take you to the wild, forested mountains of the
Casentino (where you may still see the white oxen grazing), the serene vineyards of Chianti, the gentle Mugello – home of Giotto and the Medici – or
the flat coastal plains of the Maremma, backed by those bruised and battered
mountains of the Carrara *massif* that provided the marble for Michelangelo in
the 16th century just as they have for Henry Moore in the 20th.

And then there are the buildings. In no other comparable area on the surface of the earth will you find so many cities, towns and villages that are themselves works of art. Florence, inevitably, stands by itself; but Florence is only the beginning. Siena and Arezzo, Lucca and Pisa, Pistoia and Prato, Volterra and San Gimignano, Pienza and Montepulciano – the list is endless. Each has its own colour. Florence itself is predominantly brownish-grey, from the local *pietra forie* of which the greater part of it is built; Siena is a characteristic dark, burnt brick; Volterra is the colour of pale mountain honey.

As with colour, so with character. One must never forget that Italy was not united until the later nineteenth century; this means that all her cities and towns – or, at least, all those north of Rome – have widely differing histories, and that each in consequence has a very individual personality and atmosphere of its own, quite apart from the treasures that it almost certainly contains. That is why, wherever you go in Tuscany and however rich the museums or glorious the paintings that await you, you should never allow yourself to be dragged indoors too quickly. Remember that here, time and time again, the *ensemble* of a city is infinitely greater than the sum of its parts. The first thing to do on arrival, therefore, is to take an hour's – even a half-hour's, if time is really short – stroll through the town's historic centre. Again and again you will find that this is the greatest masterpiece of all.

Laura Raison knows these cities and towns – and the countryside that lies between them – like the back of her hand; what is more, she loves them and she understands them. Indeed, this is the second book on Tuscany that she has written. We first met when it was suggested that I might write a foreword to an anthology she had compiled about the region: it is an enchanting book, and one to which I still find myself returning again and again. Her love of literature informs this volume also, as does her love of food and wine, both of which are given the attention which is their due in the pages that follow; for she is also fully aware of just how exhausting sightseeing can be – especially in a Tuscan August – and how important it is to relax in the evening with, perhaps, a dish of pasta in a sinfully rich game sauce and a bottle or two of Chianti, to talk over the day's discoveries and to plan tomorrow's campaign. She is, in short, the perfect guide: never bullying, never pressing too hard, but always ready with the information you need, the illuminating anecdote, the perfect quotation, the ideal restaurant. Put yourself confidently into her hands. It is given to few of us to travel in such delightful company.

John Julius Norwich

1. INTRODUCTION

Recently it has become fashionable to insult Tuscany, to remark how crowded the towns have become, how spoilt the countryside, how much more beautiful Umbria always was. But sitting on the veranda of an old Tuscan farmhouse with a glass of Chianti, looking out over terraced hills that rise and fall into the distance is an unforgettable pleasure. As the evening deepens the swallows give way to bats – *pipistrelle* – which swoop and quiver between the barn and the tall dark cypresses that guard the house. Nearby are rustling silver olive trees, vines and dry scratchy grasses, interrupted here and there by crumbling stone walls. Further away the pattern continues, growing hazier into the distance, with small crooked villages that cling to the top of the steepest hills.

Despite the widespread ravages of modern life, much of the Tuscan country-side has remained irresistibly seductive – the combination of cultivated and wild hills that grace the paintings of Simone Martini, Piero and Leonardo. But while many of us have in our minds a picture of the typical Tuscan scene, the real thing is a good deal more varied. There are the chestnut-clad mountains of the north, the rolling ochre hills of the southern Sienese, the flat plain of the Maremma and, sad to say, the generally dismal and charmless coast. Of course, in each area the villages differ. From the almost too pretty villages of 'Chiantishire', one discovers the sprawling townships of the Maremma, the remote alpine dwellings of the mountains or the rock settlement of Pitigliano in the south, clinging tenaciously to its sheer escarpment.

And then we come to the towns. Tuscany has some of the loveliest and most fascinating towns in Italy. Even the bigger cities seem always to keep in the centre an atmosphere of their previous smaller identity, however sur-rounded they may be by dreary modern flats and ring-roads. Protected by solid medieval walls, the old town in the middle usually remains dominated by the cathedral and the town hall – sturdy emblems of religious and civic power holding sway since the Middle Ages. The palaces and houses that line the narrow streets have also remained surprisingly intact: brick in Siena, faded ochre and pink in Pisa, honey-coloured stone in San Gimignano. In these ancient settings the life of today bustles on, somewhat changed by television, cars and good health, but still with many of the same preoccu-pations: food and wine (many Tuscans still have two big meals every day); a strong appreciation of beauty; and an almost fanatical loyalty to the local area – the all-important *contrada*. *Contrada* life has somewhat diminished over the

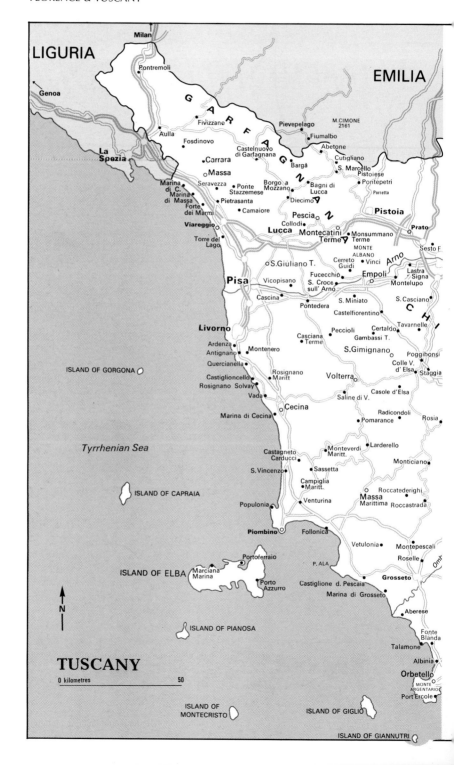

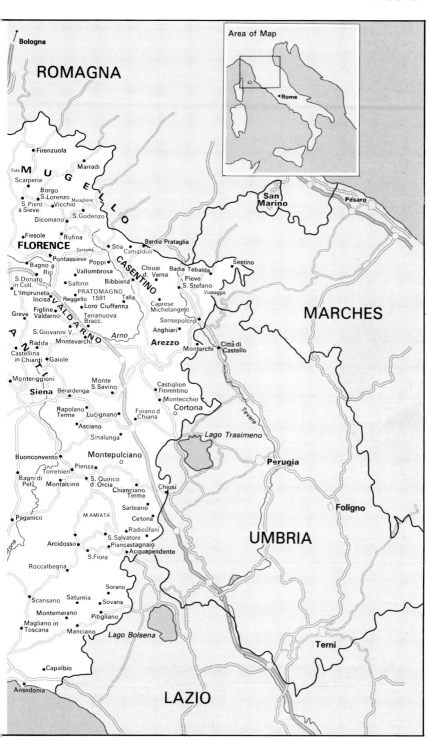

years, but all the most important events of life – birth, marriage, and death – are still officiated over by the *contrada* members in the *contrada* church.

Another thing that has not changed, except in Florence, is the daily routine, which still operates around the *siesta*. Tuscan towns take on an almost ghostly quiet in the afternoon. But in the space of ten minutes they change dramatically when the evening *passeggiata* begins and the noise of footsteps, talk and laughter reverberates round the streets and squares. And then suddenly all is quiet again. Periodically throughout the day – to say nothing of the night – there are plenty of other noises to contend with. Even in the last century, before the days of roaring Fiat trucks, power tools, sirens and angrily buzzing Vespas, Fyodor Dostoevsky was driven nearly mad in Florence:

> . . . the population of Florence spends the whole night on its feet, and there's a terrible deal of singing. Of course we had the windows open at night; then about five o'clock in the morning, the people began to racket in the market, and the donkeys to bray, so that we never could close an eye.

The early morning noise in Florence is still bad – it is the time when people work hardest. Exhausted visitors will be forced awake at six by road works or delivery vans noisily unloading replicas of the David and cute alabaster *putti* into the more expensive tourist shops. With some accuracy, Dylan Thomas described Florence as 'a gruelling museum'. It *is* exhausting – overloaded with fine paintings, architecture and sculptures, standing around in squares and niches with a casual magnificence. More than any other art form the statues are the heart of the city: they are the citizens of the past, with the familiar Tuscan faces, still found in the postcard seller on the corner and the man from the tripe stall in the market. Perhaps because of their accessibility to the public, the statues are regarded by the Florentines with a fierce admiration and pride as the most potent symbol of their ancestors' greatness.

Another strong source of local pride lies in the Tuscan language, the purest in Italy, made famous by Dante in the 13th century. It is conveniently forgotten among Florentines that their most famous son spent most of his life banished from the city under pain of death. The Tuscan pride in the language has lasted many centuries and shows little sign of dying. In an obituary written after the death of the last Count Rucellai in 1983 this typical anecdote was told:

> Motoring in Florence some years ago he was held up by road works and heard one of the roadmenders swearing. Getting out of his car he went up to the man and said to him, 'Sir, we are Tuscans, so we have to set an example of good speech. That is our duty, so we shouldn't use swear words however cross we may feel or however provoking the circumstances.' This was said in so serious yet friendly a tone that the road mender apologised, thanked him and promised to try and remember his duty better in future.

In the country, particularly, the Tuscans tend to speak with a gentle, slightly guttural dialect using a soft 'c' which transforms *casa* into *hasa*. For the traveller, Italian is an easy language to pick up and, while the tourist-weary waiters in the towns may look at their watches if you decide to practice on them, in the country you will be received with smiles of encouragement and slaps on the back. In fact the roots of the Italian language derive in part from the ancient Etruscan language spoken in the Tuscan hills.

History

The Etruscans

It is partly due to the fact that their language has remained to a large extent undeciphered that the ancient Etruscans enjoy a reputation for mystery. Another factor is that no one is quite sure where they actually came from. Ancient sources point to various explanations, many of which are contradictory. The 5th-century BC Greek historian Herodotus maintained that they came over from Lydia before the Trojan war in the 13th century BC. Dionysius of Halicarnassus, writing during the reign of the Emperor Augustus, had it on good evidence that they were indigenous to central Italy. These theories were probably based on two of the main pointers still used to argue the matter: that of the undoubted oriental influence in much of their art, and the opposing fact that their language seems not to be taken from any other recognisable area. The issue is confused still further by later theories which suggest that they were Villanovans from the north of Italy, or perhaps from other parts of Asia. Recent theorists have looked at the problem in a different light, emphasising a developmental approach as opposed to simply establishing one place of origin. The problem of the Etruscan language is also complex. From the 10,000 or so remaining texts it is clear that their alphabet was derived from Greek, probably brought over by colonising Euboeans (c.7BC); but the meanings and the grammatical structures have to a large extent remained unclear. The extensive study at Perugia University of the famous *Cippus* stone may bring the whole thing to light, but until it does the language must remain nearly 80 per cent undeciphered.

What do we know about these people? In their pottery, tombs and carvings we can see banquets, athletes, musicians, warriors and a fascination with classical mythology. Perhaps because much of the evidence comes from funerary urns, we see also a preoccupation with death – chariots bearing the deceased, and eerie figures returning from the after-life to terrorise their loved ones and claim new victims. The Etruscans were also keenly religious, and when the Romans began to supersede them in the 4th century BC the Etruscan holy men quickly became successful as Roman soothsayers. Cicero, Seneca and Livy all testify to their cleverness at divination using animal livers. In Piacenza there is a bronze liver dating back to the 2nd century BC, neatly divided into 16 parts for the 16 areas of heaven, each one inscribed with the name of a god whose domain it was. The Romans also adopted other Etruscan ways, and some say that present day Tuscany owes as much to the Etruscans as to their Roman successors.

Volterra – Arco Etrusco

The Romans

By 90BC Rome had granted citizenship to virtually the whole of Italy. Sulla, in an act which combined gratitude and political shrewdness, gave land in Tuscany to 120,000 of his soldiers, finally eroding the power of the last of the big Etruscan landowners. It was at this point that the Tuscan holiday villa was born. The Romans held sway for the following three centuries. For us today, perhaps their most significant contribution lay in their new roads *Aurelia*, *Clodia*, *Cassia* and *Flaminia* which crossed different parts of the province. They also developed a small new town in the valley below Etruscan Fiesole, where the Arno was easiest to cross. Florentia was founded by Julius Caesar in 59BC and proceeded to grow rapidly – even during the decline of the Empire and the subsequent chaos of the Dark Ages.

The fall of the Empire

After the final collapse of the Roman Empire, Tuscany, like the rest of Italy, was subjected to a seemingly never-ending stream of invasions by the Germanic races of the north – Huns, Visigoths, Vandals and Ostrogoths. Towards the close of the 6th century it fell under the dominion of the Lombards, who set up their local headquarters at Lucca. The town remained the centre of government when Charlemagne annexed central Italy to his Empire in 774, installing a system of imperial Margraves (military governors). All these changes probably affected the main rural population very little – the main difference was that they were subservient now to lords of Lombardic, as opposed to Italian, descent. It was around this time that the church, which had been in decline, began to gain in power and religious houses began to spring up around Tuscany. Also at this time, the southern abbey of San Salvatore was first built, 40km south-east of Siena, although little remains of the 8th-century building apart from its imposing crypt.

The Middle Ages: Guelphs and Ghibellines

In the Middle Ages much of the Tuscan countryside was still dominated by fierce feudal landlords such as the Aldobrandeschi, the Malaspina and the Conti Guidi of Poppi. After the death of Countess Matilda, last of the Germanic Margraves, in 1115, Tuscany saw the rise of the free city communes governed by the townspeople and a visiting *podestà* or magistrate. But Matilda's death had other repercussions. By bequeathing her immense property to the Papacy she re-awakened the earlier fierce quarrels between supporters of the Pope (known as the Guelphs), and those of the Holy Roman Empire (called Ghibellines – after Weiblingen castle, home of the Hohenstaufen supporters of the Empire). When in 1213 the Emperor Frederick II formally renounced his claim to Matilda's lands, the situation seemed briefly more promising, but the old troubles were sparked off again by a family feud between the Buondelmonte and the Amidei and degli Uberti families in Florence. Though the fighting was initially between factions within the city, it soon spread outside the walls, providing yet another reason for other power-hungry city-states to fight one another. Among these, Guelph Florence was growing increasingly powerful, and by the 12th century had started a campaign to subdue the other cities of the province. Partly in reaction to Florence, many of the other major cities (including Siena, Pisa and Arezzo) were Ghibelline. The wars were seemingly endless, with victory going first to one side and then another, but increasingly with Florence getting the upper hand.

Amidst all these troubles was born one of Italy's greatest men, Dante Alighieri (1265–1321). Dante, an exiled Florentine Guelph, wrote his masterpiece *The Divine Comedy* in pure Tuscan dialect, establishing written Italian as a beautiful and powerful language. Dante's *Commédia* is peopled by the men and women of Tuscany he knew, including his beloved Beatrice, and it fiercely depicts his country's troubled times.

Ahi serva Italia, di dolore ostello,
  nave sanza nocchiere in gran tempesta,
  non donna di provincie, ma bordello!

Cerca, misera, intorno dalle prode
  le tue marine, e poi ti guarda in seno,
  s'alcuna parte in te di pace gode.

Purgatoria VI

O enslaved Italy, a place of grief,
  a ship without a master in a great storm
  not mistress of provinces, but a brothel!

Wretched country, look around your shores,
  on every coast, and then into your heart
  and see if any part enjoys peace.

Even amid perpetual fighting and feuding (eventually the Guelphs split into 'white' and 'black' factions and fought each other) a flourishing economy was developing in many of the towns – based initially on the cloth trade but developing into extremely lucrative banking. Towns now saw the development of artisan classes and the rise of the merchants who made their fortunes in trade, travelling to far-off places to sell their goods. These merchants became the first real bankers in Europe and the foremost families in Florence – the Rucellai, the Albizzi, the Strozzi and, of course, the Medici.

The Medici and the Renaissance

The first of the great Medici, Cosimo, had his first real taste of power after the death of his father, Giovanni, in 1429. But in 1434 he was exiled to Venice under pressure from the powerful Albizzi clan. Without the huge Medici loans to the government, the economy of Florence almost collapsed and the populace, who saw in Rinaldo degli Albizzi all the symptoms of a dictator, increasingly regretted Cosimo's expulsion. Within a year the government of Florence (the *Signoria*) had asked Cosimo to return. From then on his power in Florence was assured, despite the inevitable dissenting voices from other parties. Cosimo was a shrewdly intelligent man, with a sensible dislike of ostentation and a brilliant talent for making money. As well as to the Florentine government, he leant huge sums of money to the Pope, which meant his taxes were minimal and even the most powerful were in his debt. He was also a great reader, with a passion for classical texts, as well as being a generous patron of the arts. He had a particular affection for the crusty sculptor Donatello and also for the devout Fra Angelico and the convent of San Marco. When the friars at San Marco began politely to protest at his almost overwhelming generosity he would reply: 'Never shall I be able to give God enough to set him down in my books as a debtor.' Throughout his life he held few official public offices, but he was recognised everywhere as

Pater Patriae, the supreme ruler of Florence. 'He it is who decides peace and war,' said Aeneas Piccolimini, later Pius II, 'He is King in everything but name.'

Cosimo, though the most powerful and one of the most cultured of the Florentine merchants, was in some ways typical of his species. He was extremely wealthy and well educated, as befitted a widely-travelled banker and merchant, with a desire to appease God for his immense – and not always well-gotten – riches through the endowment of beautiful buildings and religious art. It was partly the patronage of men like Cosimo which made possible the development of what has become known as the Renaissance.

The term Renaissance usually refers to the period of around 250 years beginning at the start of the 15th century and ending some time after the death of Raphael in 1520. Italy at this time saw a staggering development of the arts, the first part of which took place almost exclusively in Florence. The convenient label 'Renaissance' was finally stuck firmly into every art history book in the 19th century by Jacob Burckhardt, but the idea of a rebirth of a Classical golden age had long been fixed in the minds of the Florentines themselves. As the great Humanist Marsilio Ficino wrote in the 1490s:

> This century, like a golden age, has restored to light the liberal arts, which were almost extinct: grammar, poetry, rhetoric, painting, sculpture, architecture, music, the ancient singing of songs to the Orphean lyre, and all this in Florence. Achieving what had been honoured among the ancients, but almost forgotten since, the age has joined wisdom with eloquence, and prudence with the military art . . . And in Florence it has recalled Platonic teaching from darkness into light.

This fascination with the classical texts was central to the movement – the term 'Humanist' derived from *humanitas*, a word used by Cicero to describe studies which deserve the attention of humans. Man, instead of being a mere speck of dust in the eyes of God, is seen to have a new dignity and power to create beauty using science and logic. It was not that God was brought low, but that man was exalted. This feeling found its way into all the arts and produced a wave of experimentation in proportion, perspective and realism. In architecture, the text of Vitruvius – which states that the circle and square are the two units most appropriate to man – received special attention, and reverberate throughout the works of Brunelleschi and Michelozzo. Leonardo's drawing of Vitruvian man within a circle and a square is to be found on every postcard stand in Florence. Painting and sculpture too leapt forward, pushed along by the genius of Masaccio, Donatello, Leonardo and, of course, Michelangelo.

Important as Cosimo was to the Renaissance, his death in 1464 did not seriously interrupt the surge of activity in the art world. He was succeeded by his son Piero, *il Gottoso* (the Gouty), a cautious man lacking the talents of his father and the brilliance of his son. Ever sickly, having been afflicted by chronic arthritis since childhood, he survived his father by only a few years, quickly making way for his son Lorenzo who was then in his twentieth year. Like his grandfather, Lorenzo had a passion for the arts and he soon became known as *'il Magnifico'* ('the Magnificent'), giving support and employment to Verrocchio, Botticelli, Leonardo da Vinci and the young Michelangelo. Also like his grandfather, he was a keen reader of philosophical and classical texts, and often invited the members of his 'Platonic Academy' to Cosimo's beloved villa at Careggi where they would talk, sing and write poetry late into the night. But, unlike Cosimo, Lorenzo also loved pageantry, carnivals, and tournaments: the streets of Florence were continually witness to some great show or other. But the Medici still had many enemies and in 1478 Lorenzo's brother, the bright young Giuliano, was murdered in Florence Cathedral by Francesco dei Pazzi and his followers. Lorenzo himself managed to escape, wounded, into the sacristy. Needless to say the Pazzi paid heavily for their crime: a series of vile atrocities were performed by the people on the bodies of the implicated. Lorenzo himself died 14 years later, aged only 42, but his name has remained inextricably bound up with the great days of the Florentine Renaissance.

After the death of Lorenzo de' Medici, much of the city's creative impetus moved with Michelangelo to Rome. Florence fell ever deeper under the influence of Girolamo Savonarola, a friar from Ferrara whose pessimistic ranting temporarily returned the city to the Middle Ages. Savonarola's power was increased still further in 1494 when Charles VIII of France joined forces with Pisa and occupied Florence, expelling Lorenzo's son and forming a new republic under the guidance of the blood-and-thunder monk. But Savonarola's days of popularity were numbered and four years later he was hanged, his corpse burned in the Piazza Signoria in front of an excited crowd. By 1512 the Medici were back, supported increasingly by the Vatican (there were to be two Medici popes in the following years). In 1532, after more trouble, Alessandro de' Medici became the first Grand Duke of Tuscany. After his assassination, his son Cosimo I took over, erecting fortresses round the province, starting a new chivalric order of Santo Stefano and building the new port of Livorno. Cosimo's work can be seen all over Tuscany: he firmly re-established a dynasty that was not finally to die out until two hundred years later, with the death of the pathetic and debauched Gian Gastone in 1737.

Unification

After Gian Gastone's death Tuscany became part of the great Duchy of Lorraine, with a brief interval at the end of the 18th century when it was occupied by Napoleon. Lucca and Massa-Cararra, however, were still independent: Lucca was ceded to Tuscany only in 1847. 1859 saw the beginning of the unification of Italy and in 1861 Victor Emmanuel became the first king of the united nation, with Florence gaining importance as the capital from 1865 to 1871.

The age of the tourist

By the 18th century British visitors in Italy were already common. Increasingly they chose Tuscany, along with Naples and Rome, as their destination, lured by the warm climate, the beautiful landscape and the wealth of art. Many invalids also started to arrive in the hope of recovery, or at least of the alleviation of their symptoms, in the warm Italian sunshine. Inevitably the class system established itself, but the main division was between those who were just passing through and those who were permanent – a distinction that is still in evidence today. The real Anglo-Florentines took tea every afternoon in their drawing rooms, introduced Michaelmas daisies into their Italian gardens and, like most expatriates, remained in some ways more English than those at home. On the other hand, many developed a passionate and genuine love of their surroundings and basked happily in Tuscany's warmth and beauty. This delight is shown in their writings (they tended to be a literary crowd) which often flowed freely in letters, stories and poems. Even the pale and sickly little poetess Elizabeth Barrett Browning (who would lie for weeks on her sofa in Wimpole Street) was transformed in Italy.

> . . . Did you ever see this place, I wonder? The coolness, the charm of the mountains, whose heart you seem to hear beating in the rush of the little green river, the green silence of the chestnut forest, and the seclusion which anyone may make for himself by keeping clear of the valley villages; all these things drew us. Robert and I go out and lose ourselves in the woods and the mountains, and sit by waterfalls on the starry and moonlight nights . . . Robert is better, looking better, and in more healthy spirits, and we are both enjoying this great sea of mountains and our way of life here altogether.

Elizabeth, like Walter Savage Landor and many other of her compatriots and their dogs, lies buried in the Protestant Cemetery in Piazzale Donatello.

Later came other well-known Britons: Arthur Acton, who created a glorious garden in his villa La Pietra, and the Sitwells. The American art critic Bernard Berenson was frequently to be seen bicycling around Florence and the marvellous writer Iris Origo grew up in the Medici villa at Fiesole. To some this influx of English and Americans greatly reduced the charm of the area. When Aldous Huxley complained that Florence had become merely a 'third rate provincial town, colonised by English sodomites and middle-aged lesbians,' he was far from alone in his views. Nevertheless, the visitors had become so firmly entrenched that when the Second World War struck many of them refused to be repatriated, saying they had no other home, and stayed put throughout the fighting. Some of these families are still there. And in the English Church in Via Maggio a few Anglo-Tuscans still line the pews, elderly and dapper in neatly pressed flannels and polished shoes – a race apart from the sweating, underdressed tourist, clutching hymn book and Baedeker. Though worlds apart, each in his way bears witness to the magnetism of the province – a fascination which has drawn outsiders to Tuscany for over 25 centuries and shows little sign of abating.

Poppi – a typical Tuscan street

2. FOOD AND WINE IN TUSCANY

For July, in Siena, by the willow-tree,
I give you barrels of white Tuscan wine
In ice far down your cellars stored supine;
And morn and eve to eat in company
Of those vast jellies dear to you and me;
Of partridges and youngling pheasants sweet,
Boiled capons, sovereign kids; and let their treat
Be veal and garlic, with whom these agree.

These lines were written in the early 14th century by a well-known Tuscan poet called Folgore da San Gimignano. Folgore tells us what we had already suspected – that good food has long been a priority in Tuscany. In fact this preoccupation with eating goes back a great deal further than the 13th–14th centuries – indeed to the beginnings of Italian civilisation. As early as the 8th century BC, the Etruscans were carving scenes on their funerary urns showing the hunting and cooking of game, the olive harvest and the preparation and enjoyment of great banquets. We also know that the Romans were notorious gluttons, although perhaps their most important contribution was the spread of wine-growing that followed their colonisation. Needless to say, the Etruscans had already been making their own wine for centuries, but the Romans did introduce some new varieties of grapes to the area.

Little has been recorded about Tuscan eating habits during the Dark and early Middle Ages, and it is not until the 12th century that we begin to learn more. At this stage, as well as a growing interest in what was eaten, there was a new fussiness about table manners. In his book *Il Galateo* the poet Giovanni della Casa gave strict instruction not to put one's feet on the table, sniff somebody else's plate or offer another person food one had already bitten into. Furthermore he exhorts:

When you are eating do not masticate loudly or crouch gluttonously over your food without raising your head. That is not eating but devouring, and then you soil your hands and even your elbows and dirty the cloth.

This fussiness was precocious by comparison with the other Mediterranean countries. It was not until the mid 16th century, when Catherine de' Medici married the Duke of Orleans, that the Florentine habit of eating with a fork was taken up in France.

With the onset of the Renaissance and the rise of the great merchants of Florence, the tables of the wealthy grew heavier and heavier as the assortment of fashionable delicacies became increasingly rich. The Crusades, followed by decades of foreign trading, had introduced a variety of spices to the region and these were added to almost all dishes. Partridges, peacocks, veal and wild boar were frequently stuffed with a mixture of fats, almonds, sugar, onion, garlic, cinnamon and other spices. As well as meats there would be course after course of other foods: sweetbreads and fish, puddings and pies. Even the series of 'sumptuary' laws did little to prohibit the excesses of those great banquets. These laws dictated that no more than forty guests were allowed to sit down together, and that meals must be limited to no more than three courses. The result was that each course took on new, grander dimensions. Staple to the new, officially abstemious, approach was the *torta*, a single dish which often contained pork, capons, sausages, ham, veal, dates, onions, almonds, saffron, cheese, eggs, flat pasta and pastry. At Lorenzo il Magnifico's wedding – where 'food and drink were as modest and simple as befitted a marriage' – there were five vast banquets at which, among other things, over 2,250kg of sweetmeats were eaten. Lorenzo's son, Pope Leo X, had even more extravagant taste than his father and was known to have at his table as many as 65 courses, including such delicacies as peacocks' tongues and pies containing live nightingales.

Happily for the 20th-century health-conscious traveller, the days of such intense, highly spiced, gluttony are well and truly over. The first 'tourists' predictably found much of the Italian food coarse and unpalatable and many stuck as nearly as possible to home favourites which, needless to say, were 'never quite the same abroad'. But some travellers were bolder and more appreciative. Thomas Jefferson developed such a liking for *polenta* that he had his cook specially trained to make it and later produced it at dinner parties back home in Virginia, to the polite amazement of his guests. There were some things however which were quite beyond the pale and of which even Bohemians like Shelley could not approve.

> There are *two* Italies . . . The one is the most sublime and lovely contem-
> plation that can be conceived by man; the other is the most degraded,
> disgusting and odious. What do you think? Young women of rank actu-
> ally eat – you will never guess what – *garlick*!

Now garlic is almost universally appreciated as are most of the other staple Tuscan foods – tomatoes, olive oil, bread, and pasta. The emphasis is on simple food made with good local ingredients and the result is generally delicious. Surprisingly, tomatoes have become widespread in Tuscany only relatively recently having been brought by Garibaldi from Sicily where they had long been popular. Olive oil has been used since the time of the Etruscans, and silver olive groves are still to be found all over Tuscany, although perhaps the best oil comes from the area around Lucca. The olive harvest begins around November and the finest oil comes from the first pressing; to be absolutely supreme, it must be pressed cold. The best oil is not cheap even in Tuscany, but it is worth it. There is nothing more delicious than tomatoes with good olive oil and plenty of fresh basil.

Traditional Tuscan dishes

Much of the best and most authentic Tuscan food can be found in the cheap *casalinga* restaurants, particularly in rural areas where local specialities have not yet been abandoned in favour of international-style Italian food. *Casalinga* simply means 'housewife' and home cooking is exactly what the best of these small restaurants provide. Here the meal may begin with *crostini* – usually chicken livers or spicy tomatoes and oil on bread, or an *antipasto* of salami and *prosciutto*. There will be delicious home made pastas and soup – *ribollita* or *aquacotta* made with vegetables and often thickened with bread. The main course will probably be simple grilled or roast meat, veal or chicken, and there may be a stew made with rabbit or *cinghiale* (wild boar). Near the sea, there will obviously be fish – *fritto misto* or, if you are lucky, *cacciucco*. This is the Tuscan answer to *bouillabaisse* – a glorious spicy fish stew, traditionally made from whatever has been caught that day. The best versions are to be found in the rougher restaurants in and around Livorno. Favourite Tuscan puddings seem to be *zuppa Inglese* (trifle) and the beautifully named *tiramisù* (literally 'pull-me-up'). The home-made ones are rich but delicious, swimming in *Vin Santo*, but often they are the ready-packaged variety and are more like an ordinary ice-cream. Another typical pudding is *Macedonia* – fruit salad. Personally, I recommend sticking to fresh fruit and cheese – *dolcelatte* or, better still, the local sheep's milk cheese, *pecorino*. All these delights are what you might expect to find in your nearest *trattoria*, and many of them you can easily buy and prepare yourself. Of course there are also some more upmarket restaurants that genuinely concentrate on Tuscan food, and which real gourmets will want to try. Visit, for instance, the Terzo Cerchio in Istia d'Ombrone for as many courses as you can eat of excellent Tuscan food from the Maremma, for a set price, washed down with unlimited and very drinkable wine from Scansano.

Game is still popular in Tuscany, particularly in the Maremma where wild boar is still hunted. In many areas the *contadini* were not allowed to hunt for game and, until quite recently, a public whipping was the usual penalty for poachers. Despite this, stew made with *cinghiale* is a widespread and popular dish among the country people. Another popular dish is *pappardelle con lepra* – wide strips of pasta with hare. In feudal days the peasants made this by collecting the hare's blood that was left over from the local lord's meal and adding it to their supper. In Florence the favourite meat courses are *trippa* (tripe), which can be bought from stalls in the streets, and of course *bistecca fiorentina* preferably made with steak from the beef cattle of the Val di Chiana or the Maremma.

Another local food in which the Tuscans take particular pride is *funghi porcini*, the wonderful big wild mushrooms gathered in the chestnut woods of the region. In San Gimignano in the Via San Giovanni you can even buy *gelato ai funghi porcini* – and revolting it is too. If you are a mushroom fiend, one of the best places to eat is the Fonte della Galetta near Michelangelo's birthplace Caprese. Here, in rustic-chalet-style surroundings, you can try the gourmet *funghi porcini* menu which involves mushroom in each of the five courses.

Also from the woods come the chestnuts themselves, which are eaten widely in Tuscany, in biscuits and cakes. Chestnuts are a particular feature of cooking to the north of Lucca, where even the *polenta* can be made with chestnut flour – a habit that began during times of hardship when chestnuts gathered in the forest were an abundant source of free food. Also from here is the delicious *castagnaccio*, a chestnut cake made without sugar and sweetened only by the chestnuts themselves. Likewise with the traditional fragrant Pan di Romarino, which Tuscan children still love. It too derives its sweetness from the chestnuts, but it is also flavoured with rosemary – a traditional Tuscan herb. Another sweet favourite is the heavy, spicy *panforte* found, along with various other impossibly sweet pastries and biscuits, mainly around Siena and San Gimignano – the southern Tuscans seem to have a particularly sweet tooth. There are also *brigidini* (aniseed biscuits), *ricciarelli* (a type of macaroon) and the dry *cantucci*, also made with almonds, to dip in *Vin Santo*.

Tuscan wines

For many people coming to Tuscany, sampling local wines will play a major part in the enjoyment of the holiday. For Tuscans too, the subject is of never-ending fascination and always has been. In the 15th century Leonardo da Vinci maintained that there is a natural joy in people born in areas where good wine is produced. A few years later Michelangelo, combining his skill of giving life to the inanimate with a truly modern wine critic's vocabulary, described one of his favourite drinks (the yellow Vernaccia of San Gimignano) as a wine that 'kisses, bites, licks, thrusts and stings'.

Far earlier, we know that wine played an important part in the lives of the ancient Etruscans, as it did later with the Romans. Historians believe, however, that fewer grapes were grown during the Dark Ages, and the production and consumption of wine sank dramatically in the Italian hills. However, some wines were still made and a variation on the famous Brunello di Montalcino was apparently highly esteemed by the Lombards in the 8th century. By the Middle Ages things were looking up again and the white grapes of the Trebbiano Toscano vines spread widely throughout the Tuscan hills. Most of the

Tossing chestnuts

larger farms (and many of the smaller) produced their own vintage which was freely drunk by all and sundry. Drunkenness was apparently common among both men and women, and the teetotaller – known as *bevilaqua* – was rare. In the Middle Ages white wine was far more common: it was not until the Renaissance that the reds that we most commonly associate with the area really caught on. Even then the whites remained more popular. At Lorenzo il Magnifico's wedding banquets no fewer than three hundred barrels of Trebbiano and Vernaccia wine were drunk. Vernaccia – the golden yellow wine from around San Gimignano – was also popular in England and was mentioned (as 'Vernage') by Chaucer.

Another wine which became popular during the Renaissance and is now one of the most famous and highly acclaimed wines in Italy is the full-bodied red, Vino Nobile di Montepulciano. Made in the south of Tuscany from a mixture of Trebbiano, Prugnolo, Malvasia and the black Canaiolo grapes this wine acquired its reputation for excellence as early as the 14th century, though it is unclear whether the term *nobile* referred to the quality of the wine or its imbibers. Travelling in Tuscany in the 19th century, American writer Henry James found his memory of Montepulciano involved this powerful vintage:

> What we were doing or what we expected to do at Montepulciano I keep no other trace of than is bound up in a present quite tender consciousness that I wouldn't for the world not have been there. I think my reason must have been largely just in the beauty of the name (for could any be greater?) reinforced no doubt by the fame of the local vintage and of how we should quaff it on the spot. Perhaps we quaffed it too constantly; since the romantic picture reduces itself to me but to two definite appearances; that of the more priggish discrimination so far reasserting itself as to advise me that Montepulciano was dirty, even remarkably dirty; and that of its being not much else besides but perched and brown and crooked, and noble withal . . .

In the more recent Sainsbury's wine book, Oz Clarke comments:

> . . . at its best the slightly heavy sweet-sour raisiny quality is superseded by a creamy oaky softness, a good bash of acidity, and then, and then a delicious fruit mixing blackcurrant and cedar with an exhilarating dry sandalwood spice.

If you are a serious sightseer there is a very definite danger in drinking too much of this luscious wine too early in the day but it would be a minor tragedy not to taste it all.

A few miles away to the west of Montepulciano is the home of another of Tuscany's great reds, the wonderful Brunello di Montalcino. It is grown from the Brunello grape, a variation on the Chianti Sangioveto, within a small area near the town. At the end of the last century the wine was completely revamped by the Biondi-Santi producers and it has since, over some years, achieved a supreme status. Today, like the Vino Nobile and the best Chianti, it carries the DOCG initials (*Denominazione di Origine Controllata e Garantita*), the highest government classification which is held by few other wines in the country. It must be matured in old wood for four years before being released and for five years to be classified as *riserva*. Like the Montepulciano, it takes on an orange tint with age and usually needs from four to twenty-four hours to breathe before drinking. Ever the master of under-statement, Oz Clarke describes the best vintages as:

> . . . maturing over five to ten years into a marvellously individual flavour, your palate being assaulted by the pepper, acidity and tannin, yet soothed by an almost viscous richness of prunes and liquorice, meaty savouriness and bitter black chocolate.

Cheaper, but often pretty good, is the more modest wine of the area which is known simply as the Rosso di Montalcino.

Chianti

Chianti is Tuscany's most famous wine and is made in huge amounts all over the region. Every year over 170 million bottles are produced by the 100 thousand workers employed in the trade. Of course all these bottles are not of the same quality and critics maintain that over the past few decades the emphasis has been more on quantity than quality. Recently, however, with the increase in imports of cheap wines from other countries, there is new incentive to improve the quality of the more moderately-priced Tuscan wines. There is also a wide variety of taste from vineyard to vineyard depending on the soil, the production method and the different quantities of grapes in the mixture. To find out which ones you particularly like there is no alternative but to taste each one. Chianti is made with not more than 90 per cent Sangioveto grapes combined with 5 per cent Canaiolo, generally not more than 2 per cent white grapes and a maximum of 10 per cent of other varieties. In the past, vineyards from different parts of Tuscany would exchange huge amounts of wine to create popular blends, but this practice is now diminishing in favour of the more interesting single estate wines. Chianti can be drunk young but it must be matured for two years to be called *vecchio* and three to be labelled *riserva*. Most *riservas* should be drunk between about four and eight years old.

The part of Tuscany that is generally known as Chianti lies between Florence and Siena to either side of the Via Chiantigiana (SS222). This is the zone where Chianti Classico wine is produced, under the supervision of a wine consortium which dates back to the 14th century. The Chianti Classico emblem is a black rooster on a yellow ground which was apparently taken from a painting by Vasari on the ceiling of the Palazzo Vecchio in Florence. If you have a car this is a wonderful area to drive around, picking up samples as you go (see chapter 10). Good places for serious wine shoppers to stop are Greve, Panzano and Castellina, each of which has its own *enoteca*.

The other, relatively new, Chianti consortium operates outside this immediate area. Its producers are divided into the following six regions: Colli (meaning hill) Senesi, Colli Aretini, Colli Fiorentini, Rufina Montalbano and Colline

The vineyards of Chianti

Pisane. Perhaps the best of these is the Rufina zone to the east of Florence, where some of the finest Chiantis can be found. These wines are sold under the Chianti Putto label, distinguished by a plump Renaissance cherub. Although this is not so old or traditional a consortium it generally controls wines of equal quality to Chianti Classico. In addition to the two consortia some of the best producers like the Ricasoli, Antinori and Castello di Brolio vineyards have decided to branch out on their own and now operate independently of the *consorzio*.

New wines

Along with the traditional wines there has recently been a spurt of new hybrids springing up around the region, many of which use a new variety of grapes altogether. Perhaps the most striking of these is the Sassicaia, which has been made only for the last twenty years – a pure Cabernet Sauvignon, grown on the coast near Livorno. Other wines mix traditional local grapes with new imports. This is obviously not a recent idea – Montecarlo, one of the favourite wines of the 14th century, was and still is a compound of various elements which include Semillon, Pinot Grigio and Bianco and the native Trebbiano. Montecarlo continues to be made today in a small area near Lucca and can be very good if rather expensive. Other new wines include the new-look table whites made by modern methods in some of the bigger vineyards. Perhaps the most popular of these is Galestro, a very light refreshing, slightly fizzy, wine perfect for lunchtime drinking. Another new favourite among whites is the traditionally made Bianco della Lega which some estates in the Chianti Classico zone are taking up.

There are, of course, many of the old whites still in production. Among the DOC classified are the Bianca Vergine della Val di Chiana, the wines of Elba, Vernaccia, Pomino, and the delicious fortified sweet Moscadello di Montalcino which is one of the oldest recorded wines of Tuscany. Many other white table wines are also worth trying, both from the north and far south of the region, where the wines of Pitigliano (grown on volcanic soil), and nearby Scansano, can be very enjoyable. Scansano is also renowned for its red Morellino while other DOC reds can be found at Carmignano, and under the labels of Pomino and Tignanello.

Among the Tuscans the aniseed spirit Sambuca is very popular, sometimes drunk after having been set alight with a coffee bean in it. But probably the favourite drink of all is the sweet white fortified wine known as Vin Santo which can be found in almost every house. Particularly in the country, in the villages and *fattorie*, this is the drink that will probably be offered to guests – often accompanied by the hard almond biscuits known as *cantucci*. It is a delicious combination.

Food and wine festival in Montalcino

3. LUCCA AND THE MASSA-CARRARA

Lucca

The word 'Lucca' goes back a long way, and was probably the invention of the Ligurians who called the town 'Luk' meaning marshland. After the Ligurians came the Etruscans who probably drained much of the land, fast followed by the Romans, who by the 2nd century BC, developed Lucca into a thriving and popular town. Traces of the Romans can be found in the lovely oval Piazza del Mercato which was built on walls of the Roman amphitheatre, and in the name of San Michele in Foro built on the site of the town forum. Apparently Lucca was the favourite winter resort of Julius Caesar and it was here in 58BC that the triumvirate between Caesar, Pompey and Crassus was formed. History records little else until, in the 6th century, Saint Frigidanus (Frediano) arrived from Ireland and was made Bishop of Lucca in 565. Legend has it that it was Frigidanus who divided the river Serchio to stop it flooding the city during a deluge. By the Middle Ages Lucca was already a town to be reckoned with, but it was in the 14th century, under the dominating leadership of the great soldier-leader Castruccio Castracani d'Antiminelli, that her power reached its zenith. Castruccio, who, along with Cesare Borgia, had the rather dubious accolade of being deeply admired (and having his biography written) by Niccolò Macchiavelli, brought the city both glory and enslavement until his death of fever in the Maremma in 1328, aged 44. Another period that the Lucchese look back on with pride was the more peaceful and creative time under the nobleman Paolo Guinigi at the beginning of the 15th century, when many of the city's loveliest works of art were created – including Jacopo della Quercia's lovely effigy of Paolo's wife Ilaria del Carretto in the Cathedral.

Extraordinarily, although Lucca increasingly came under threat from the main powers in Tuscany, the little city state retained her independence right up to the time of the French invasion at the end of the 18th century. The massive walls that surround the city today were built in the 16th century and topped with a fine park; the park was later destroyed but the walls remain a pleasant place to walk. Lucca has long been popular with visitors: by the 18th century many English travellers stayed in the town or in nearby villas on their way to the nearby spa, enjoying the quaintness of the tiny republic. With typical condescension an 18th-century Englishwoman writes:

> . . . we must not look for great men or great things in little nations, to be sure; but let us respect the innocence of childhood and regard with tenderness the territory of Lucca . . . A great boarding school in England is really an infinitely more licentious place and grosser immoralities are every day connived at in it than are known to pollute this delicate and curious commonwealth . . .

In 1805 Napoleon gave Lucca as a principality to his sister Elisa Baciocchi who ruled until his capture in 1814, but even then it was not until 1847 that it finally and reluctantly became part of Tuscany.

The centre of 19th-century Lucca is the *Piazza Napoleone*, the large square that was laid out during the brief reign of Elisa Baciocchi. The massive **Palazzo Ducale** (also known as the Palazzo della Provincia or Signoria) runs right along the west side of the square. It was initially designed in 1578 by the Medici architect, the Mannerist Bernardo Ammannati, although there had been another council palace on the site before. The new building was left unfinished and work was not resumed until the beginning of the 18th century under the direction of an architect named Juvara. Work was finally finished in the early 19th century under Elisa Baciocchi, although various parts of the palace, including the two great courtyards, have remained incomplete. Just off the square are two churches, San Romano to the west and San Giusto to the north. **San Romano** was built in the 13th and 14th centuries by the Dominicans and houses Saint Romano's tomb which was designed in about 1490. **San Giusto** was built mainly in the 12th century and has a charming striped brown-and-white façade and ornately carved door opening into a Baroque interior. Adjoining the south-east corner of the Piazza Napoleone is the **Piazza del Giglio**, with its Neo-Classical theatre and the elegant Hotel Universo long housed in the Palazzo Paoli. Next door is the equally popular Ristorante del Giglio which has tables on the piazza.

From the Piazza Napoleone it is a short walk east to the Cathedral. On the way look in at the little church of **San Giovanni**, built on the site of the first cathedral of Lucca which was here until the 8th century. The remains of the original crypt are said to date back as far as the 5th–6th century. The church itself was rebuilt in the 12th century but completely remodelled in 1622. The lovely door still preserves a carved lintel of the Virgin between Angels and Saints, which dates back to 1187. The domed baptistery was added in 1422.

Lucca's cathedral square, *Piazza San Martino*, is rather less grand than that of the more central church of San Michele in Foro. The origins of the **Cathedral of San Martino** are uncertain, but it is thought that it was possibly first founded as a parish church in the 6th century by the Irish saint, Frigidanus (San Frediano). It was rebuilt in the 11th century by Bishop Anselmo, later Pope Alexander II, and enlarged again in the 13th. The ornate, peculiarly asymmetrical façade was added by the Lombard architect Guidetto da Como. Above the doors are a series of marvellous carved friezes, probably dating back to the

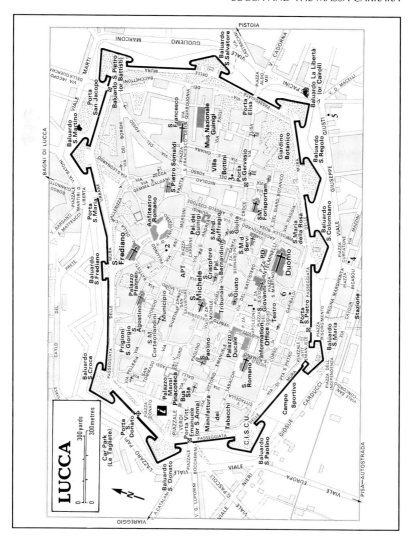

mid 13th century, by a variety of Lombard sculptors including Guido da Como. Above the main door is depicted the Ascension of Christ above a frieze of Mary and the Disciples. The left-hand door shows the Descent from the Cross, which may have been carved in the workshop of the great Nicola Pisano, possibly even by the master himself. The right hand door tells the story of San Regolo, his missionary works and subsequent martyrdom. Between the doors are stories from the life of San Martino and a frieze of the months of the year beginning with people sitting by a fire in January and ending with the killing of the Christmas pig.

Compared to the Romanesque exterior, the inside of the cathedral has a

The asymmetrical façade of Lucca Cathedral

high Gothic feel about it. The Englishman Fynes Moryson, travelling in the early 17th century, described it as being:

> . . . stately paved with marble but very dark, as most of the Papist churches are built, either because they think darkness increaseth religion, or to make it an excuse for their burning candles in the day.

Immediately inside the main door is a really fine Romanesque sculpture from the 13th century of St Martin giving his cloak to a beggar, brought in from its original position on the façade to protect it from the weather. The pulpit is by Matteo Civitali, a native of Lucca, as are the two tombs in the right-hand transept, of Pietro di Noceto and Doménico Bertini. Civitali was also responsible for the altar of San Regolo and the two angels in the adjoining chapel. The windows in the apse are by Pandolfo da Ugolino and were made at the end of the 15th century. The Chapel of the Sanctuary houses an extremely beautiful *Madonna and Child* between SS Stephen and John the Baptist, which dates from around 1310 and is probably the best work of Fra Bartolomeo. To the left of the sanctuary is a rather bland *St John the Evangelist* by Jacopo della Quercia, a sculpture which no way shows the sculptor's true capability. To gauge this we must go to the loveliest work in the building – the remarkable tomb of Ilaria del Caretto, wife of Paolo Guinigi, who died in 1405. John Ruskin, like countless others, was deeply impressed by this graceful and time-less piece.

> The hair is bound up in a flat braid over the fair brow, the sweet and arched eyes are closed, the tenderness of the loving lips is set and quiet; there is that about them which forbids breath; something which is not death nor sleep, but the pure image of both . . . such a lesson of love as no coldness could refuse, no fatuity forget, and no insolence disobey.

But for the Lucchese the most important object in the Cathedral is the crude wooden Crucifix known as the Volto Santo, housed in an ornate *tempietto* carved by Civitali. The Volto Santo was supposedly carved in cedar wood by Nicodemus after the Ascension of Christ. Before finishing the task, however, Nicodemus grew weary and fell asleep, whereupon the work was finished by angels who carved the miraculous face with their own hands. The Crucifix was said to have been brought to Lucca via Livorno in the 10th century amid much rejoicing and has worked miracles here ever since. Every September (and on various other occasions) the great simple Christ is dressed up in gold and finery until he looks like an absurd puppet and paraded around the streets of Lucca. There are various other works of art in the Cathedral, but perhaps none as moving as the tomb of Ilaria. Before leaving look at the Tintoretto's swirling *Last Supper* in the third chapel on the right and, in the Sacristy, the delightful *Lives of the Saints*, probably painted in Ghirlandaio's workshop.

On the site of the Roman Forum is the magnificent if absurd church of **San Michele in Foro**, built mainly in the 12th century. Both its magnificence and its absurdity are centred around the same thing – the high, ornate Pisan façade, embellished with every sort of decorated pillar, which rises a full two storeys about the building it fronts, like a great Pinewood Studios set. Its final gesture is the big, charmingly misproportioned Archangel Michael who perches clumsily on the top between two diminutive colleagues. The whole effect is extremely joyous and slightly crazy.

Inside, the original flat roof was replaced in the 16th century by a vaulted ceiling, but the rest of the church has been little altered. Among San Michele's works of art you will find a gentle blue-and-white della Robbia *Madonna and Child*. The picture of the martyrdom of St Andrew was painted by the Lucchese Pietro Paolini, who was born in the city in 1435. Over the high altar is a rather splendid painted wooden crucifix made in the area in the 12th century. The painting I like best here, however, is the exquisite work by Filippino Lippi of SS Helen, Jerome, Sebastian and Rocco, painted towards the end of the 15th century.

The lovely oval Piazza del Mercato was built in the Middle Ages on the ruins of the great Roman amphitheatre, constructed between 1 and 2AD. Much of the theatre, which could seat well over 10,000 people, is still buried some 2m underground. After its decay in the Dark Ages, the area was used as a sort of central supply for anyone who needed ready-cut stone. Now, cracked and dilapidated, it still has immense charm, with its irregular medieval dwellings and a few shops and cafés on the ground floor. Just south of the square is another good example of medieval building, the double Palazzo Guinigi, with its high slender tower, crowned by a holm oak. If you are energetic, you can climb the Guinigi tower and will be rewarded for your efforts by a wonderful view of the city's red roofs.

On the north side of town, past the oval amphitheatre square, is another fine church – the 12th-century basilica of **San Frediano**. There has been a church on this site since the 6th century, when the Irish missionary Bishop Frigidanus founded a church here dedicated to San Vincenzio. At the top of the otherwise plain façade is a large restored Byzantine mosaic which has been attributed to Berlingo Berlinghieri. It shows Christ seated in Glory between two angels, with the Apostles below. In the surprisingly large and beautiful interior of this church there are many treasures. Of the two fonts, one was carved by Matteo Civitali, while the other dates back to the 12th century and was probably by a craftsman known as Maestro Robertus. It has a large basin for total immersion and a smaller one in the centre, finely carved to depict the months of the year. Round the base are some sturdy carvings showing the Life of Moses and Christ the Shepherd. In the Trenta Chapel to the left of the church is a marble polyptych by della Quercia. It shows the Madonna and Child surrounded by saints, and has a particularly fine carved predella. The nearby tombs of a husband and wife belong to the donors of the Chapel. Before leaving look in at the Chapel of St Augustine and the series of frescoes by the minor 14th-century artist Amerigo Aspertini, showing the life of Frigidanus and the bringing of the Volto Santo to Lucca.

To the east of the amphitheatre is the small church of **San Pietro Somaldi**, set in a triangular piazza surrounded by 16th-century palaces. As with many of the local churches, the façade is a combination of sandstone and white limestone, though the top of the beautiful campanile is of brick. Above the central door is a fine 13th-century carved architrave attributed to Guido Bigarelli, showing Christ giving the keys to Saint Peter. Inside are various 16th-century paintings of fairly moderate interest. A short distance east of San Pietro, the Via del Fosso runs north–south, parallel with a picturesque canal – an area sometimes referred to with an amazing lack of originality as 'Little Venice'. East again is the church of **San Francesco**, which was first founded only two years after the saint's death in 1226 but rebuilt in the 14th century. It contains a slab monument to Lucca's most famous ruler Castruccio Castracani d'Antelminelli, as well as some interesting 15th-century Florentine frescoes.

Museums and galleries

Just south of San Francesco is one of the town's main museums, housed in the early 15th-century **Villa Guinigi**. The villa was built by Paolo Guinigi to celebrate his second marriage after the death of his first wife, the beautiful Ilaria. It has an interesting collection including sculptures by della Quercia and Civitali and paintings by Berlinghieri, 'Il Vecchietta', and Filippino Lippi. Lucca's **National Gallery** is housed in the sturdy **Palazzo Mansi** to the west of the town. The palace itself is 17th-century, though with an interior belonging to the most extravagant phase of the 18th. Amid exuberant *trompe-l'oeil* and fantastically gilded stucco (particularly splendid in the main bedchamber), is a rich collection of Italian pictures. Paintings include works by Beccafumi, Veronese, del Sarto, Tintoretto, Guido Reni and others, collected mainly by Grand-Duke Leopold II and donated to the city in 1847 when Lucca finally joined the rest of Tuscany.

Perhaps the most sumptuous of Lucca's town palaces is the large **Palazzo Pfanner**, located close to the church of San Frediano and built in 1666 on an earlier design. On the façade is a grand staircase leading up to a fine loggia which overlooks the spectacular formal garden complete with statues, topiary and a charming octagonal pond.

The villas of the Lucchese

The Lucchese countryside is also famous throughout Italy for its elegant villas. Many of these are still privately owned and not open to the public, but a few may be visited by those who are interested. Most were built by wealthy Italians in the 16th century, and a number were later taken up by the British and the French as fashionable summer retreats. Three of the finest (which can be visited) are in the area a few kilometres to the north-west of Lucca towards Péscia. The nearest – and probably the most famous – is the **Villa Reale** at

Marlia. The Villa Reale was created by Napoleon's sister Elisa Baciocchi by the joining together of two earlier palaces of the 16th and 17th centuries. The villa is set in a lovely garden decorated with statues, fountains, lakes and a small water theatre surrounded by trees.

Equally splendid is the **Villa Torrigiani**, a few kilometres away near Segromino. It was built in the 16th century but enlarged by Alfonso Torrigiani a century later, when it was given an extravagant new façade. The result is a stunning mixture of statues, balconies and loggias constructed in a rich variety of stone and marble. The Torrigiani also has a magnificent formal garden best visited in late spring or early summer. Nearby, the **Villa Mansi** is surrounded by a fine garden with a small ornamental lake. Like the other two, this villa is fundamentally 16th-century, revamped once in the 17th century (when the façade was added) and again a century later. The second refurbishment was carried out by the well-known 18th-century architect Juvara, who also improved the grounds by adding the so-called lake of Diana. For those with a car the villas can easily be visited in a morning, but it is worth checking opening times before you go.

The Garfagnana

Directly north of Lucca lies the mountainous area known as the Garfagnana. This is another region that was popular with British travellers in the past, though more for the cool climate, hot springs and healthy mountain air than for its works of art. To reach the Garfagnana, take the main north road out of the city which follows the river Serchio upstream into the hills. At Borgo a Mozzano is a strange asymmetrical bridge, called the Ponte della Maddalena but because of its strange history usually known as the **Ponte del Diavolo** or Devil's bridge. Legend has it that in 1322 when it was built the mason was unable to build high enough to withstand the Serchio in full spate so he asked the Devil to help him. The Devil agreed in return for the soul of the first traveller across it, and completed the bridge the same night. The following morning the builder sent a dog across which so enraged the Devil that he cast the animal to the ground with such force that the bridge broke and the dog was washed away. Apparently there is still a hole under the pavement in the middle of the bridge confirming the story. A few kilometres further on the road branches away from the river past the hideous industrial site at Fornoli and onto the still functioning spa of Bagni di Lucca, where a few of the less fashionable Italians come to take the waters.

Bagni di Lucca has the feeling of a place that has long passed its hey-day, but despite this (or perhaps because of it) it retains a definite charm of its own. Nestling amid chestnut trees in the high hills of the Garfagnana, the little town still has an air of faded 19th-century elegance with a small public garden, a disused casino and an overgrown English cemetery, all hinting at days when Bagni bustled with the importance of a fashionable Spa-town. The local hot springs were already famous in the Middle Ages under the name Bagni di Corsena but it was not until the 18th and 19th centuries, with the arrival of Napoleon and the Bourbons, that the little resort really took off. Soon it had become the summer haunt of such celebrities as Byron, Shelley, Heine, Montaigne, the Brownings and Ouida. The Casino (supposedly the first in Europe) was built in 1836, by Mathis and Ginestet who later moved to Monaco where they built a bigger and more famous one in Monte Carlo. Most of the little town runs along the edge of the river Lima, (a tributary of the Serchio) but perhaps the nicest part is up the steep shady road leading to **Bagni Caldi**. Here there is a small piazza, with a bar where the locals drink and the large, shabby Hotel Savoia which, like the town itself, has seen better days.

The wooded hill country around Bagni is peppered with fine villas and, further into the mountains, crumbling unspoilt villages reached by long drives up endlessly twisting roads. In the little village of **Benabbio**, dominated by its *rocca*, the 13th-century church contains a Renaissance triptych and two statues carved by Jacopo della Quercia's father Pietro d'Angelo di Guarnieri. Many of the little *pievi* in these lovely villages have something of interest tucked away, and, if the drive is long, the air is fresh and there is nearly always a small and friendly bar where you can slake your thirst.

A few miles north of Bagni, perched above the new town, is the small medieval city of **Barga**. In the Middle Ages Barga became important as a fortress, jealously guarding the narrow Serchio valley route through the mountains and, as such, a constant target for the bigger towns to the north, east and south. The best way to enter the old town is to go through the fortified Porta Reale, decorated with a della Robbia Virgin and Child, and walk up the narrow streets towards the Duomo. The biscuit-yellow cathedral was begun in the 9th century, but its austerely plain façade shows the influence of the Lombard Romanesque. Above the main door is a charming old carved frieze showing the pleasures of the wine growers. After an earthquake at the beginning of this century much of the little cathedral had to be rebuilt, but luckily its greatest treasure – a superb 12th-century pulpit – has remained intact. Exquisitely carved and delicately decorated with red and black, it depicts scenes from the lives of Mary and Christ and stands on fine columns supported by lions and an old man squatting. Another fascinating object is the primitive wooden polychrome St Christopher, possibly carved around the year 1000.

Further up the Serchio pass, through more dramatic countryside, is the town of **Castelnuovo di Garfagnana**, slightly claustrophobically hemmed in by mountains. Castelnuovo has a restored 13th-century castle, and a cathedral belonging to the beginning of the 16th century which contains various works of art including a della Robbia *St Joseph*.

The Lunigiana

Driving still further to the north-west, you come to the small mountain range of the Lunigiana which, although officially part of Tuscany since 1859, has a different feel to the rest of the province. Some of the region is rather dominated by the two great north–south roads that run parallel through Pontremoli to La Spezia, but high in the hills are plenty of shy villages, refreshingly cool in summer but bleakly cold in winter: Bagnone, Pieve di Monti, Montereggio and Rossano.

Between the mountains of the Lunigiana and those of the Alpi Apuani lie the biggest and most successful of the marble quarries grouped around the industrial marble towns of Carrara and Massa, capital of the province. Although **Carrara** still preserves a lovely Pisan-style Romanesque cathedral, the town is generally modern and of interest mainly to those who wish to look into the marble-quarrying business. The best quality marble from these mountains is the snow-white *statuario*: it was this that Michelangelo used to create his masterpieces. Sometimes, on receiving a commission, he would come and stay in the area so that he would be on hand at the quarries to pick out the blocks he wanted. The quarrying itself was, and is, exhausting and occasionally dangerous work, and visitors who arrive with a romantic view of the proceedings are invariably disillusioned by the reality. Even the most indefatigable Tuscanophile of this century, Edward Hutton, found Carrara and the quarries a disappointment:

> . . . busy with the frightful labour among the stones in the heart of the mountains, where no green thing has ever grown or even a bird built her nest, where in summer the sun looks down like some enormous moloch, and in winter the frost and the cold scourge them to their labour in the horrid ghostly twilight, the people work . . . Here, cut by the most hideous machinery with a noise like the shrieking of iron, the mantelpieces and washstands of every jerry-built house and obscene emporium of machine-mad furniture are sawn out of the rock. There is no joy in this labour, and the savage, harsh yell of the machines drowns any song that of old might have lightened the toil. Blasted out of the mountains by slaves, some 13,000 of them, dragged by tortured and groaning animals, the marble that might have built a Parthenon is sold to the manufacturer to decorate the houses of the middle classes, the studios of the incompetent, the streets of our trumpery cities.

A few kilometres away, **Massa** too is dominated by quarries, marble yards and workshops. Like Carrara, though, it has an old part of town worth visiting for those who take the time to find it. The centre is the Piazza Aranci, where the descendants of the great feudal family of Malaspina built their bold 17th-century palace, the Palazzo Cybo Malaspina. A few minutes' walk from here is the Duomo, which was begun in the 15th century and contains the sunken burial chapel of the Cybo Malaspina. Just outside the town is their 16th-century Renaissance-style palace which was built on the site of the medieval castle. Another mining town is **Pietrasanta**, also close to the sea, whose main interest

Carrara – the Fantiscritti marble quarry

lies in the annual festival of marble-carving which runs every year from July to September in the Consorzio Artigiano. Though these towns lack the grace of much of Tuscany they do have a certain fascination.

The northern coast

These days the northern coast of Tuscany has little to recommend it. Traditionally the smartest resort is **Forte dei Marmi**, right in the north of the province, which has a good beach and rather more upmarket facilities than some of the other areas but is still dismally overcrowded in summer. The fort after which it is named was built by grand Duke Leopold I in 1789. Travelling south down the sweltering coast road one passes the slightly scruffier areas of Marina di Pietrasanta and Camaiore, coming soon to the biggest and most popular of the seaside towns: **Viareggio**. In 1920 the writer Norman Douglas visited Viareggio and was moved to make the following comment:

> For this is a modern town built on a plain of mud and sand, a town of heartrending monotony, the least picturesque of all cities in the peninsula, the least Italian. It has not even a central piazza! . . . The people are birds of prey: a shallow and rapacious brood who fleece visitors during those summer weeks and live on the proceeds for the rest of the year.

To my mind it still has little to recommend it, dominated as it is by the busy coast road and with a pocket-handkerchief of a public beach where almost every inch is taken up by the oiled brown bodies of the Turin Fiat workers in tiny black trunks. But Viareggio does have historical importance, particularly to the British, for it was less than a mile north of here that Shelley's body was washed up after his ill-fated sailing trip in 1822. Later his remains were burnt on the beach, in accordance with the quarantine laws, a dismal ceremony attended by his close friends Byron, Leigh Hunt and Trelawny.

A few miles away is the home of another great artist; the Italian composer Giacomo Puccini. He lived by Lake Massaciúccoli at what is now called **Torre del Lago Puccini**. The lake is actually far more pleasant than the coast and has a couple of reasonable seafood restaurants on its shores. It is possible to visit the villa where Puccini lived until his death in 1924, and where he wrote these mournful words:

> Non ho un amico
> Mi sento solo,
> anche la musica
> Triste mi fa.
> Quando la morte.
> Verrà a trovarmi
> Sarò felice di riposarmi.

I have no friend
I feel alone:
Even my music
Fills me with sadness.
When death finds me
I shall be happy to rest.

Practical Information

Hotels and Restaurants

LUCCA   *Hotel Universo* (tel. 43678) Piazza Puccini 1 (otherwise known as the Piazza del Giglio), Piazza Napoleone. Traditionally Lucca's grandest hotel, central and fairly elegant. As in most of Lucca's hotels, advance booking is a must. The hotel has a reasonable restaurant although the Giglio next door is perhaps more interesting.
La Luna (tel. 42236) Via Fillungo Corte Compagni 12; *Ilaria*. Via del Fosso 20. Both of these are small, pleasant, reasonable and very central. *La Luna* is slightly more upmarket and has its own car park.

CAMAIORE   *Peralta* (tel. (0584) 951230) Beautifully situated in the hills above Viareggio, a small group of old buildings attractively turned into a charming informal hotel with a swimming pool.

BAGNI DI LUCCA   *Bridge Hotel* (tel. (0583) 97147) Ponte a Serraglio. A well run hotel near the river. A few minutes walk along the river is a good, small *casalinga* restaurant.
Up in Bagni Caldi is the large crumbling (rarely full) *Hotel Savoia*, extremely cheap, and with an air of having seen better days.

FORTE DI MARMI   *Hotel di Tirreno* (tel. (0584) 83333) Viale Morin 7. A family hotel with a good clean beach and nice garden.

VIAREGGIO   *Principe di Piemonte* (tel. (0584) 50122) Piazza Puccini 1. Large, smart and Edwardian.

Museums

LUCCA
Museo Nazionale   Villa Guinigi, open weekdays 09.00–14.00; Sun and holidays 09.00–14.00; closed Mon.
Pinacoteca Nazionale   Palazzo Mansi. Via Galli Tassi 43, open weekdays 09.00–19.00; Sun and hols 09.00–13.00; closed Mon.

VILLAS OUTSIDE LUCCA
Villa Torrigiani   2km south of Segromino, open April–Oct daily 09.30–

11.30 and 14.30–19.30; winter, weekends only 09.00–11.30 and 14.30–17.00.

Villa Imperiale   Marlia, open July–Oct Tues, Thurs and Sun 09.00–12.00 and 15.00–18.00; Nov–June Tues–Sat 09.00–12.00 and 15.00–18.00.

Villa Mansi   4km east of Marlia, open summer 09.00–13.00 and 15.30–20.00; winter 10.00–12.30 and 14.30–17.00.

CARRARA

Mostra Nazionale Marmi e Machine (mining museum)   Viale XX Settembre, open Sat 10.00–13.00 and 16.00–19.00; Mon, Thurs and Sun 10.00–13.00

Casa Puccini   Torre del Lago Puccini, open summer 10.00–12.00 and 15.30–18.00; winter 10.00–12.00 and 14.30–17.00; closed Mon.

4. THE PROVINCE OF PISA

Pisa is one of the most visited towns in Italy. It is also one of the most underrated. The vast majority of tourists never get beyond the Cathedral square, with its famous tower, and perhaps the railway station. The scores of lovely Romanesque churches, the faded ochres and pinks of the old town and wide elegant sweep of the Arno all remain unnoticed except by a small proportion of visitors who have time on their hands and are not prepared to rush like madmen from one 'major site' to the next.

The early history of Pisa is somewhat obscure. The indications are that it was probably a Greek trading colony, founded by the Phoceans some time between the 7th and 5th centuries BC. Later the Etruscans settled there but the town only became important under the Romans, who established it as one of Italy's main ports. In the 1st century AD, it was greatly enlarged under the Emperor Octavian. Pisa's harbour continued to thrive throughout the next thousand years despite repeated Saracen raids. When Pisa (aided by the Normans) defeated the Saracens at Messina in Palermo in 1063, this battle marked the start of the town's greatest period when it was to become briefly the most powerful republic in the Mediterranean. The 11th century was characterised by a tremendous spirit of success and expansion. Pisa's great seafaring rivals Genoa, Amalfi and Venice were all conquered, as were the islands of Sardinia, Corsica and the Balearics. Much of the city's enormous wealth came from trade with the Orient which had been built up since the First Crusade when, as well as accumulating huge amounts of booty, the Pisans set up invaluable trading posts along the coast of the Levant. It was at this time that the great buildings of the Piazza dei Miracoli were begun. Money was to be no object and the new buildings were designed to reflect the magnificence of the town's achievements. Towards the end of the century, Pisa also became one of the first towns in central Italy to be successfully governed by ordinary citizens, who were formed into a Council of Twelve.

There followed 200 years of prosperity. Pisa, which had taken up the Ghibelline cause, was rewarded by the Emperor Frederick Barbarossa with still more territory, made up of huge tracts of the Italian mainland. But these conquests constantly needed defending, and in 1284 Pisa suffered a catastrophic defeat by Genoa at Meloria. It was a blow from which the town

Pisa – Campo dei Miracoli with the cathedral and Leaning Tower

could not recover. And as the neighbouring land cities of Lucca, Siena and, particularly, Florence, grew ever more powerful, the maritime port of Pisa started to decline. The town's heyday was over. Gradually the colonies fell away while, within the walls, chaos broke out. The Council of Twelve was no longer a stable institution and the great families of the town – the Appiani, the Uguccione della Faggiola, the Gherardesca and the Gambacorti – all vied for supremacy. The most powerful of these families, the Appiani, were finally the victors and held the town in uneasy sway until the Visconti from Milan took over. But in 1406, after a long siege, Pisa fell to her greatest rival, Florence. After the town, the port also capitulated and, apart from a brief period around the beginning of the 16th century, Pisa never really regained her independence.

Every tourist who comes to Pisa starts in the same place, the green sward of land near the city's northern walls known, not without some justification, as the **Campo dei Miracoli**, the Field of Miracles. It is here that you will find some of the most beautiful buildings in the world and, of course, one of the most bizarre – the lovely **campanile** known to everyone as the **Leaning Tower of Pisa**, unfortunately now closed to the public for its own protection.

However casually or conscientiously visitors study Pisa's most famous building, they all come away preoccupied by the same thing. The fact that it is a lovely graceful Romanesque building remains of secondary importance; what really grips the attention is the undeniable fact that it really does lean quite alarmingly, at an angle that increases at the rate of roughly 1mm every year. The American writer, Mark Twain, describes the thrill of fear he experienced

38

after climbing the 294 steps which spiral endlessly around the hollow interior, at the end of the last century.

> Standing on the summit, one does not feel altogether comfortable when he looks down from the high side; but to crawl on your breast to the verge on the lower side and try to stretch your neck out far enough to see the base of the tower, makes your flesh creep, and convinces you for a single moment, in spite of your philosophy, that the building is falling. You handle yourself very carefully, all the time, under the silly impression that if it is *not* falling, your trifling weight will start it unless you are particular not to 'bear down' on it.

In the past there has also been much dispute as to *why* it leans, and why the bottom storeys lean more heavily than the rest. Travelling some years earlier than Mark Twain, his countryman and fellow writer James Fenimore Cooper was convinced that the architect deliberately designed it at an angle because

> an architect silly enough to erect such a monstrosity would be as likely to begin his folly at the bottom as anywhere else . . . Caprices of this sort are not unknown; most men, indeed, fancying it a greater achievement of genius to make a thing that is extravagant than a thing whose merits consists in exquisite fitness.

Incredibly, this was actually quite a popular theory at the time. It is now fairly certain that in fact the tower was begun in 1174 by the great Bonanno Pisano who continued it for three storeys but then halted construction because one side of the 3m foundations had severely sunk. The building was then left incomplete for around 100 years before another Pisan, Giovanni di Simone, built the next four storeys at a slightly more upright angle in an attempt to right the building's incline. The top gallery was finally added in 1350 and houses the seven bells. The oldest bell, known as La Pasquareccia, was installed in 1301 and was rung on special public occasions. It rang to record what was perhaps Pisa's most famous act of injustice, the starving to death of the traitor Ugolino della Gherardesca and his innocent children, so bitterly mourned by Dante. In the 16th century the great astronomer Galileo Galilei made better use of the tower, dropping objects from it to establish the principles of gravity.

The Cathedral and Baptistery

The **Cathedral** was the first building to be started in the Piazza. It was begun in 1063, on the design of the architect Buscheto, in thanksgiving for Pisa's victory over the Saracens at Messina and Palermo. It was consecrated, although still unfinished, in 1118. Built in white marble decorated with grey stripes and inlaid geometrical designs in soft-coloured stone, it was the first real example of the Pisan–Romanesque style, taking over where hitherto most of the city's churches had followed the influence of the Lombardy school.

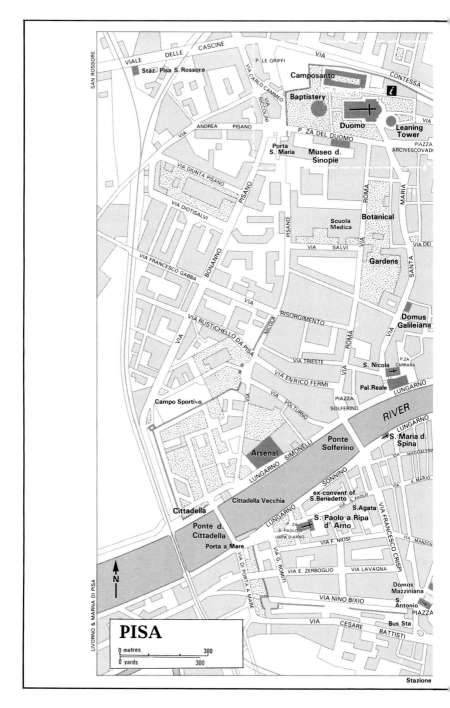

PISA

0 metres 300
0 yards 300

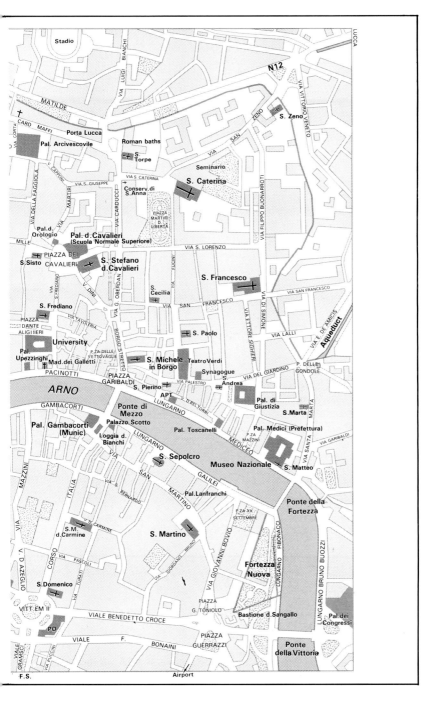

41

The new style owed much to ideas picked up in the east, from the Crusades and subsequent trading. The façade is a classic example: it was designed in the 13th century by Rainaldo, with pillared galleries rising on top of one another, four storeys high. This style quickly caught on in other parts of Tuscany particularly in neighbouring Lucca where many of the churches are designed in the Pisan– Romanesque genre. The original doors in the façade were by the sculptor Bonanno Pisano, but these were lost in the terrible fire of 1595 and later replaced by the school of Giambologna. The main door, flanked by two ornately carved pillars, depicts scenes from the life of the Virgin, divided by charming reliefs of plants and animals. The two side doors tell the story of the life of Christ. On the top of the façade perches a Virgin by Andrea Pisano, between two angels from the school of Giovanni Pisano. (Andrea (1270–1348) was unrelated to the great Pisan father and son Nicola (c.1220–1284) and Giovanni (c.1245–1314) but much of his work shows Giovanni's influence.)

Walking round the Cathedral to the right, we come to the Porta di San Ranieri, the entrance to the south transept. These doors are the original ones by Bonanno, cast in 1180 and illustrating scenes from the life of Christ. The 24 panels are worth looking at closely. They have a wonderful lively simplicity and naïveté about them and a strong Byzantine feel.

The interior of the cathedral is very lofty and grand. The ceiling, which was burnt in the fire of 1595, has since been replaced with a fine carved ornamentation of blue and gold wood. The fire also irreparably damaged the original paintings in the nave; there is now a collection of 17th- and 18th-century works of varying interest and charm. At the end of the centre aisle hangs the bronze chandelier known as the Lamp of Galileo because it was traditionally believed that Galileo first developed the theory of pendulums from watching it swing from side to side. Actually the lamp was first installed in 1587, some six years after Galileo's discovery – which rather detracts from the legend. Behind the lamp in the apse is a large mosaic of Christ between the Virgin and St John the Evangelist. The mosaic dates back to the early 14th century, and it is thought that it was worked on by the great early Florentine painter, Cimabue. Recent critics suggest that the master's contribution is apparent only in the face of the Evangelist, which does seem to show a superior quality to the rest. Below the apse are various works by Domenico Beccafumi (1489–1551) and on the altar a bronze crucifix by Giambologna. On the side pillars hang two good oil paintings, a gentle *Madonna and Child* by Antonio Sogliani (1492–1544) on the left, and del Sarto's St Agnes with a lamb on the right. St Agnes, in beautifully painted garments of orange and rose, looks pensively heavenward against a Leonardesque landscape of a castle on a hill.

In the left aisle of the right transept is the fine sculptural tomb of the Emperor of Luxembourg Henry VII by Tino da Camaiano. The Emperor was much admired by Dante who referred to him as 'Alto Arrigo' (Tall Harry). Around the sarcophagus is a frieze of the 12 apostles. The life-size sculptures of the Emperor and his followers which used to surround the tomb have for some reason been relocated in the Camposanto, destroying the intended effect.

Undoubtedly the greatest treasure in the cathedral is the magnificent pulpit of Giovanni Pisano, which was begun in 1302 and took around eight years to complete. The pulpit is built as an octagon but the general effect is round. It is supported on a mixture of coloured marble columns, some of which are supported by lions, and allegorical figures. The scenes in the eight panels are taken from the New Testament, starting with the birth of John the Baptist, following the life of Christ, and finishing with the Last Judgement. This was Giovanni's fourth and final pulpit and was finished a few years before his death. In it we can see clearly the advances he had made since helping his father Nicola on the pulpit in the Baptistery some 40 years earlier. His success in fusing the classical elements that so captivated his father with the prevailing Gothic style marks a giant step towards Renaissance sculpture.

The **Baptistery** was begun in 1153, about 100 years after the start of the cathedral. The inscription by the main door names Diotisalvi as the founding architect. Like the other buildings in the square, the Baptistery took a long time to complete and various eminent artists worked on it. The sculptor Nicola Pisano became master of works in 1260, followed by Giovanni. The building was finally finished at the end of the 14th century.

The Baptistery is a three-storey circular building with four portals. The most important of these opens towards the cathedral and has round it some fine carvings by an unknown 13th-century artist. On the right-hand pillar are the Apostles, the Descent into Hell and David, while on the left are the months of the year. The carved architrave above the door shows Jesus between Mary and John the Baptist surrounded by saints, above some scenes from John's life. In the lunette above is a copy of Giovanni Pisano's *Madonna and Child*, the original of which can be found in the Cathedral Museum. Most of the other statues on the second storey of the building are from the school of Nicola Pisano, but many of them have been replaced by copies. Some of the originals have been put inside the Baptistery and others have gone to the Museo di San Matteo. On the top of the dome perches a 2m high John the Baptist, installed at the end of the 14th century.

Inside, the Baptistery has a spacious simple feeling. Around the walls are the weatherbeaten statues by Nicola Pisano and his school, which were brought inside to protect them from further damage. In the centre is Guido Bigarelli da Como's huge inlaid marble font. Around the edge are four small basins for baptising infants while the main area is for the total immersion of adults. But by far the most important thing in the Baptistery is Nicola Pisano's magnificent pulpit, carved with the aid of his son Giovanni and others between 1255 and 1260. The figures on the corner pillars represent the Virtues while, somewhat squashed into the sides of the arches, are the Prophets. The main panels show episodes from the life of Christ. The pulpit shows the full extent of the classical influence on the sculptor who had carefully studied Roman and Greek sarcophagi found in the locality. Nicola's faces are, in general, stylised and expressionless, with little of the dramatic intensity of his son's work. Even so, the pulpit is extremely powerful and leaves one with a clear impression of an unforgettable, if rigid, beauty.

If you are inside the Baptistery for any length of time you will probably hear the Sacristan demonstrate the building's remarkable echo. As he sings various notes in succession (luckily they seem to employ Sacristans with good voices in Pisa) a harmony builds up from the echoes that reverberate around the dome. At the end of the performance he collects a tip and the magic dissolves as the crowd shuffles out of the door, blinking in the sudden bright sunlight.

The Camposanto

Running along the city wall to the north of the Piazza is another dazzling white edifice – the long marble building of the **Camposanto**. In 1204 the Pisan Archbishop Ubaldo dei Lanfranchi returned from the Holy Land bearing sacred earth taken from the hill of Golgotha where Christ was crucified. The earth apparently had miraculous properties and could reduce fresh corpses to bare skeletons within a day. It was placed in the piazza, and in 1270 the Camposanto was begun to gather together the graves which were accumulating around the Cathedral. It was started by Giovanni di Simone in 1270 but, like the surrounding buildings, took centuries to complete. As time passed, more sepulchral monuments and ancient sculptures were collected beneath the cemetery's low roof. The walls were frescoed by the leading painters of Tuscany: Benozzo Gozzoli, Spinello Aretino and Taddeo Gaddi. The building remained thus, a rich gallery of painting and sculpture, until 1944 when the air raids of the Second World War melted the roofs and the lead ran down the walls, destroying many of the pictures. During the extensive and painstaking restoration that followed, many of the preliminary sketches or Sinopie came to light. Some of these are now in the little **Museo delle Sinopie**, housed in the 13th-century Spedale di Papa Alessandro IV on the far side of the Piazza and give an idea of what the paintings were originally like.

One enters the Camposanto through a plain door beneath the Gothic tabernacle of the *Madonna and Child with Saints* by the school of Giovanni Pisano which perches uneasily on the edge of the roof. Once inside, one is immediately struck by the beauty of the long cloistered interior, with its graceful mullioned windows looking over a rectangle of perfect lawn. Charles Dickens describes them better than I can:

> . . . such cloisters, with such playing lights and shadows falling through their delicate tracery on the stone pavement, as surely the dullest memory could never forget.

On the walls are the sad remains of Gozzoli's Old Testament stories and Taddeo Gaddi's Life of San Ranieri and Job. Below them are a collection of Greek and Roman sarcophagi and other sculpted monuments, the great hanging chains were used to close the city gates in the days when Pisa was a great Marine Republic.

In the large Salone degli Affreschi is great 14th-century fresco cycle known as *The Triumph of Death* by an unknown master (known as the Maestro del Trionfo della Morte). The paintings show The Triumph of Death (look at the noble onlookers shuddering and holding their noses), the Last Judgement and Hell, followed by stories of the anchorite hermits. There are also some fine sculptures in this room, most notably a striking *Madonna* by Giovanni Pisano and an elongated *Baptist* from his father Nicola's workshop.

From the Duomo to the Arno

Just south of the Campo dei Miracoli are the **Botanic Gardens**, laid out by Cosimo I in 1543. Nearby in Via Santa Maria (No.26) one comes to the house of Pisa's most famous son, the great scientist and astrologer Galileo Galilei. Galileo was born in Pisa in 1564 and by the age of 25 was already a mathematics professor at the university. His house now has a library and study centre but is open to the public most mornings and afternoons. Further down the road is the restored 12th-century church of **San Nicola**, also with a bell tower which leans, though much less dramatically than its grander neighbour.

A few minutes' walk away, on the site of the Roman forum, is Pisa's second most interesting square – the **Piazza dei Cavalieri**. In 1561 Grand Duke Cosimo I decided completely to redevelop the square (known previously as the Piazza delle Sette Vie – the meeting place of seven roads) as the centre for his newly founded chivalric order, the Knights of Santo Stefano. The central building, the **Palazzo dei Cavalieri**, was remodelled by Vasari in 1562 as the initiation and training school for prospective knights. In the high niches are busts of the Medici Grand Dukes. The lovely *sgrafitto* decoration is mainly original but was restored at the beginning of this century. Next to the Palazzo dei Cavalieri is the **Palazzo dell'Orologio** – two towers joined by an arch by Vasari. It is from the weathered clock above the gateway that the palace took its name. The left-hand side was previously a prison, known as the Gualandi tower, where the traitor Ugolino della Gherardesca and his children were shamefully starved to death. This act of injustice towards innocent children was fiercely described by Dante in his *Inferno*.

> Oh Pisa, you thing of shame among the people of this beautiful country. Since your neighbours are slow to strike, let the islands of Gorgona and Capraia move and choke up the mouth of the Arno, so that every one of your citizens is drowned. For even if Ugolino did betray his country, his children should never have been tormented.

On the other side of the Palazzo dei Cavalieri is the elegant church of **Santo Stefano dei Cavalieri**, also built by Vasari, on the shell of an earlier church. Above the entrance is the Medici crest, the balls known as Le Palle, that bear witness to the great family all over Tuscany. The Maltese cross above was the emblem of the Order of Santo Stefano. Inside, the walls are hung with Islamic flags and tapestries, loot from the Crusades. On the ravishingly decorated wooden ceiling are Mannerist paintings showing episodes from the history of the Order, which became increasingly piratical in its activities. The tempera paintings on the walls showing the life of St Stephen are attributed to Vasari, and the 17th-century Baroque altar is the work of Silvani and Foggini.

The area around the piazza is rich in lovely Pisan churches. Immediately to the north-west is the restored Romanesque church of San Sisto, built in 1073 on the site of the earlier church of San Rocco. North-east of the square, in the **Piazza Santa Caterina**, is the church of the same name with a fine, typically Pisan, Romanesque façade. Inside is the tomb of Archbishop Salterelli, and an *Annunciation* spanning the altar carved in the 14th century by Nino Pisano. The wonderful altarpiece of Thomas Aquinas was probably done in the same century by Francesco Traini. Another fine church can be found at the north-east corner of town – the restored 10th-century San Zeno on the site of a Roman temple just near the city wall. Heading back towards the river and the centre of town, one reaches the Piazza San Francesco. This rather strangely-shaped church was probably built by Giovanni di Simone in the 13th century. Inside are the remains of the unfortunate Pisan Ugolino della Gherardesca and his sons. There is a 14th-century polyptych carved in marble by Tommaso Pisano and, in the sacristy, some good Saints by Taddeo di Bartolo. In the Piazza San Paolo all' Orto is a 12th-century church much altered in the 15th century and with the addition of a 17th-century façade.

The whole of this part of Pisa is charming and fascinating and surprisingly free of tourists. The main street to the north of the river is the **Borgo Stretto** (Narrow Street), a lively arcaded alley where shops and bars mingle with fine houses and palaces. Terraced between two buildings is the charming 10th-century church of **San Michele in Borgo**. Like most of the Pisan churches it was revamped in the early 14th century when Fra Agnelli designed the beautiful marble façade. Inside is a 13th-century painting of St Michael which was discovered during rebuilding, after the ravages of the Second World War. Across the street is the colourful market which meanders back through narrow streets and small piazzas selling fruit and vegetables, meat and fish. Here also are various cheap family restaurants and cafés.

Near the river at the corner of Vie Cavour and Palestro stands **San Pierino**, sometimes called San Pietro in Vinculus (St Peter in Chains). San Pierino was built around the turn of the 12th century with another good façade, a fine aisled interior, and a long crypt which runs under the whole church. Also inside is a 13th-century *Crucifixion* and a 14th-century *Annunciation* over the door.

Near the 13th-century Medici Palace on the Lungarno Mediceo is the Civic Museum, the **Museo Nazionale di San Matteo**. It is housed in a pleasant cloistered building that was formerly a Benedictine Convent and then, briefly, a prison and a military barracks. The Museum was originally conceived in the late 1940s to house works from the town's artistic heyday in the 12th and 13th centuries but has recently become more general in scope. The ground floor is mainly devoted to sculpture. In the first rooms are early Romanesque statues (11th–13th century) taken from the cathedral complex. In the rooms dedicated to Giovanni Pisano one finds a touching grandeur in these powerful blocks of stone worn down by centuries of exposure to the elements. In Room No.8, the Hall of the Wooden Sculptures, is Andrea Pisano's simple but delicate polychrome *Angel and Virgin Annunziata*. Like the sculptures, the paintings are arranged chronologically, beginning with splendid early Pisan crucifixions and Madonnas, some dating back to the 13th century, with stern Byzantine faces and writhing, strangely defined bodies.

Many of the later paintings come from other parts of Tuscany; they date from a time when Pisa was no longer an important marine republic, and her spurt of artistic creativity had all but ceased. There are also Sienese pictures by Simone Martini and Taddeo di Bartolo, Florentine ones by decorative International Gothic painters, Gentile di Fabriano and Benozzo Gozzoli. Among the most interesting of the pictures is a polyptych panel of St Paul, painted in 1426 for the Carmine Chapel by the brilliant Masaccio. Among the museum's other treasures are illuminated manuscripts, armour and ceramics — all in all a formidable collection and very worth seeing.

Outside the museum flows the Arno, wider and perhaps more elegant than at Florence, lined with houses, shops and palaces washed in pale ochres, corals and yellows. Next to the museum is the 13th-century **Medici Palace** with its double and triple mullioned windows, now used as the Prefecture. Further down on the Lungarno Pacinotti is the early 15th-century **Agostini Palace**, richly decorated in the style of the day with raised terracotta. Once this type of decoration could be found all over Pisa, but now the Palazzo Agostini is the only surviving example. Further along the Lungarno Pacinotti is the **Giornata Palace**, a fine Renaissance building now attached to the University.

South of the Arno

On the other side of the river, on the Lungarno Galileo Galilei, is the octagonal church of **San Sepolcro** built in 1153 by Diotisalvi, later much restored. Just beyond it is the **Scotto Palace** which appears to have fallen on hard times since Shelley inhabited it in 1820–22. Walking seawards one reaches the *Lungarno Gambacorti*, with the 14th-century family palace where the one time ruler of the city Piero Gambacorti was murdered by his enemies in 1393. Facing the palace is the 17th-century **Loggia di Banchi** where an antique market is regularly held. Further along the river is the amazing little church of **Santa Maria della Spina**, built to house a thorn from Christ's crown brought back from a crusade to the Holy Land. The little oratory was substantially rebuilt in the ornate Pisan Gothic style by Lupo Capomaestro in 1323. Its initial position was even closer to the river but in 1871 it was dismantled stone by stone and pinnacle by pinnacle and reassembled here to prevent any more water damage. Some of the sculptures in the many niches are now in the museum and have been replaced by copies, but the little structure still feels complete and unspoilt.

The little church of Santa Maria della Spina by the Arno

Another fine church in this area is **San Paolo in Ripa d'Arno** near the Ponte a Mare. It was begun in 805 but substantially enlarged in the 12th and 13th centuries, when a truly lovely Romanesque façade was added. In the fine simple interior are some of the original columns from the old church, and there is a 14th-century stained glass window in the apse. The 12th-century tomb of the Archbishop Burgundio is made from an important Roman sarcophagus. Another early sarcophagus has actually been built into the wall in the left transept. Next to the church is the 12th-century octagonal brick chapel of St Agatha, probably by the prolific Pisan architect Diotisalvi who was also responsible for the Baptistery.

The **Ponte a Mare** spans the river on the edge of old Pisa and has a good view of the city particularly in the evening sun. It was here, one evening, that Shelley watching the city's reflection, wrote these haunting lines:

> *Within the surface of the fleeting river*
> *The wrinkled image of the city lay,*
> *Immovably unquiet, and forever*
> *It trembles, but it never fades away; . . .*

Just over the bridge is the old city Citadella (fortress) rebuilt by the Florentines when they conquered the city in the 15th century. Next to it are the low buildings of the Arsenale delle Gallee, built by Grand-Duke Ferdinando I as a military shipyard for the Knights of Santo Stefano.

In general, the south of the river is less interesting than the north. Much of it is modern, dominated by busy one-way streets where the traffic roars ceaselessly. Around the railway station is the usual paraphernalia of boring hotels, postcard shops and bars. But towards the river things improve; leaving the Corso Italia, you will find the churches of the Carmine and San Martino and some small forgotten alleys in which to wander.

The environs of Pisa

For those tired of the city there are various, not very wonderful, beaches along the Pisan coast where it is possible to swim and sunbathe. Otherwise you can climb into a car or bus (heading for Marina di Pisa, on the coast) and visit the old church of **San Piero a Grado** in a village of the same name about 8km south-west of town. Legend has it that it was here that St Peter landed on his journey from Antioch to Rome, and since that day there has been a church here. The present church was built in the 11th century and is a marvellous building: sturdy Romanesque with four apses, made from glowing, honey-brown tufa. In the lovely, simple interior are some 14th-century frescoes that have been attributed to Deodato Orlandi. Recently the crypt has been excavated and parts of a 6th-century church exposed. On the nearby coast are various fish restaurants; but for the best family restaurant try Ugo, a bit further north at Migliarino.

Another excursion can be made to the **Certosa di Pisa** about 15km out of town near the little village of Gabella. Set in attractive countryside on the edge of the Monte Pisano, this Certosa (charterhouse) was originally founded by the Carthusians in 1366. In the 17th–18th centuries it was completely remodelled and is now an elegant Neo-Baroque complex in a tranquil setting. Near the Certosa in the village of Calci is a 12th-century *pieve* or parish church with a two-storey Pisan façade. Inside are the remains of a lesser known Saint, Ermolaio, Patron of the valley.

Picking up the main road to Florence which passes nearby, one is soon at the little furniture-manufacturing town of **Cascina**, where the Florentines defeated the Pisans in a great battle in 1364. The 14th-century Oratory of

St John contains frescoes attributed to Martino di Bartolommeo and painted in the 14th century. The church of Santa Maria dates back to the 1100s and has been little altered since. In neighbouring Vicopisano is an old *fortezza* that was restored by the great Florentine architect Brunelleschi in the first part of the 15th century.

Midway between Pisa and Florence is the town of **SAN MINIATO AL TEDESCO**. Its name, San Miniato of the Germans, is a throwback to the days when the town was a base of the German Holy Roman Empire which claimed the allegiance of the Ghibellines. Under Emperor Otto I, from 936 to 973, San Miniato became the seat of the Imperial Vicars. It was here that the last, and possibly the greatest, of the German Margraves in Tuscany, Countess Matilda, was born in 1046. It was also thought to be the ancestral home of a later but equally great European family – the Bonapartes. In 1796 Napoleon visited the town to meet a certain Filippo Buonaparte whom he believed to be the last surviving member of the original family.

San Miniato is situated on a hill 156m above the edge of the Arno plain. It is dominated by a 12th-century *rocca* of Emperor Frederick II (known as Barbarossa) which was rebuilt after its destruction in the Second World War. The great tower has a sad and sinister history related by Dante in his *Inferno*. Apparently Piero della Vigna, most brilliant of the chancellors of Frederick II, killed himself here in despair at having been falsely accused and then blinded by the Emperor. The shorter tower, the **Torre di Matilde**, has been turned into a campanile for the Cathedral. The **Cathedral of Assunta e San Genesio** was itself begun in the 12th century but subsequently much altered. The extravagantly decorated Neo-Baroque interior was added in the 19th century. To the left of the building is the 13th-century **Bishop's Palace**, now housing the Museo Diocesano, which has an excellent selection of Tuscan paintings, ranging from Fra Bartolomeo to Filippo Lippi and Verrocchio. Outside in the square are lovely sweeping views over the Arno valley.

A short walk away in the Piazza del Popolo is the 14th-century church of **San Domenico**, with a rough, unfinished façade. Inside are various 17th–18th century frescoes and a fine carved 15th-century tomb attributed to Bernardo Rossellino, perhaps from a design by Donatello. Over the second altar on the right is a powerful early 14th-century Crucifix. Good churches abound in San Miniato. There is the church of San Francesco, built in 1276 on the site of an earlier building. There is also the 14th-century **Lorentino church** which has good Giottoesque frescoes. Up some steps opposite the 14th-century Palazzo Communale with its modern façade is the 18th-century **Sanctuary of the Cross**. San Miniato makes a pretty good stopping-place on the otherwise rather dull road to Florence.

In the province of Pisa, as in most regions of Tuscany, it is impossible to generalise about the landscape which changes dramatically from place to place. There is the flat Arno plain dotted with sprawling villages, the small mountain range known as the Monte Pisano, and industrial towns like Pontadera (the birthplace of the sculptor Andrea Pisano). Also some of the loveliest countryside in the whole of Tuscany is to be found in this province, in the high and rolling Volterran hills dotted with farms and settlements (like the pretty little town of Castagneto Carducci where the mournful 19th-century poet Giosué Carducci was born). The great hills roll on and on, growing steeper towards the Colline Metallifere, and plummeting sharply down to the sea near Cecina.

Volterra

Right up on the tufa crags that separate the Val d'Elsa and the Val de Cecina perches the ancient town of Volterra. **VOLTERRA** is a fascinating place, but tourists on a limited time schedule generally prefer to visit Volterra's ancient rival, the more picturesque hill town of San Gimignano, some 20km away. To visitors San Gimignano is more immediately accessible with its picture-book towers and its best-kept-village aura. But while San Gimignano belies its violent and war-ridden past, Volterra shows its sterner nature to all. Guide-books from the last 200 years describe the town as dour and windswept, a forbidding fortress settlement, eking out its time on crumbling rocks, and dominated by a huge prison.

Like most Tuscan towns Volterra has lived through both boom and decline. As an Etruscan settlement it was extremely wealthy, establishing a profitable trade in alabaster, which was mined from the nearby quarries and then taken to *botteghe* to be carved. Even now the *alabastro* is still the town's major industry. The settlement was called *Velathri* and was one of the powerful Etruscan League of Twelve. The remains of the Etruscan walls show a town that was initially over twice its present size, powerful and well-defended – the walls were 14m high and over 4m deep. However, in 298BC, the town was captured and made to join the Roman league.

Volterra's history in the Dark Ages is somewhat obscure, but predictably dominated by attacks from marauding Barbarians, Goths and other Germanic tribes. Apparently in the 6th century Volterra gave refuge to a band of African Christians escaping from the Berber tribes in North Africa. In gratitude for shelter, the group's leader saved Volterra from siege by Totila who was on the rampage. The story goes that the townspeople threw huge quantities of bread over the walls, convincing the marauders that the town was so well stocked that there was no point in trying to besiege it.

In the 9th century Volterra fell under the sway of the Bishops who had been given power of government by the Emperors. The most notorious of these was tyrannical Bishop Pannocchieschi, who eventually pushed his luck so far that the people rose against him and he was assassinated. The next two Bishops did little to pacify an increasingly hostile populace and in 1239, after years of fighting and unrest, the Bishops lost power altogether. Battles ensued between the Guelph and Ghibelline factions within the town, further compli-cated by a long and bloody feud with San Gimignano and the major powers of Pisa and Florence. The beginning of the 14th century saw a brief period of calm under the wise guidance of Ottaviani Belforti. After his death chaos returned as his sons fought for leadership. Things became so bad eventually that in 1348 the Belforti family called in Florence to arbitrate.

For the Florentines this was too good an opportunity to miss; within a year they had taken control of the city. From then on, despite constant friction, the Volterrans were never really independent again, and in 1470 they were reduced to total subjection by Lorenzo de Medici. Lorenzo, worried that Florence was losing her hold over Volterra, hired the Duke of Urbino to attack the town. The result was a siege of terrible bloodiness that sits uneasily with the rest of Lorenzo's generally sophisticated diplomatic approach. Later Lorenzo built the new fort, **Il Maschio**, near the 14th-century one above the city, which now serves as a prison. One of its first prisoners was a Volterran who had been involved in the Pazzi plot that succeeded in killing Lorenzo's brother Giuliano.

The main square in Volterra, the **Piazza dei Priori**, has been the centre of civic life in the town since the Middle Ages. It is one of the loveliest squares in the region. Dominating it, the **Palazzo dei Priori** is one of the oldest civic buildings in Tuscany – its foundations were laid as early as 1208. Until the 15th century, when the town eventually fell to Florence, the building had a large loggia and a *ringhiera* (literally a haranguing place) for public addresses and meetings. The various terracottas and coats of arms on the façade commemorate Florentine governors of the city. The clock was added later. The top section of the crenellated tower replaced a wooden bell-tower dislodged in the earthquake of 1846. Inside the palace is a fine frescoed council chamber with a vaulted wooden ceiling. The frescoes have been rather uncertainly attributed to the 14th-century Florentine painter Orcagna. The building also houses an excellent picture gallery, with mainly Florentine and Sienese pictures. Look out for Luca Signorelli's *Madonna and Child* and *Annunciation*, and Rosso Fiorentino's dramatically sculptural *Deposition*. From the tower there are good views of the town and the sweeping Volterran hills.

Back in the square, one faces (to the north-east) the restored 13th-century **Palazzo Pretorio**, also built in the soft biscuit-coloured *panchina* stone that characterises the piazza. Protruding near the top of the otherwise fairly plain tower is the rather peculiar stone piglet that gives the tower its name **Il Torre Porcellino**. To the left are the Maltrasi family palaces. It was in the squat tower that prisoners were held under the beady eye of the Captain of Justice and his guard, who lived in the small palace next door. The Piazza dei Priori is also the headquarters of another of Tuscany's banks, the *Cassa di Risparmio di Volterra*, housed in the much altered 13th–14th century Inghirami building which was initially used as a Bishop's Seminary. The **Bishop's Palace** itself is next to the Palazzo dei Priori. In the 14th century it had a huge arch leading to the grain market, and for many years was used as a granary. Between the Palazzo dei Priori and the Bishop's Palace one can see the low striped marble wall of the back of the cathedral.

In contrast to its striped rear end, the front of the little **Cathedral** is simple, with three round windows and a series of blind Romanesque arches to the

Volterra – Palazzo dei Priori

top. Only the main portal has been dressed in Pisan inlaid marble, cut in simple but delicate geometric patterns. The cathedral was first consecrated in 1120 by Pope Calixtus II, but was enlarged in the Pisan style in 1254. Vasari attributes the façade to Nicola Pisano, but there is no other evidence to support this theory. The Campanile is to the left of the church at the far end of the Chapel of the Santissimo Nome di Gesú. It was rebuilt in the 15th century after collapsing, but the top storey was removed later because it appeared unsafe to a population who had at various times been the victim of earthquakes.

In the 16th century the interior of the cathedral underwent a transformation which destroyed the atmosphere of Romanesque simplicity that the outside has retained. There are various interesting examples of Tuscan sacred art here; a larger-than-life 13th-century *Deposition*, a marvellous pulpit reassembled from 12th-century carvings and a 15th-century tabernacle sculpted by the sweetest of Tuscan sculptors, Mino da Fiesole. Mino was also responsible for the two angels on either side of the altar, perched on 13th-century columns. In the Oratory are two painted terracotta groups, *The Nativity* and *Epiphany*, which were done in the 16th century, probably by the Volterran artist Zaccario Zacchi, a student of the della Robbia school. Behind the *Nativity* is a faded fresco by the decorative Florentine painter Benozzo Gozzoli in the 15th century.

The fine octagonal **Baptistry** facing the cathedral was built between 1278 and 1283 on the site of a much earlier building, possibly (as in Florence) a pagan temple. If it is locked, the sacristan of the cathedral will usually let you in to see the carved arch above the high altar which is attributed to Mino da Fiesole. The marble octagonal font, echoing the shape of the building, is 16th-century, by Andrea Sansovino. On it can be seen representations of Faith, Hope, Charity, Justice and the Baptism of Christ.

The large 14th-century building on the edge of the square is part of the **Hospital of Saint Mary Magdalen**, built by Bishop Pagani in 1383 to unite the existing small hospitals dotted around the city. At the beginning of Via Roma is the cloistered building which holds the **Museum of Sacred Art**. The contents of this museum were sadly depleted in the air raids of the Second World War, but it is still worth visiting. Among its treasures is a glazed terracotta bust of a gentle, mournful, St Linus by Andrea della Robbia. St Linus, a native of the town, became the second Pope after the death of St Peter. Also of note is a 15th-century beaten silver reliquary bust by Antonio del Pollaiuolo and a gilded bronze crucifix by the 16th-century artist Giambologna.

Following the Via Roma to where it meets the Via Ricciarelli, you find the best examples of medieval tower-houses in the city, notably the gaunt 13th-century **Palace of the Buomparenti**, joined to its neighbour by a high arch. The Via Riciarelli has other fine palaces, the **Palazzetto della Sbarba** at No.24, and the houses of the Ricciarelli further along at No.34. Many of Volterra's streets seem narrower than they really are, forced together by these gloomy towers and palaces of the Volterran nobility, the Bonaguidi, the Martinoli, the Inghirami and the Incontri. The Via di Sarti passes between more palaces. No.1, the **Palazzo Solaini**, is attributed to Antonio Sangallo the elder. Further down at No.37, the **Palazzo Viti** was designed by the great Florentine Mannerist Bartolommeo Ammannati in the 16th century. On the corner of Via di Sarti and Via Guarnacci is the little Pisan-fronted, Romanesque church of San Michele which houses a terracotta Madonna and Child thought to be by Luca della Robbia. Carrying straight on, through the Piazza XX Settembre, into the Via Don Manzoni one reaches the famous Etruscan treasure house, the **Museo Guarnacci**.

In 1785 a local prelate and fanatical archeologist, Mario Guarnacci, left the *commune* his massive collection of local finds. This, with another smaller collection, became the basis of today's museum. The collection is stupendous: some 650 Etruscan funerary urns, many in fabulous condition, mainly dating from 4th–1st centuries BC. The urns generally follow the same pattern, with a sculpted lid depicting the deceased and a detailed frieze around the base showing Etruscan customs and popular mythology – much of it Greek in origin. The result is a repetitive but fascinating look at Etruscan customs, beliefs and lifestyles. Various items stand out. There is the touching double portrait known as *degli Sposi*, (of the married couple), which has traditionally been thought to be an elderly woman and her husband who looks past her towards the afterlife. Recent archaeologists have suggested however that the woman is actually a she-devil trying to tempt the ruler away from his duty. I prefer the original interpretation; the relaxed intimacy of the couple, combined with the woman's look of sorrow, seem more fitted to husband and wife. Another much reproduced object is the Giacometti-thin bronze figure, known by the name that the poet D'Annunzio gave it: *l'ombra della sera* – Evening Shadow. The museum also contains objects from the Villanovan and Roman eras and from its leafy garden is a view over the Val d'Era.

Across the town is another fine Etruscan monument, the gate known as the **Porta all' Arco**. Much of the arch was rebuilt by the Romans after the siege of Volterra by Sulla in 80AD, but the three worn heads are thought to be original and probably date back to around the 4th century BC. More recently the gate escaped destruction by the Germans in an attempt to stop the Allied advance in the Second World War. The citizens were so determined that the arch should be saved that they worked day and night digging up the road and blocking the entrance so that the gate's destruction would be unnecessary.

The Porta all' Arco is part of the original city wall that the Etruscans built to protect the small city state of Velathri. The walls, which measured up to 12m high in places, surrounded a far bigger area than the later medieval ones, giving an indication of the size and importance of the Etruscan settlement. Both walls follow the same line to the south, but to the north and north-west of the town they diverge, with the old Etruscan walls ambling far out onto the precarious crumbling cliffs known as the **Balze**. The best stretch is to be found near the little church of Santa Chiara. If you have time, it is worth walking out to the great scarred ruins of the Balze, a jumble of continually corroding stone which has, even quite recently, swallowed up churches, abbeys and anything that anyone was optimistic or foolish enough to build there. Also to the north of the town, just outside the medieval walls, is the **Roman amphitheatre** whose impressive remains date back to the 1st century AD. Lower down are the remains of the Roman baths (3rd century BC).

West of the amphitheatre is the medieval fortified gate of **San Francesco** near the 13th-century church of the same name. The church is worth visiting for its interesting early 15th-century frescoes in the Croce di Giorno chapel. They are by Cenni di Francesco di Sercenni and show the Life of Christ and the Legend of the True Cross. There are various other churches for those with time on their hands to visit in the area – the 17th-century **San Giusto Clemente** with its austere but elegant façade, and **Sant' Agostino** with its 13th-century carved crucifix. Off the Siena road (which continues from the Viale dei Ponti) is the 15th-century church of **San Girolamo**, attributed to the great Florentine Renaissance architect, Michelozzo. Inside are two Giovanni della Robbia terracottas and some fine paintings, notably a beautiful *Annunciation* on gold by Benvenuto di Giovanni, a painting by Santi di Tito, and a fine *Madonna Enthroned with Saints* by an unknown 15th-century artist.

Livorno

A few kilometres to the west, through sweeping hilly countryside, is the big industrial port of **LIVORNO**. Livorno is the second biggest container port in Italy. It is fundamentally a modern industrial city attracting few tourists, apart from those using the giant ferry ships to Elba, Sardinia and Corsica. Strangely, it has had a long association with the British, who traditionally call it Leghorn from the old Italian word *Legorno*. It is here that the novelist Tobias Smollett is buried in the oldest protestant cemetery in Italy; here also Byron lived and Shelley wrote his 'Ode to a Skylark'. Even the cathedral, which was rebuilt after the war to its original design, had a façade by Inigo Jones. However, in the early 19th century much of the old town was demolished in an attempt to clean it up and the narrow streets were replaced by wide boulevards and grand houses so that in 1876 Augustus Hare was able to say that there was 'nothing whatever worth seeing in Leghorn'. This was not altogether true; and even now, after the catastrophic air raids of the war when up to 90 per cent of the city was demolished, Livorno still has some things to offer the tourist.

It is known as Tuscany's youngest city. The first official mention of a settlement in the area was not until the 10th century when Livorno was described as a small fishing port attached to Pisa, little more than a village. In 1405, after Pisa's defeat by Genoa, the harbour became part of the Genoese Republic, but it remained insignificant and only after it was sold to Florence in 1421 did it begin to develop as a town. It was over one hundred years later, under the Medici Grand-Dukes, that things really started to move. The reason for this sudden spurt of activity lay mainly in the silting up of the port of Pisa – a new port was therefore vital if the Florentines were to continue their highly lucrative trading activities. With this in mind Cosimo I set to draining the malaria-infested marshes that surrounded the area and revamping the little town. The **Fortezza Vecchia** (old castle) near the port was amalgamated into a sturdy Medici fortress by Guiliano da Sangallo. The squat 11th-century watchtower known as the **Mástio di Matilde** rises above the port. In 1577 the architect (and firework-maker for the Medici) Bernardo Buontalenti was commissioned to design an ideal city to encourage people to live there. He used a hexagonal plan and a grid system centred on the Piazza Grande. The town walls were surrounded by a moat-cum-canal called the Fosse Reale. In 1590 the new fortress (La Fortezza Nuova) was built just to the north of the town. But the actual harbour was still not functioning efficiently, and in 1621 the English navigational expert, Sir Robert Dudley, son of the Earl of Leicester, came to the rescue. He built the great wall, known as the **Mole**, enclosing the harbour.

The real problem in Livorno was lack of population, so in 1593 Grand-Duke Ferdinand I declared it an open city, exempt from taxation and with absolute religious freedom. The result was a population explosion as Turks, Armenians and Jews flooded the area. In fifty years the population rose from 800 to 8000 and kept on growing. Another element that soon started to flourish was the slave trade. Travelling in 1644, John Evelyn described the scene in the Piazza Michele as

> such a concourse of slaves, Turcs, Moors and other nations, that the number and confusion is prodigious; some buying, others selling, others drinking, others playing, some working, others sleeping, fighting, singing, weeping, all nearly naked and miserably chained. Here was a tent where an idle fellow might stake his liberty against a few crowns, at dice or other hazard; and, if he lost, he was immediately chained and led away to the galleys, where he was to serve a term of years, but from whence they seldom returned . . .

Already in Evelyn's time Livorno's most interesting monument stood in the **Piazza Michele** – the statue of Ferdinand I surrounded by *I Quattro Mori*, the four black slaves chained and straining. Ferdinand is by Bandini, but the bronze Moors were cast by Tacca in 1626 and have an undisputed raw energy and power. Now, obviously, the real slaves are no more, but the city has retained its feeling of tough trade and maritime goings-on. Even at the height of its popularity with travellers it never became a really elegant resort. In 1836 James Fenimore Cooper found

> a certain absence of taste, a want of leisure and tone; a substitution of bustle for elegance, care for enjoyment, and show for refinement.

Today the want of refinement is even more pronounced in this modern container port which, like Marseilles and Piraeus, has its share of drunken brawls and sinister dealings.

Though parts of the city may be jostling with soldiers, sailors and prostitutes, Livorno is still worth a brief visit. For lovers of modern painting there is the **Museo Civico G. Fattori**, housed in the Villa Fabricotti to the south of the city. Here are paintings by two of Livorno's most famous sons – Giovanni

Fattori and Amadeo Modigliani. Fattori was an excellent painter, the leader of the 19th-century Italian Impressionist movement known as the *Macchaioli*. As well as many pictures by him and his followers, there are also some fine works by Modigliani who was born into the Jewish community of the city. Nearby is the Museum of Contemporary Art which has occasional special exhibitions.

The **Lungomare**, overlooking the sea, is in parts fairly elegant, with various 18th-century villas and, further along towards Ardenza, a racecourse and the wide *Terazza Mascagni* looking out towards the islands. Among the modern buildings on the nearby hills are the villas where such celebrities as Byron, Shelley, Lamartine and Napoleon III once stayed.

For the food-lover there is another reason to visit Livorno – the best real seafood in Tuscany. The most authentic and roughest seafarers' dish is the delicious *cacciuco*, the Livornese answer to bouillabaisse, a marvellous spicy fish stew swimming in garlic, tomatoes and olive oil, to be mopped up with coarse bread and washed down with local wine. In Livorno, as elsewhere, the best restaurants are not the smartest or most expensive. Many are down by the port and can be identified by the crowds of locals and sailors guzzling and arguing. Sergio's, unpromisingly situated next to a petrol pump, is a good bet if you don't mind a rather boisterous, rough and ready atmosphere. There are also a couple of good *trattorie casalinghe* near the Fortezza Nuova.

Practical Information

Hotels and Restaurants

PISA   *Hotel Royal Victoria* Lungarno Pacinotti. A large hotel with a restaurant, housed in an elegant building overlooking the Arno.
Hotel Leon Bianco Piazza Garibaldi. A modest but clean *pensione* near the river and the old town.
Sergio. This restaurant on the Lungarno Pacinotti has a very high reputation and is correspondingly expensive. For less grand meals there are various small family restaurants in the market area behind the Borgo Stretto.
About 7km north of Pisa by the tiny hamlet of Rigoli is the marvellous *Villa Corliano* (tel. (050) 940186) 56017 Pisa. It is situated in its own park and while it cannot be said to be luxurious it retains the charm of a grand country house hotel.

LIVORNO   There are various good fish restaurants towards the harbour including *La Parmigiana* in Piazza Luigi Orlando and *La Barcarola* in Viale Carducci. The smarter restaurants are in Ardenza of which *Oscar* in Via Franchini is one of the best.

VOLTERRA   *Nazionale* (tel. (0588) 86284) Via dei Marchesi 2. A reasonable choice in the centre of town though without a restaurant.

Albergo Villa Nencini (tel. (0588) 86386) Borgo S. Stefano. Just on the edge of town with a sumptuous garden but no restaurant.
In the Via delle Prigioni are two good family restaurants *Da Beppino* and *Il Pozzo degli Etruschi*. There is also an excellent self-service on the road leading up to the Nazionale with good *casalinga* cooking.

Museums

PISA
Baptistery   open summer 09.00–19.00; winter 09.00–17.00.
Campanile   Closed.
Camposanto   open daily as Baptistery.
Duomo   open daily 07.45–12.45 and 15.00–18.45 (16.45 in winter).
Museo delle Synopie   open 09.00–12.30 and 15.00–sunset.
Museo Nazionale di San Matteo   Lungarno Mediceo; open weekdays 09.00–19.00; Sun and hols 09.00–13.00; closed Mon.

SAN MINIATO AL TEDESCO
Museo Diocesano   open 09.00–12.00 and 14.30–17.30 (winter Sat and Sun only); closed Mon.

LIVORNO
Museo Civico G. Fattori   Villa Fabbricotti: open daily 10.00–13.00; Thurs and Sat also 16.00–19.00; closed Mon.

VOLTERRA
Museo di Arte Sacra   Temporarily closed: due to re-open 1993.
Museo Etrusco Guarnacci   Via di Minzoni 15: open daily summer 09.30–13.00 and 15.00–18.30; Oct–March 10.00–14.00.
Galleria Pittorica/Palazzo dei Priori   Piazza dei Priori: open weekdays 09.00–13.00.

5. PRATO AND PISTOIA

Prato

Entering **PRATO** by car is an experience to forget. No sooner have you quit the sprawling suburbs of western Florence and caught a glimpse of the green Calvana hills than you are back in another modern concrete maze which is, if anything, worse than before. There are more factories, more warehouses and office blocks. The buildings are separated by busy, badly signed roads where, as on all Italian highways, indecision is regarded with the utmost contempt and fury. Don't be deterred. When you are finally within the walls, you will almost certainly feel that your raised blood pressure and sweating palms were worth it. (Alternatively there is a quick and regular train service from Florence right to the centre of town). True, the narrow streets with their tiny pavements are lethal places to wander, with buses, taxis and motorbikes hurtling crazily round corners, but this is all part of the atmosphere, and the atmosphere of Prato is very strong. It is, and always has been, predominantly a manufacturing town and, unlike some of Tuscany's more beautiful places, it makes few concessions to tourism. Its success lies not in its beauty or its geographical position as a suburb of Florence, but in its independence and commercial know-how.

Prato lies half way between Florence and Pistoia in the basin of the Bisenzio river. Like many other towns, it probably began as an Etruscan settlement; but it was not until the Middle Ages that it rose from obscurity with the development of the trade that has remained its life-blood — the wool and textile industry. Strangely for a wool town, the local hills do not make particularly good sheep country and the sheep that do graze there have coarse, poor-quality coats — so most of the raw wool is imported, much of it from England. But, being on a river, Prato does have an abundance of the other vital element necessary to the production of cloth — water.

For a long time Prato managed to stay clear of its powerful neighbour Florence but in 1312, after fierce feuding between local families, the town gave itself over to the superpowers — joining the forces of the Guelph leader, Robert of Anjou, King of Naples, whose family later sold the whole town to Florence for 17,500 florins. But the Florentines never really brought the increasingly successful little town to heel, despite ploys like rationing its cloth production in the 16th century, in an attempt both to improve their own trade and to weaken Prato's. Recently Prato has again boomed, with the population more than doubling since the Second World War, and around 75 per cent of the workforce in the cloth trade. Many of the old roads bear witness to the town's manufacturing heritage – such as the Via dei Cimatori, Via de Tintori or Via dei Lanaiuoli named after the clippers, dryers and woolmerchants. And even now Prato's relationship with Florence is more competitive than seems realistic for towns of such different sizes. Florentines still, with some acrimony, refer to Prato as 'la coda che muove il cane' (the tail that wags the dog).

In the Piazza Duomo is the small but immensely rich **Cathedral** dedicated to St Stephen. It was built in 1211 by Guido da Como, though the transept and five chapels were added later in the mid 14th century. It was not until 1653, when Prato was made a separate see, that it actually became a cathedral, long after all the works of importance had been completed.

The façade, dating from 1384–1487, is simply but charmingly striped in white and the dark blackish-green local marble, occasionally broken up by a block of pink or brown. To my mind, its only blemish is the decorative open stone-work balustrade along the top, which I cannot believe would have been intended in that crude form. In the lunette above the main door is a typically sweet *Madonna and Child with Saints* created in 1489 by Andrea della Robbia. To the right of the door is one of the loveliest things in Tuscany, the famous open-air pulpit by Donatello and Michelozzo, finished in 1439. The general opinion seems to be that Michelozzo designed the beautiful and graceful structure while Donatello carved the *putti*, who race like street urchins round the seven panels of the pulpit, shrieking, laughing and banging drums. Donatello's *putti* were always wilder and more fun-loving than those of the rest of his contemporaries.

The pulpit was built to display Prato's most famous relic, known as the Virgin's Girdle (actually more of a belt). The legend behind this sacred object is that St Thomas, true to form, was not convinced by the story of the Assumption of Mary, at which he had not been present. To alleviate his uncertainty the Virgin herself leaned down from Heaven and passed him her girdle. The girdle found its way to Prato in 1141 with a crusader whose new wife, a descendant of a friend of St Thomas, had it in her dowry. It is kept inside the Cathedral in the Capella del Santo Cingolo (1385–95) which is frescoed by Agnolo Gaddi with the legend. Over the altar in the chapel is a powerful *Madonna and Child* carved by the great Giovanni Pisano in 1317.

Other treasures inside the cathedral include the fine 'Sweet-style' pulpit in the nave, carved in 1473 by Mino da Fiesole and Rossellino. The bronze crucifix on the high altar was cast by Ferdinando Tacca in the early 14th century. But the main reason to enter the cathedral is to see the masterpiece of the Florentine painter Fra Filippo Lippi: the wonderful series of frescoes painted from 1452–66 on the walls of the choir. The paintings on the left depict episodes from the life of St Stephen, while those on the right show the life of John the Baptist. Vasari in his inimitable style tells the story of the rather unconventional painter monk:

Prato cathedral – The famous open air pulpit of Michelozzo and Donatello

It is said that Fra Filippo was so lustful that he would give anything to enjoy a woman he wanted if he thought that he could have his way; and if he couldn't buy what he wanted, then he would cool his passion by painting her portrait and reasoning with himself. His lust was so violent when it took hold of him he could never concentrate on his work.

While working at a convent in Prato Fra Filippo met the young novice who appears in the wonderful fresco of Salome dancing before Herod. Vasari recounts:

Fra Filippo made advances to the girl, who was called Lucrezia and who was very beautiful and graceful, and he succeeded in persuading the nuns to let him use her as a model for the figure of Our Lady in his painting. This opportunity left him even more infatuated, and by various ways and means he managed to steal her away from the nuns on the very day that she was going to see the exposition of the Girdle of Our Lady, one of the great relics of Prato. This episode disgraced the nuns, and Francesco, the girl's father, never smiled again.

Lucrezia eventually married Filippo, who was released from his vows, and produced a son Filippino – another superb painter.

On either side of the choir are two more chapels containing 15th-century frescoes. Those to the right of the altar were possibly begun by Paolo Uccello, or a follower, and finished a short time after by Andrea di Giusto. In one of the left hand chapels is the tomb of Filippo Inghirami, by the 15th-century sculptor Niccoló de' Bardi.

To the left of the cathedral is the **Museo dell' Opera del Duomo**, with the originals of Donatello's dancing *putti* from the outside pulpit. Almost equally exquisite are Maso di Bartolomeo's cherubs on the delicately-carved reliquary of the Sacred Girdle also to be found there.

In the nearby Piazza Commune is the rather strange-looking **Palazzo Pretorio** which now houses the town art gallery. The earlier part of the building, the red brick corner, was enlarged in grey limestone in the 14th century, but the battlements and the small bell-tower were not added until the 16th. Inside is a good selection of Tuscan paintings, with some excellent Renaissance works by the Lippis and others, as well as some fine 14th-century pictures by Bernardo Daddi. Nearby to the south of the Piazza Comune, is the house of the great merchant and banker of Prato, Francesco Datini, immortalised in Iris Origo's excellent book, *The Merchant of Prato*. Datini was one of the wealthiest merchants of the 14th century, who although 'grasping and wilful', gave much to the city. On the day of his death Mass is still said for him every year in the cathedral, and his lamps still burn in the Chapel of the Sacred Girdle. He was buried near his home in the 13th-century church of San Francesco, which has a green and white striped façade and a fine interior and cloisters.

South-east of the square is the Emperor Frederick II's hefty **Castello dell' Imperatore** built in the mid 13th century to guard the route south. Near it

63

stands one of the city's loveliest buildings, the Renaissance church of **Santa Maria della Carcerie**, named after a painting of the Virgin on the wall of the prison which previously stood there. The church was designed by Giuliano da Sangallo in 1484, and was one of the earliest centrally-planned churches in Tuscany. But the Greek Cross form, considered so perfect by Renaissance architects, was never popular with the clergy, who preferred a long nave for preaching; and few were ever completed in the region. The two other main examples in Tuscany are Brunelleschi's Pazzi Chapel in Florence, and the marvellous church of San Biagio near Montepulciano by Antonio Sangallo the elder. In the beautifully proportioned interior of Santa Maria are some graceful terracotta roundels by Andrea della Robbia, who also decorated the Pazzi chapel.

To the south-west of the old town in the Via Silvestri is the church of **Santo Spirito** near the Convitto Cicognini (now an exclusive boarding school). In Santo Spirito is a painting of the Presentation of Christ in the Temple, painted by Filippo Lippi's pupil, improbably named Fra Diamante, on a design by the master. Northwards on the Via Vincenzo is the 13th–14th century church of **San Domenico**, with a fine north portal and an unfinished façade. Inside is a large crucifix which dates from the beginning of the 15th century. Off the 15th-century cloisters is a small museum of frescoes and *sinopie* (preliminary sketches).

The Pratoiese in general eat well, though surprisingly some of their best restaurants concentrate on fish, like the excellent Il Scoglio near the centre or the more expensive Il Pirana, unpromisingly situated amid factories on the outskirts of the town.

Five miles south of Prato at the base of Monte Albano is the important Medici villa of **Poggio a Caiano**. It is a lovely Renaissance building designed by Giuliano da Sangallo in 1480 for Lorenzo de Medici, based on the idea of an antique Roman villa. Usually only the gardens are open to the public, but it is sometimes possible to go inside and see the great *Salone* which replaces the central courtyard and frescoed by Andrea del Sarto, Franciabiagio and Pontormo. It was finally completed by A. Allori in 1582. The stairs leading up to the first floor were added in the late 16th century.

Pistoia

Pistoia is, if anything, even more fascinating than Prato, though with a reputation for violence and brutality unparalleled even in Tuscany. The town was probably founded by the Romans, and it was near here that the fearsome counter-revolutionary and warrior Catiline was finally defeated and killed by the Roman army in 62BC. But it was in the Middle Ages that the town's reputation really plummeted. After the death of Countess Matilda in 1115, Pistoia belligerently declared itself an independent Ghibelline commune, a staunch rival of her Guelph neighbours Lucca, Prato and, of course, Florence.

Despite warring factions within the city, Pistoia just managed to retain its independence until 1329 when Florence finally moved in. But even Florence could not stop the dreadful feuding and fighting between rival families within the now supposedly Guelph town. Dante maintained that it was due to the enmity between the two powerful families, the Cancellieri and the Panciatichi, that the violent feud between the Black and the White Guelphs began. The squabbles quickly spread to Florence and became the cause of Dante's life banishment from his native town in 1301. The poet never forgave Pistoia for this, hating the town and its inhabitants until the end of his days. In the eighth Circle of his *Inferno* we meet a Pistoian thief caught stealing from the church of San Zeno who says:

> . . . *Son Vanni Fucci*
> *Bestia, e Pistoia mi fu degna tana.*

> . . . *I am Vanni Fucci*
> *A beast, and Pistoia is a fit den for me.*

Some years later the Florentine Niccolo Macchiavelli, in his widely read book *Il Principe*, accused the Pistoiese of further viciousness, saying that they raised their young merely for slaughter and fighting. And in the 17th century, when the Germans named the pistol after the small but lethal iron dagger that the Pistoiese were known to carry in their clothes, the town acquired a new name: 'Pistoia la ferrigna' meaning both pitiless and of iron.

Entering Pistoia by car is initially rather like entering Prato – a depressing modern jungle of buildings and busy roads. Once inside, you will find that Pistoia has a fine and spacious cathedral square in which the buildings of religious and civic power stand side by side. The **Cathedral**, dedicated to the saints Zeno and Iago, is a charming Romanesque building rather dwarfed by the splendid 65m bell-tower that stands next to it. It is thought that the tower was originally an old Lombard watch tower which was enlarged in the 13th century. Its brick top was not added until the 16th century; the clock, by Giuseppe Ansinelli, is of 1712. The cathedral itself was also fundamentally rebuilt on to an older church, and a typical Pisan style striped arched façade was added in 1411. Under the tall central arch are majolica roundels, and in the lunette above the door is a Madonna and Child between two angels by Andrea della Robbia.

Inside, the roomy nave is divided from the aisles by fine columns with richly worked capitals. Near the right hand door is the tomb of Cino di Pistoia, the town's most famous poet and friend of Dante. The font was designed by the Renaissance sculptor Benedetto da Maiano. Before the main altar is a mid-13th century bronze candle holder by Maso di Bartolomeo. In a chapel on the left is a painting of the Madonna Enthroned, probably by Leonardo da Vinci's teacher Andrea Verrochio who may also have been responsible for the monument to Cardinal Niccolo Forteguerri who died in 1473. Near the painting of the Madonna is the carved figure of Bishop Donato di Medici, generally thought to be by Rossellino although some think it may also be by Verrocchio.

The 15th-century façade of Pistoia's cathedral

From the right aisle be sure to enter the Capella di San Jacopo to see the fabulous silver altar of Sant' Iago, made between 1287 and 1456 by a variety of Tuscan sculptors including Brunelleschi, who is thought to be responsible for two figures on the extreme left. If you study the piece carefully it is possible to trace the differences in styles through the years.

Outside in the square opposite the cathedral is the lovely octagonal **Baptistery** completed in 1359 by Cellino di Nese and based on a design by Andrea Pisano. It has a tiny external pulpit and carvings depicting the life of John the Baptist over the door. The inside is rather bare, but it does contain its original 13th-century font by Lanfranco da Como.

There are many other fine buildings in the square. At one end, running between the cathedral and Baptistery, is the 14th-century **Bishop's Palace** with mullioned windows and coats of arms decorating the front. On the other side of the cathedral is the **Palazzo del Commune**, begun in 1294 at the command of one of Pistoia's most successful governors, Giano della Bella from Florence. After Giano's death building stopped, but was resumed again in 1334 and finally finished in 1385, although the bridge linking the palace with the cathedral was not added until the 17th century. It is a fine, regular, if austere, building, with mullioned windows and a shady portico. On the corners and over the main door is the Medici crest, the six balls known as Le Palle. To the left of the central window is a negroid marble head, thought to be a portrait of the exiled black King of Majorca, Musetto, though some sources suggest that it is a portrait of the traitor Tedici who sold the city to Castruccio Castracani of Lucca in 1315. The palace houses the Museo Civico with its collection of Tuscan paintings. On the ground floor is an exhibition of the works of the modern sculptor Marino Marini, who was born in Pistoia in 1901. There are also occasional visiting exhibitions.

In front of the palace is the small well, generally known as the **Leoncino** after the little lion on the top. It was commissioned by the Neri Capponi from Florence, where the *Marzocco* lion is the city's symbol of justice.

On the other side of the square from the Palazzo Comune is the **Palazzo Pretorio** or **Palazzo del Podestà**, constructed mainly in 1367 as the home of the Florentine governor, but later turned into a palace of justice. The building has been heavily restored, but in the courtyard one can still see the old bench where the judiciary sat to mete out justice to the populace. On the bench is an inscription in Latin which, roughly translated, reads:

> This place hates wrongdoing, loves law, punishes crimes, conserves the right, honours the righteous.

Pistoia's principal gallery may be somewhat disappointing, but spread round the town is plenty of wonderful Tuscan art hidden away in fine old churches. For lovers of sculpture, Pistoia has three of the finest early pulpits in Tuscany. The earliest of these is to be found in the 12th-century church of **San Bartolomeo in Pantano**, built on an area of reclaimed marsh (*pantano*) to the northeast of the Piazza Duomo. The church has a lovely old façade with a relief of Christ sending forth the Apostles. It was carved in 1167, probably by the sculptor Gruamonte, who did a lot of work on local churches at that time, and whose rather formal compositions recall early Roman and Etruscan sarcophagi with which he would almost certainly have been familiar. Inside is the pulpit, carved by Guido da Como, who was also responsible for the font in the Pisa Baptistery. Finished in c.1250, it has the naïve, rather wooden charm of the days before the influence of the great monumental sculptor Giovanni Pisano was felt.

Across the town, in the beautiful church of **San Giovanni Fuorcivitas** (St John outside the city) is the second of the three great pulpits, this time the work of Fra Guglielmo da Pisa, dating around 1270. On it is a frieze with 11 sections showing the life and death of Christ. The holy water stoup has carvings of the Seven Virtues (four cardinal which were possibly an early work of Giovanni Pisano – and three theological). To the left of the altar is a fine polyptych by Taddeo Gaddi, while the terracotta *Visitation* is from the della Robbia school. The church itself is a magnificent building begun in the 12th century but not finished for another 200 years. The south side, arcaded in the Pisan style, is, unusually, far more decorative than the brick front. It has three tiers of blind arches and is splendidly striped in white and the blackish-green marble of Prato. Over the south door is a 14th-century St John above a frieze of the Last Supper carved by Gruamonte in c.1265.

The latest and perhaps the most spectacular of the three pulpits was begun in 1298 by the father of modern sculpture – the great Giovanni Pisano. It is to be found in the attractive church of Sant' Andrea, which has another lovely arcaded façade and also a frieze by Gruamonte (possibly with the help of his brother Adeodato), this time showing the Three Kings before Herod. Inside, Giovanni's pulpit depicts scenes from the New Testament: the Annunciation, the Nativity, Joseph's Dream, the Slaughter of the Innocents, the Crucifixion and the Last Judgement. Dividing the panels are figures from the Old and New Testaments. Giovanni's figures have a dynamic power and grandeur that is absent from the earlier pulpits – one can see immediately just how great his contribution to sculpture really was. In the 13th Chapel to the left is a strong wooden crucifix also carved by Giovanni.

To the west of Sant' Andrea in a large leafy piazza is the church of **San Francesco d'Assisi**, built during the course of the 14th century. Despite sustaining a lot of damage through different uses (it was at one time an army barracks – a rather inappropriate transition considering its patron saint) the church still contains some fine 14th-century frescoes. There are works here by Lippo Memmi and also Pietro Lorenzetti from Siena, and the less well-known Puccio Capanna who studied under Giotto. Most of the frescoes show scenes from the life of Christ and many of them have been substantially restored.

Perhaps the most unusual building in Pistoia is the late Renaissance church of the **Madonna dell' Umilità**, designed around a domed octagonal centre by Ventura Vitori in 1490. Over the altar is an image of the Virgin which was said to perform miracles and was the reason for the church being built.

Pistoia has countless other treasures that the visitor with time on his hands will want to explore, but for those with limited time there is one more thing that absolutely must be seen. A few minutes' walk north-east from the Piazza Duomo is the **Ospedale del Ceppo** with its splendid majolica frieze. Even those (or perhaps especially those) who find the gentle works of the della Robbia family to be of limited excitement should make the effort to look at this fascinating and charming series. The frieze depicts the seven works of mercy: clothing the naked, looking after pilgrims, caring for the sick, comforting prisoners, interring the dead, giving food to the hungry and giving drink to the thirsty. It was created under the direction of the della Robbias in the early 16th century, and is more original and less sentimental than the pretty blue and white virgins that the Victorians adored but which modern critics tend to find bland and too sweet.

Environs of Pistoia

Outside the town, the countryside of the province of Pistoia is extremely varied. Travelling to the north, one soon finds oneself in the high (for Tuscany anyway) mountains known as the Appenino Tosco-Emiliano – an area with a very different character from much of Tuscany. Right at the top of the province, perched on the edge of Monte Gomito, is the town of **Abetone** – a popular and fairly well equipped ski-ing resort with some of the best and most difficult runs in Tuscany. Other popular winter resorts nearby include **Cutigliano**, which also has a 14th-century *Palazzo Pretorio*, and the rather bigger town of **San Marcello Pistoiese**. Much of the surrounding area has also become popular in the summer for the more strenuous kinds of walking holidays. If you are travelling that way, try the popular mountain restaurant **da Bizzino**, 10 minutes' drive from Abetone on the Via Secchio, which specialises in fresh mountain mushrooms and delicious home-made pasta.

If you leave Pistoia on the southbound road towards Empoli you will come, after much picturesque twisting and turning, to the little town of **Vinci**, birthplace of Leonardo in 1452. At the top of the old town is a heavily restored 13th-century castle, which now houses a museum to the great man with interesting models of some of his amazingly varied inventions, made by students using Leonardo's designs. Outside the town at Archiano, in a lovely setting amid acres of ancient silver olives, is Leonardo's family house – which is worth visiting more for its fine situation than its meagre contents.

Off the main Florence–Lucca road some 16km west of Pistoia, surrounded by gentle hills, is the popular spa resort of **Montecatini Terme**. The spa of Montecatini was probably in existence in Roman times and has slid in and out of fashion ever since. Towards the end of the 18th century, under Grand Duke Leopold I, it began to flourish on a vast scale and now the healing springs have become so popular that there are said to be over 500 hotels in the area. The five main thermal establishments are situated in the leafy Parco delle Terme in the new town. Some 260m above is the beautifully situated old town, **Montecatini Alto**, which can be reached by a funicular and has a little museum of sacred art next to the completely re-vamped Romanesque church. From here it is a short drive (perhaps two or three kilometres) to the little walled castello of **Buggiano**, with its 13th-century Palazzo Pretorio and a *pieve* begun in the 11th century. In the church at Ponte Buggianese are some frescoes by the modern painter, Annigoni, famous in England for his portraits of the Queen.

To the west of Montecatini lies the market gardening town of **Pescia**, famous for its asparagus and huge flower market. Pescia is divided into two parts by the River Pescia – on one side is the rather muddled Cathedral, built on to a Romanesque church but with an early 18th-century campanile, a 19th-century façade and a Baroque interior. Another church worth looking at is the Gothic church of San Francesco, which contains a wonderful 13th-century panel of scenes from the life of St Francis. It was painted by the artist Berlingo Berlinghieri only ten years after the death of the saint, and is thought to be his truest likeness extant. The 14th-century church of San' Antonio preserves 15th-century frescoes of the life of St Anthony Abbot.

Across the river is the civic centre, the Piazza Mazzini: a hotch-potch of buildings dating from the 13th to the 19th century. At one end is the fine 15th-century Oratorio della Madonna di Piè, perhaps designed by a local artist known as *il Buggiano*, the adopted son of Filippo Brunelleschi. The little Civic Museum is in the nearby Piazza Santo Stefano.

Outside the town, some few kilometres to the east, is the high perched medieval village of Uzzano and, further north, the lovely Romanesque *pieve* of Castelvecchio.

Another popular pilgrimage is to the nearby village of **Collodi**, home of the author of the childrens' book *Pinocchio*, the story of a living wooden puppet whose nose grows when he tells lies. It is possible to visit the rather dismal **Parco di Pinocchio**, but the real point of this expedition is to see the 17th-century gardens of the Villa Garzoni. Here it is possible to relax and find the odd patch of shade, in fine surroundings made pleasant by cool fountains and formal hedges where elegant statues vainly pose or glance coyly out at the hot tourists.

Practical Information

Hotels and Restaurants

PRATO *Stella d'Italia* (tel. (0574) 27910) Piazza Duomo 8. A very central hotel and restaurant with tables in the main square. Prato has various good restaurants including the excellent but expensive *Il Pirana* (tel. (0574) 25746) in the Via Valentini 110 in a dismal suburb. In the centre is another fish restaurant, *Il Scoglio*, cheaper and also good.

Between Prato and Pistoia on the Via provinciale Pratese 58, is the *Osteria di Contadino* with sturdy Tuscan cooking and some good wines.

PISTOIA *Il Convento* (tel. (0573) 452651) Via San Quirico 33. At Pontenuovo in the hills about 4km from town, a simple and quiet converted convent with a cosy restaurant.
The *Chiavi d'Oro* Via Pacini 19 in the centre of town is an unpretentious and pleasant restaurant.

Museums

PRATO
Museo dell' Opera del Duomo   Piazza Duomo: open weekdays 09.00–12.30 and 15.00–18.30; Sun and hols 09.30–12.30; closed Tues.
Galleria Comunale   Piazza Comune: open weekdays 09.30–12.30 and 15.00–18.30; Sun and hols 09.30–12.30; closed Tues.
Castello dell' Imperatore: open weekdays 09.00–12.00 and 15.00–18.00; Sun and hols 09.00–12.00; closed Tues.

PISTOIA
Palazzo del Comune   Piazza Duomo: open weekdays 09.00–13.00 and 15.00–19.00; Sun and hols 09.00–12.30, closed Mon.
Medici Villa a Poggio a Caiano   Gardens open 08.30–sunset.

PESCIA
Museo Civico   Piazza Santo Stefano: open Mon, Wed, Fri and Sat 09.00–13.00; Wed also 15.00–19.00.

VINCI
Museo Vinciano   open daily 09.00–18.00.

COLLODI
Villa Garzoni   Gardens open 08.00–sunset.
Parco di Pinocchio   open 08.00–sunset.

6. CENTRAL FLORENCE

In 1818 Shelley wrote:

> Florence itself, that is the Lung'arno (for I have seen no more), I think is the most beautiful city I have yet seen. It is surrounded with cultivated hills and from the bridge which crosses the broad channel of the Arno, the view is the most animated and elegant I ever saw.

By the 19th century this sort of letter home was commonplace. For a hundred years Florence had been a popular stop on the way to Rome and Naples for the wealthy Britons who made the Grand Tour an important part of their education. In 1740 the English envoy in Florence, Sir Horace Mann, found he had so many visitors that he had to commission a separate guest-house to accommodate them all. Many of these travellers stayed on, hiring villas outside the city or apartments in town or even palaces, whose great dark chambers they turned into cosy English drawing rooms. They held tea parties and balls to which they invited the new arrivals, the expatriates and a few fashionable or eccentric Italians. In general their attitude to the Florentines was predictable – a combination of the attraction of opposites and a rather patronising sense of superiority. A fourteen-year-old English girl's diary of 1817 reads:

> Last Saturday Walter gave his ball here. Everybody thought it splendid and all in all it was so for this country . . . I often half envy the happy life of an Italian free from care and brought up so as to be almost devoid of conscience, indulging in every inclination natural to man loving to be loved, and all without restraint. Yes I sigh after such happiness.

But times and fashions change and travelling about a hundred years later, Aldous Huxley had this to say:

> We came back through Florence and the spectacle of that second-rate provincial town with its repulsive Gothic architecture and its acres of Christmas card primitives almost made me sick. The only points about Florence are the country outside it, the Michelangelo tombs, Brunelleschi's dome and a few rare pictures. The rest is simply dung when compared to Rome. The Florentine country is, of course as good as anything in the world; but the town . . . pooh.

Florence on the River Arno

Florence is still out of fashion today; slandered by those who find Venice more beautiful, Rome more sophisticated, Naples more exciting. The critics are right – Florence *is* provincial, and remains so despite the ever-increasing numbers of visitors from America and Japan. It is this overwhelming characteristic that dominates everything. You can come, in theory, just to see the great Dome, the Giottos, the Massaccios, or the Michelangelos. But in practice, it is impossible to see them in isolation – they are irrevocably bound to their surroundings – their history is the town's history. The painters, architects and sculptors who shaped Florence were nearly all from the province, and if they travelled it was after serving an apprenticeship in their home city, forming their ideas under the careful eye of another Florentine. It is partly this that makes Florence hard work – nothing can safely be ignored. But other factors contribute to its current lack of popularity. It is noisy, there is a ghastly traffic problem and it can be stiflingly hot. Dostoyevsky, who lived here in the summer of 1868, complained that for six weeks it was 'hot as Hell'. He was probably not exaggerating. Equally it can be absolutely freezing in winter or, if you are really unlucky, raining bitterly at Easter. The best time to go is late spring or early autumn, when it is less crowded and everything is at its best.

It is impossible to stay long in Florence without learning the names of the great Florentine families. Their names crop up again and again in streets, chapels, portraits and tombs. Frescobaldi, Strozzi, Capponi, Bardi, Pazzi and, everywhere you look, the six *Palle* (balls) of the Medici. The streets are made dark by their massive palaces, and in the narrow alleys, now blocked by the

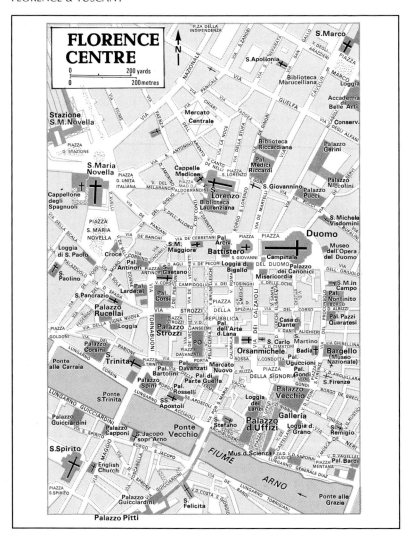

ubiquitous Fiats, it is easy to imagine the fighting and the revelry of the Middle Ages. In those days the city was dominated by feuds and faction fights – Guelph against Ghibelline and, later, Black Guelph against White Guelph. There was a constant jostling for power; everyone, it seems, walked in fear of their lives.

It is odd that in such a troubled and violent place the other great fear was of banishment. However dangerous and fraught with difficulty life became, there was no pain to compare with that of being sent away from the mother city. At the beginning of the 16th century, the Florentine historian Francesco Guiccardini gave this warning about the perils of ambition:

In Florence he who has not the qualifications for becoming head of affairs were a fool to involve himself so far with any government as to peril his whole fortune or success; since what he may gain is as nothing to what he may lose. Nor let any man incur the risk of exile. For since our city is not divided into factions like the Adorni and Fregosi of Genoa, none will come forward to take his part, and he will be forced to lie abroad without money or credit; nay, may be reduced to beg for a livelihood.

One has only to read the letters of Macchiavelli to understand the bitterness of spirit of these political refugees. Two hundred years earlier, Dante, perhaps the city's most famous exile, attacks Florence with all the hostility of a jilted lover:

> I would have had my Florence great and free
> Oh Florence! Florence! Unto me thou wast
> like that Jerusalem which the Almighty He
> Wept over, 'but thou wouldst not'; as the bird
> Gathers its young, I would have gathered thee
> Beneath a parent pinion, hadst thou heard
> My voice; but as the adder, deaf and fierce,
> Against the breast that cherished thee was stirr'd
> Thy venom, and my state thou didst amerce.
> And doom this body forfeit to the fire.

Despite the constant friction, flood and plague, Dante lived through one of Florence's great periods. There were the paintings of Giotto (1266), and the commencement of the great buildings of Florence: the Cathedral, the Town Hall and churches of Santa Croce and Santa Maria Novella. It was also at about this time that the other two major Tuscan writers, Petrarch and Boccaccio, were born.

By the end of the 14th century Florence had become a rich city. Her principal wealth lay in the lucrative cloth trade and subsequently in international banking. The town, which had been a Republic for over 150 years (apart from a few short interruptions), began to fall more and more into the hands of the increasingly wealthy *Signori*, the merchant banking families of Florence. The most prominent of these were the Medici. But in 1434 Cosimo de Medici, *il Vecchio*, was driven out of the city. His power had become too obvious, and he had made enemies among other powerful Florentine families. Within a year he was called back; the finances of the city had collapsed and the people could no longer do without him. From then on his power in Florence was assured. In fact it would have been hard for the Florentines to find a pleasanter or more cultured tyrant. Cosimo *Pater Patriae* was a wise man who knew the power of envy and consistently sought to avoid it. He was also a great art-lover and, along with the other great humanists of the time, an avid reader of classical texts.

These (often newly translated) writings by the early Greeks and Romans played a great part in the massive upsurge of creativity in Florence during the period that hundreds of years later was to become known as the Renaissance. Their subject was the dignity and excellence of man, the assertion summed up by the Greek theorist Protagoras, that man, and not God, was 'the measure of all things'. Until this time the general feeling had been the medieval one epitomised by Francis of Assisi, that man was worthless in the eyes of God. By the 15th century this was no longer the case. In 1451 the Florentine humanist Gianozzo Manetti described man as 'lord and king and emperor in the whole orb of the world and not unworthy to dominate and to reign and to rule . . .' He continues:

> Ours then, are every thing that you see, all the homes, the fortresses, the cities, all the buildings in the entire world which are so many and such that they seem the work of angels rather than of men . . . Ours are the pictures, ours the sculptures, ours the arts, ours the sciences, ours the wisdom.

And so, in architecture, we see the end of the great soaring Gothic churches, where man hardly seemed to exist, replaced by the smaller, perfectly-proportioned churches of the Renaissance, designed around man rather than God.

In sculpture and painting, too, these ideas took hold – there was no problem, either of technique or composition, that the artist could not hope to solve. Pictures took on a new tone as painters showed off their skills and tested new ideas. Religious pictures started to include portraits of well-known Florentines (often the donor of the painting and his family). In some cases they were given almost the same importance as the holy subjects. A typical example of this can be found in Benozzo Gozzoli's Journey of the Magi, in the Palazzo Medici-Riccardi, where the Three Kings and some of their train are depicted as members of the Medici family. Cosimo's grandson, Lorenzo il Magnifico, was another devoted patron of the arts. Under his patronage worked Verocchio, Botticelli, and the young Michelangelo. Other wealthy families followed suit, and commissioning works of art for religious or civic buildings became an important part of the rich merchant's budget. It was important on three counts. Firstly it illustrated the tremendous wealth and generosity of the donor. Secondly it showed devotion to God. Thirdly, it satisfied the Florentines' genuine love of beauty and creativity.

In 1494 artistic development received a blow with the expulsion of the first batch of the Medici and the brief rule of the fire-and-brimstone monk from Ferrara, Girolamo Savonarola. But within a few years he too had fallen out of favour, his body burnt to ashes in the Piazza della Signoria. The golden period of Florentine art lasted for 250 years, ending in about 1550 when the grossly stylised works of the high mannerists became fashionable and the real artistic impetus moved to Rome.

The cathedral of Santa Maria del Fiore

The Duomo and Baptistery

Undoubtedly the pride of Florence lies in its **Duomo**, or **Cathedral**, Santa Maria del Fiore. Rising a massive 60m above ground, it could be seen as far away as Pistoia. Because of its size and the smallness of the Piazza it is impossible ever to see the whole thing in its entirety. But, approaching it down the narrow neighbouring streets, one is constantly aware of it flashing in and out of sight, splendid in white, red and greenish-black. Matthew Arnold found both the building and its setting enchanting, likening it to 'a hen gathering its chickens under its wings'; but some years earlier another British traveller, James Johnson, had been distinctly less taken with it. To him the Duomo and its belfry suggested:

> . . . the grotesque similitude of a huge architectural zebra and its keeper – the former with a coating or skin, consisting of alternate stripes of black and white marble, the latter exhibiting, on its exterior, all the colours of the rainbow, all the chequers of a gigantic harlequin! Is there no mitigation of the penalty due to this Gothic and tasteless idea?

Johnson was in Florence some years before the present, controversial, façade was added in 1875 by de Fabris and Conti. I suspect that he, like many, would have found that even harder to take.

The first plans for the Duomo were drawn up at the end of the 13th century by the sculptor and architect Arnolfo di Cambio. At that time the cathedral was the old church of San Lorenzo. A more central site was chosen where the old church of Santa Reparata had stood, surrounded by a clutter of medieval houses and shops. The Florentines, jealous of the beauty and grandeur of the cathedrals of the nearby towns, (particularly their old rival Pisa), were determined that, whatever the cost, theirs should be the most magnificent of all. A document exempting Arnolfo from tax stated that

> . . . by reason of his industry, experience, and genius, the Commune and the people of Florence from the magnificent and visible beginning of the said church, commenced by the same master Arnolphus, hope to have a more beautiful and honorable temple than any other which there is in the regions of Tuscany.

It was this tremendous civic pride that motivated the flow of competitions over the following centuries, resulting in the square's appearance today.

In 1420 architects and craftsmen were called together from all over Europe to give their views on the dome that was being planned for the new building. It was to be 45m across – easily the biggest in Europe at that time – and its construction was obviously going to be a problem. Endless different options were put forward, ranging from making it out of pumice stone so that it would be light, to supporting it on a huge mound of earth filled with coins, so that after it was built the people would remove the earth to get the money. After much argument the commission was finally given to Filippo Brunelleschi, initially in conjunction with the sculptor Lorenzo Ghiberti. The two men had been rivals since Ghiberti had received the commission for the Baptistery doors, and there was little love lost between them. According to Vasari, Ghiberti's involvement in this project was solely the result of how 'affectionately he was regarded by certain men who were very influential in the government of Florence'. The partnership did not last and the credit of the dome must go almost completely to Brunelleschi. His structure, with eight ribs dovetailed together at the lantern, was built in two layers – the inner one being the stronger, and the outer shell mainly a protection against the elements. Some of the tools and devices he used can be seen in the Cathedral Museum. After another competition he was allowed to design the lantern but did not live to see it completed. The bronze orb on top was executed by another master of all trades, Andrea Verrocchio. Filippo Brunelleschi is buried under his dome – perhaps the greatest honour that could be conferred on a Florentine citizen.

Before entering the great building it is best to walk right the way round it, looking particularly at the different sets of doors. The big bronze doors at the front are 19th-century but the church's other doors are of considerable interest. To the south of the building near the Campanile one finds the oldest entrance which has a carving from the studio of Nino Pisano, known as 'Our Lady of the Pigeons', in the tympanum above. The smaller of the northern doors is similar in style but with the addition of twisted columns supported by medieval lions. Chronologically the next door is back on the southern side – the Porta dei Canonici – richly decorated with plants and beasts. In the tympanum by Lorenzo di Giovanni d'Ambrogio, is a *Madonna and Child* and above is a rather fine *Pietá*. But the loveliest of the Duomo doors is without doubt the early 15th-century Porta della Mandorla. In the lunette is a mosaic of the Annunciation by Domenico and Davide Ghirlandaio. The lovely carved Virgin in the almond shaped frame is known as the *Madonna della Cintola* and is perhaps the most beautiful work of Nanni di Banco (c.1419). The busts of a Prophet and Sybil are thought to be by the young Donatello.

On entering the Duomo one's first impression is of a large, sombre, rather too empty space. Santa Maria is apparently the fourth largest cathedral in the world. The feeling of emptiness is due to partly to the fact that many of the best of the artworks were removed from the building in the mid 19th century. However this rather austere feeling is not unpleasant: the space itself is impressive and clearly defined – grey against white – with sturdy pillars and domed cross-vaulting separating each bay. The whole effect is given balance by an unbroken cornice which gives a strong horizontal pull stopping the ceiling from soaring too wildly upwards.

In the left aisle are the fine painted equestrian monuments (cheaper than sculptures) to two of the most famous *condottieri* of the region. Niccolo da Tolentino was painted by Andrea Castagno and the English mercenary John Hawkwood by Paolo Uccello. Both men served the Florentine Republic at critical times and Hawkwood, who died in 1394, had the distinction of being described by Saint Catherine of Siena as '*Carissimo e dolcissimo fratello di Cristo Gesù*'. Further along is Michelino's painting of *Dante illuminating Florence with his Divine Comedy*. In the 14th and 15th centuries, during Lent, readings of the great book were regularly given in the Duomo.

In the cupola are some pompous Mannerist works showing the Last Judgement by Vasari and Zuccari. But around the base of the dome are some beautiful windows taken from drawings by Donatello, Ghiberti, Uccello and Castagno. The octagonal choir stall and the high altar are the works of Bandinelli over which hangs a wooden crucifix by Benedetto da Maiano. Above the sacristy doors are some typical terracotta lunettes by Luca della Robbia. More interesting are his wonderful bronze doors for the New Sacristy, probably the only work in bronze he ever completed. It was in the New Sacristy that Lorenzo il Magnifico hid after the murder of his brother Giuliano by the Pazzi family in the terrible conspiracy of 1478.

There are several other less important works of art to be found dotted around the building but, perhaps more interesting for those with limited time, is a visit to the crypt of the earlier church which can be entered from the left aisle. The crypt contains early Christian and Roman remains as well as various 14th-century tombs and fragments of frescoes. For the energetic there is also the punishing walk up to the top of the dome to Verrocchio's lantern from where one has a fabulous view of the city and surrounding buildings.

Standing nearby is one of the oldest and most beloved of Florentine churches – the **Baptistery** – dedicated to the city's patron saint, San Giovanni Battista. Throughout the Renaissance, it was generally believed that the octagonal building was Roman – a pagan temple dedicated to Mars. The Classical columns inside seemed to confirm this theory. Although the building is obviously of a much later date, it may have been modelled on the Pantheon, and possibly stood on an ancient site. In 1293 Arnolfo di Cambio encased it in dark greenish-black and white marble, but the white roof was not added until some time after, and is a sad substitute for terracotta tiles.

The real glory of San Giovanni lies the three sets of bronze doors, lovely in themselves, and also a concise illustration of the development of Gothic into Renaissance art over a period of about 100 years. The idea of bronze relief doors was taken from the Campo dei Miracoli in Pisa. Fittingly, it was a Pisan who won the commission for first set of doors.

Andrea Pisano, although unrelated to the great Nicola and Giovanni, had worked in their studio and inherited from them something of the mighty figural tradition they had embarked upon. He began the south doors in 1328, and they took ten years to complete. Of the 28 panels, twenty depict episodes from the life of John the Baptist and the remaining eight show the cardinal and theological virtues. The panels are simple and uncluttered; the figures, modelled in a uniform depth of relief, have a static, almost childlike quality.

The next set of doors was not begun until 1403 following the competition of 1401 which is sometimes described, with baffling simplicity, as 'the beginning of the Renaissance'. The competition required the designing of a bronze panel of Isaac and Abraham. There were entrants of the quality of Brunelleschi and della Quercia, but the commission was finally given to the young and relatively obscure craftsman Lorenzo Ghiberti, then aged 23. The two finalists' panels by Ghiberti and Brunelleschi are now side by side in the Bargello museum and are fascinating to compare.

The north doors are also divided into 28 panels and the narrative is again contained within the rather restrictive Gothic quatrefoils. Between the panels a variety of human heads have replaced the earlier symbolic lions' heads and they are linked by what Ghiberti called a 'most grand ornamentation of leaves and many kinds of plants, all conducted with the greatest invention and discipline'. The panels themselves, showing the life of Christ and various saints, bear little stylistic resemblance to Pisano's – Gothic has subsided into Renaissance. Look at the different depictions of scenery and architecture; and increasingly lifelike figures and drapery. Ghiberti also experimented with different depths of relief as additional aids in the portrayal of perspective and space. In his words, he

> sought to understand how forms strike upon the eye, and how the theoretical part of graphic and pictorial art should be managed. Working with the utmost diligence and care I introduced into some of my compositions as many as a hundred different figures, which I modelled upon different planes, so that those nearest the eye might appear larger and those more remote smaller in proportion.

Ghiberti's comments are typical of the time, combining a scientific approach with an intense awareness of beauty, and a strong belief in his ability to achieve his aims.

But it is not until the third set of doors that we really become aware of

Ghiberti's mastery in the techniques of bronze relief. Dubbed by Michelangelo as 'the gates of Paradise' these ten splendid panels are, in all senses, the culmination of Ghiberti's art. By using many of the skills he had learnt from earlier doors and by removing the constrictions of the quatrefoil frames, he was able to combine all the central episodes of each Old Testament figure's life into single panels. It is worth looking at these doors very closely to see how carefully the master has observed the human situation and, particularly, the way in which small groups of people interact. At the moment the panels are being systematically removed for restoration but one can usually see the missing panels in the Duomo Museum. Between the second and third panels up, Ghiberti himself looks beadily out – a shrewd balding fellow, more like a craftsman than an artist, with a touch of wry humour in his face.

Inside the Baptistery there is still an aura of paganism and a surprising feeling of space. In former centuries baptisms were held infrequently and, consequently, on a massive scale. Sometimes literally hundreds of babies were baptised in succession. The noise of these new little Christians, echoing round the church, must have been quite phenomenal. The original huge font has now disappeared, replaced by the Gothic one to the right of the entrance. Between two of the Roman pillars, taken from an earlier building, is the Renaissance tomb of the Anti-Pope John XXIII by Donatello and Michelozzo. Michelozzo was probably responsible for most of the tomb but the fine portrait of the old man is Donatello's. The lovely black-and-white mosaic pavement was begun in 1209 – the oldest part is by the font. The ceiling mosaics are also rather magnificent; a huge and fierce *Last Judgement* attributed to Coppo di Marcovaldo and, in the cupola, some of San Giovanni himself, the earliest of which are possibly by Cimabue.

Return to the Piazza for a look at one of Ruskin's favourites – the elegant **bell-tower** of Giotto. The gentle painter, who began life as a shepherd in the Mugello countryside, laid the first stone in 1334 but he died three years later and the work was continued by Andrea Pisano, who, being a sculptor himself, added the niches which later housed Donatello's prophets and sibyls. The tower was finally completed in 1360 by Francesco Talenti, but he omitted Giotto's tall spire because, as Vasari tells us, it was thought to be 'a German thing and of antiquated fashion'. In Ruskin's view the combination of beauty and power

> occurs more or less in different buildings, some in one and some in another. But all together, and in all their highest possible relative degrees, exist, as far as I know, only in one building in the world, the Campanile of Giotto.

Around the bottom of the tower are copies of a series of reliefs: *The Creation of Man*, *The Arts* and *The Industries*. It is thought that these were designed by Giotto himself but mainly carried out by Pisano, Arnoldi, and Luca della Robbia. The originals are in the Duomo Museum, as are the brilliant Donatello sculptures, copies of which are in the niches above the reliefs.

The small but intensely rewarding **Museo dell' Opera del Duomo** is at No. 9,

Piazza del Duomo, behind the cathedral. Since the early 15th century the Duomo's affairs have been managed from this building. It was also periodically used to store marble, stone and other building materials for artists. It was in this courtyard that Michelangelo carved his massive David. Now the museum houses all the works taken from the cathedral buildings – many of the most important sculptures in Florence.

On the ground floor there is a facsimile drawing of Arnolfo di Cambio's original Duomo façade, and some of the sculptures that adorned it, by various sculptors including Andrea Pisano, Arnolfo and Nanni di Banco. The adjoining rooms have been made over to the cathedral's construction with various wooden models of projected façades that were never realised. Here also is Brunelleschi's death-mask, blunt-nosed, with a protruding upper lip.

But to find the real treasures of this museum it is necessary to climb the stairs. On the half landing is the first real treat – the moving *Pietà* carved by the elderly Michelangelo for his own tomb. The awkward dead-weight of the Christ seems about to slither uncontrollably out of the grasp of the sufferers and on to the ground. The deeply mourning Nicodemus at the back of the group is probably a self-portrait. Michelangelo was, however, so dissatisfied with the work that he deliberately mutilated it, smashing off Christ's leg and arm, and it had to be repaired by one of his pupils.

Room No.1 on the first floor holds more treasures. There are the two triumphant singing galleries, both completed at the same time, by Luca della Robbia and Donatello. If you are tired of Luca's pretty glazed terracottas these beautiful marble children cannot fail to revive your admiration for his skill. Opposite, Donatello's *putti* tear between pillars with hysterical gaiety like naughty children at a party.

Around the rest of the room are the statues from the Campanile, the best unquestionably being those by Donatello. Donatello's prophets are no idealised heroes. Sunk in thought, troubled and stern, it seems that they alone understand what is happening and what is yet to come. The most moving of these is *Habakkuk*, Donatello's favourite, nicknamed the *Zuccone* (Marrowhead; baldy). Habakkuk is portrayed magnificently as a wise fool with a slight squint in his kindly eyes. Vasari tells us that

> whenever Donatello wanted to swear convincingly to the truth of anything he used to protest 'by the faith I have in my *Zuccone*'. And while he was working on this statue he would look at it and keep muttering, 'Speak, damn you, speak.'

Another stunning piece is Donatello's ravaged Mary Magdalen. Carved in wood, she belongs to the last period of his life, after his return from Padua. These late works are characterised by a new spirit of pessimism and a veering away from the flesh, as if the body has become merely a shell for the spirit. The Magdalen has tremendous pathos. At first glance she is little more than a gaunt animal but there are traces of her lost beauty in her fine hands and the hint of blue in her sunken eyes. It is hard to imagine the effect that these highly expressionistic sculptures must have had on the Florentines at a time when the 'Sweet-style' of Desiderio and della Robbia was all the rage.

The small adjoining room houses the lovely original bas-reliefs from the base of the Campanile (see p.81). In Room No.2 is the magnificent silver-gilt altar from the Baptistery, begun in 1366 and decorated with scenes from the life of John the Baptist. The panels were designed by a variety of artists, including Antonio del Pollaiuolo and Verrocchio. It is frustratingly badly lit, but I find Verrocchio's panel of the *Beheading of Saint John* the liveliest. Also in this room are sometimes exhibited the newly cleaned bronze panels from the Ghiberti's Baptistery doors. Other treasures include some wonderful early 14th-century Byzantine mosaic tablets and a few interesting Florentine paintings and sculptures taken from the Duomo and Baptistery. Though small, this is one of the best museums in the city. It can be explored, superficially at least, fairly quickly, but it would be a real pity to miss it altogether.

Before leaving the square, don't forget to look at the little Gothic **Loggia of the Bigallo**, on the corner of Via Calzaiuoli. It was probably built in the 1330s by Alberto di Arnoldo, and became part of the charitable institution of the Misericordia. In the loggia, foundlings were displayed to the public for three days before going to institutions or foster homes. Now it houses a tiny but interesting museum with works by Bernardo Daddi, Jacopo del Sellaio, Arnoldi and others.

The Piazza della Signoria and Orsanmichele

The Via Calzaiuoli links the cathedral to the city's other main square, the Piazza della Signoria. Built on the route of a Roman road, it became the stamping ground of one of the most volatile of Guelph families, the Adimari. They were described by Dante as an 'outrageous tribe, who played the dragon to those who ran away, but were as quiet as lambs to those who showed them tooth or purse'. Now the street has become a pedestrian zone with expensive shops and buskers playing to the tourists on warm evenings. Here the tall Africans spread out their wares on plastic sheets: fake Gucci handbags, Lacoste shirts or RayBan sunglasses; and one eye on the police.

In this busy commercial street stands the market church of **Orsanmichele**, the pride of the Florentine guilds. In the 13th century the original church of St Michele in Orto (St Michael in the Garden) was demolished to make way for a corn and grain market, for which Arnolfo di Cambio designed a loggia in 1280. On one of the pillars was hung a painting of the Madonna which, by the end of the 13th century, had acquired a reputation for working miracles; healing the sick and ridding the possessed of their devils. Every day the market would be jostling, not only with *contadini* and corn sellers, but also with the devout and the crippled hoping to be cured.

But in 1304, Villani tells us, in one of the most terrible of the faction fights between the black and white Guelphs, the loggia and all the buildings around it as far as the river were set alight. For many years it remained ruined but in

1336 it was decided to rebuild it, combining the features of market place and religious building, to honour the Madonna, who had survived the blaze. The *commune* delegated the task of rebuilding and filling in the remains of the open loggia to a powerful guild, the Arte di Por Santa Maria. The new building was designed by Francesco Talenti, Neri di Fioravante and Benci di Cione. The outside decoration was to be the responsibility of the Parte Guelfa and the other major guilds. Each of the chosen guilds was to provide a statue of its patron saint in a tabernacle on the outside walls, before which its members would make offerings on feast days. The whole ethos of the building was typical of Florence — a combination of tremendous civic and commercial pride, with a great show of religious fervour.

The plan for the external sculptures was put forward in 1339 but nothing much was done until the beginning of the following century, when a time limit was put on the project to speed things up. Surprisingly, and to their eternal credit, the great guilds chose three of the younger, less established, artists to do most of the work: Ghiberti, Nanni di Banco and the young Donatello, then in his twenties. It is worth looking at these statues closely, for it is here that one becomes aware of the new monumentality and realism that characterised the early part of the Florentine Renaissance. Only Ghiberti's Baptist on Via Calzaiuoli still bears witness to the Gothic movement. This figure, the largest to be cast in bronze to that date, won great popular acclaim for its magnificence and elegance. But, despite its undoubted energy, the strange face and great, swooping draperies are unrealistic and seem to be from another world. In contrast, Nanni's four soldier saints have a great weightiness and simplicity about them. Their garments and rather expressionless features echo their Classical predecessors. In Ghiberti's next offering, *St Matthew*, he shows a much greater Roman influence than before in posture, draperies, and, most strikingly, in the very different face he gives his work. His last statue, *St Stephen*, is on similar lines, and shows disappointingly little progression from the earlier ones.

Donatello's *St Mark*, begun when he was 25, also shows a strong classical influence. But even at this stage in his career one is constantly aware that he is interpreting and developing earlier ideas — never merely copying. His *St George*, placed slightly forward in his shallow niche, stands assertively with his weight on both feet and a look of concentration on his otherwise idealised boyish face. Underneath is a relief, also by Donatello, of the slaying of the dragon with the Princess looking on primly. Donatello was also commissioned by the Parte Guelfa to make a *St Louis* in bronze for the central niche in Via Calzaiuoli. The Guelphs were determined to have the grandest statue of all. They ordered it to be cast in bronze and then gilded, to set it apart from the others. This ostentation inevitably aroused much envy, and the *St Louis* was taken down a few years later when the Parte Guelfa finally fell out of favour. The statue is now in the Sante Croce Museum. It does have a certain grandeur but, to my mind, the Saint is so swamped in his cloak and outsize mitre that he looks like a small boy dressed up in grown-up's clothes.

Replacing St Louis is a marvellous group by Verrocchio of *Christ and*

St Thomas, begun in 1476. To fit the two figures into a space made for one, Verrocchio made them smaller than their predecessors, and placed Thomas outside the niche itself in a new use of space. The figures are bound together both by the intimacy of the action and by the repeating pattern of their clothes. There is exquisite sensitivity both in the gentleness of the Christ as he raises his arm and in the hesitancy of the doubter as he reaches his hand towards the open wound.

The inside of Orsanmichele is a dark rectangular hall now used solely as a church. Such natural light as exists beams gently through the fine Gothic stained-glass windows designed by Lorenzo Monaco. Many of the pillars are decorated with rather damaged frescoes of the Guilds' patron saints, painted mainly in the 14th and 15th centuries. The most interesting thing is Andrea Orcagna's amazing Gothic tabernacle, which houses the replacement miracle-working Virgin, painted by Bernardo Daddi in 1366. The Infant Jesus seems almost to be pushing his mother away, while his small left hand tightly squeezes a goldfinch. Nearby is Sangallo's marble group: *St Anne with the Virgin and Child.* The two Gothic halls on the upper floors of the building are reached by a corridor from the Palazzo dell' Arte della Lana behind the church. It was from this tower house that the City's wool trade was controlled, including some 30,000 workers and 200 shops.

Turning off the Via Calzaiuoli opposite Orsanmichele one comes to the small area traditionally associated with Dante. In Via Santa Margherita is the little church where the poet was probably married. Nearby is the **Casa di Dante**, where he may have been born, containing a collection of material, little of which is original. The Via Calzaiuoli continues its way past more shops and bars straight to the Piazza della Signoria.

In 1268 the great Ghibelline family of the Uberti were ruined. Their property was confiscated and left in ruins, a dismal pile of rubble, as an example and grisly warning to anyone whose sympathies lay away from the increasingly dominant Parte Guelfa. When the great town hall was planned some 15 years later the refusal of the Guelphs to build on the cursed land of the Uberti meant that the new square took on the beginnings of the irregular shape it has today. The **Piazza della Signoria** soon became the recognised centre of public life in the city. It was here that political speeches were made and public meetings were held, and the volatile Florentines roused to fever pitch or calmed into inactivity.

It was here that Girolamo Savonarola lit his 'bonfires of the vanities', burning jewellery and mirrors, sculptures and drawings, paintings by Botticelli and illuminated manuscripts by Boccaccio. On 23 May 1498 the final bonfire burnt the body of the Friar himself, ending the city's brief but destructive return to the Middle Ages. Eyewitnesses say that the burning corpse raised his right hand out of the flames in a sign of benediction, at which the people shrank back in horror, terrified at the damnation they had brought upon themselves. For two hundred years flowers and lights kept burning by the devout commemorated the place of Savonarola's death. Now it is marked by a simple porphyry plaque.

At right angles to the Palazzo Vecchio is the open **Loggia dei Lanzi**, built in grey stone by Benci di Cione and Simone Talenti in 1376–82. Its name comes from Lanzichenecchi, Cosimo I's Brigade of Swiss Lancers, who were stationed there to protect him. Now it is filled with statues: Roman along the back wall and later ones towards the front. On his first trip to the city, D. H. Lawrence was less than bowled over by this arrangement: '. . . Then all the statuary in the Loggia! But that is a mistake. It looks too much like the yard of a monumental mason.' Perhaps the most impressive of these statues is Cellini's bronze *Perseus* – he evidently thought so himself – which was nearly destroyed by a fire in his studio. On the back of Perseus's head another face can be made out which is thought to be a self-portrait of the artist. Under the right arch is Giambologna's *Rape of the Sabine Women* and behind it, his *Hercules fighting the Centaur*.

The sculptural theme spills out of the loggia and into the square, providing a unifying force amid the rather haphazard architectural arrangement. Larger than life is the copy of Michelangelo's *David*, standing where the sculptor placed him in front of the great palace. Here was something by which Lawrence could not fail to be impressed:

> He may be ugly, too naturalistic, too big, and anything else you like. But the David in the Piazza della Signoria, there under the dark great palace, in the position Michelangolo chose for him, there, standing forward stripped and exposed and eternally half-shrinking, half-wishing to expose himself, he is the genius of Florence.

Beside the *David* the other sculptures look rather small. There is the copy of Donatello's *Judith and Holofernes*, of which the fabulously restored original is in the Palazzo Vecchio. There is also a copy of his famous Marzocco lion. The lion was a symbol of Florentine power and justice – criminals were frequently humiliated by having to kiss its rear end in public, to the unfailing delight of the crowd. Nearby is the clumsy and lethargic *Neptune* on his fountain by Ammanatti. This was never a popular work. In the 16th century there was a rhyme in the city which ran *'Ammanato, Ammanato, che bel marmo ha rovinato'* (Ammanatti, Ammanatti, What lovely marble you have ruined). Giambologna's equestrian monument to Grand Duke Cosimo is more successful, rising arrogantly above the heads of the tourists on his magnificent green bronze charger.

Much of the rest of the square is taken up with cafés and restaurants which, as in most main squares, tend to be overpriced and crowded. The ever popular bar Rivoire still has the most style and is good for an extravagant hot chocolate on cold days. If you want a proper meal in the piazza Il Cavallino (6 via delle Farine) is your best bet. Equally popular with the Florentines is the little Buca dell' Orafo in a cellar in the Via dei Girolami just beside the Ponte Vecchio. In June the Piazza is the site of the famous *Calcio* – a football match in medieval dress which takes place between the different *contrade* of the city.

Near the eastern corner of the Piazza della Signoria stands the biscuit-brown town hall, the **Palazzo Vecchio**. It was begun in 1298, just a short time after the Duomo, and was probably also designed by the architect and sculptor Arnolfo di Cambio. In 1332 the great bell was cast by the Sienese for the tower. The bell was known officially as 'the Lion', the symbol of Florence, but its low resonance struck the citizens as being more like a cow and the bell-tower soon became known as the Torre della Vacca (Tower of the Cow). It was used to call the people to the square for meetings or in times of crisis. At the front of the building, there was a large *ringhiera* or platform, (literally haranguing place) where the *Signoria*, the town council, would address the populace. It was pulled down in 1813 and replaced by the present steps.

Inside the entrance, to the right, is Michelozzo's Cortile designed in the mid 1440s. In 1565 when Francesco de Medici, son of Cosimo I, moved into the palace with his new wife Joan of Austria, the courtyard was totally revamped by Vasari using gilt and stucco. Verrocchio's bronze *Boy with a Dolphin*, made for Lorenzo il Magnifico, was taken from the villa at Carreggi for the centrepiece. Now it has been replaced by a copy and the original is upstairs.

Inside is the huge Sala del Maggior Consiglio or Cinquecento built after the collapse of the first batch of Medici, following the expulsion of the weak and foolish Piero, Lorenzo's son, in 1494. It was designed by Simone di Pollaiuolo, (known as il Cronaca, for his endless supply of anecdotes about Savonarola), and was big enough to house the whole of Fra Girolamo's new council of 500 men. It was here that he made his most famous speech on being offered a Cardinal's hat as a bribe from the Pope:

> I want no hats, no mitres great or small; nothing would I have save what Thou has given to Thy saints – death; a red hat, a hat of blood – this do I desire.

Characteristically the friar ordered the rooms of the great hall to be left bare, and it was not until after his death that it was decided to decorate them.

In 1503 Savonarola's successor Piero Soderini commissioned two great battle scenes for the main walls of the *salone* from Michelangelo and Leonardo da Vinci. Neither of these pictures ever got much further than cartoon stage but they soon became standard texts for young artists to study. Now, sadly, they are both lost, replaced by the grandiose battle scenes of the late Mannerists, painted under Vasari's direction to exalt the Medici. More appealing is the elegant little Mannerist Studiolo di Francesco I with two fine portraits of Francesco's parents, Cosimo I and Eleanor of Toledo, painted by Bronzino. Bronzino also decorated the chapel of Eleanor of Toledo in her private apartments. To appreciate most of the rooms in the Palazzo Vecchio one needs to be an ardent devotee of the Mannerist school. Room after room is covered with the ornate, exaggerated frescoes of the late 16th century, planned and implemented by the tireless Vasari and his colleagues. A few rooms stand out: there is the lovely Sala dei Gigli on the second floor designed by Benedetto da Maiano and painted by Domenico and Davide Ghirlandaio, and the little Cappella dei Priori built in 1511 and decorated by Ridolfo Ghirlandaio. There is also Maiano's Sala di Udienza which now houses one of the best statues of the Renaissance – Donatello's *Judith and Holofernes*.

There are two marvellous statues on the second floor of the Palazzo Vecchio; the *Judith* and the original of Verrocchio's *Boy with a Dolphin* from the Courtyard, now in the Cancellaria. Verrocchio's bronze *putto* looks mischievously over his shoulder provoking his audience to walk round him – the first statue of the Renaissance designed specifically to be seen from the back as well as the front. In the Sala di Udienza, Donatello's statue in its recently restored state is breathtaking, with the slight figure of Judith towering above Holofernes as she raises her sword to slay him. Her small foot is forcing his hand down but we do not really feel that he is even trying to escape. His eyes are closed, soporifically, almost in ecstasy, while she seems unable to look at what she is doing. This statue was created in the ten years before the sculptor's death in 1466, and has something of the desperate quality of much of his later work that is epitomised in the Magdalen in the Duomo Museum.

There is one more thing to do in the Palazzo Vecchio and that is to climb the great tower. On the way up is the Alberghettino, less a small hotel than a prison, where Cosimo Il Vecchio, and later, Savonarola, were incarcerated. At the top is one of the best views of the rooftops and churches of the city. Immediately below is the Piazza della Signoria with its sculptures and people, while nearby the long twin palaces of the Uffizi stretch down to the river.

The Uffizi

The Uffizi was designed by Vasari for Grand Duke Cosimo I to be used as the central administrative offices of Tuscany (hence Uffizi-offices). Begun in 1560, it consists of two similar palaces running along a piazza so long and narrow as to be effectively little more than a passage. Unusually for the period, it is built mainly of the cool grey *pietra serena*. Generally this stone was used only for internal structural decoration, often in conjunction with white plaster as in the church of San Lorenzo. The building has niches for statues of famous citizens but, in general, Vasari's details are rather unimaginative. After his death the building was finished by another master of many skills, the aptly named Bernardo Buontalenti, who as well as being an architect, painter and sculptor, made fantastic and exotic fireworks for the Medici. The weird Porta delle Suppliche, with its pediment halved and placed end-to-end, giving the effect of a giant insect's wings, is his creation.

In summer, particularly in the morning, the queue for the picture gallery can seem endless. But usually by lunchtime it has diminished and often disappeared. Even so, for the less rigorous sightseer, the word 'Uffizi' is as likely to be accompanied by a sigh of anticipated exhaustion as of pleasure. In fact the end result is both. The Uffizi is a massive undertaking but a correspondingly rewarding one. For those with plenty of time it is best to make several shortish visits, but for the majority whose time in Florence is limited it is probably wisest just to concentrate on the Tuscan pictures of the Renaissance. The Uffizi's collection of these is staggering, with countless examples of unrivalled beauty and quality.

The main galleries are on the third floor. Before going up (there is a lift if you need one) have a look at Castagno's murals of famous Florentines, down in the remains of the old church of San Pier Scherraggio which was demolished before the Uffizi was built. On the stairs up to the galleries is also a worn but rather lovely *Annunciation* by Botticelli. The building was first used as a gallery after Cosimo I's death and originally housed a huge collection of different artefacts as well as sculptures and painting, proclaiming the massive wealth of the Medici as art patrons. The long corridors are lined with sculptures, many of which date back to classical times. In fact when Shelley visited the gallery for the first time his notebook left out paintings altogether.

In **Room No.2**, one of the greatest rooms of the Uffizi, are the three great early Madonnas by Cimabue and two of his pupils, Duccio di Buoninsegna and Giotto. Cimabue's *Maestà* was painted for the church of Santa Trinità in 1285 – the final phase of Florentine Byzantine painting. There are indications of what is to come in the shaded drapery of the angels' garments and the attempt at perspective in the Virgin's throne, but the whole effect is stylised and dreamlike – purely Byzantine. The so-called *Rucellai Madonna* attributed to the Sienese painter Duccio was painted at about the same time. Duccio worked in the same studio as Cimabue, but he also inherited the Sienese love of decorative detail that is particularly noticeable round the frame. It was only 25 years later that Giotto painted his *Maestà*, but the solidity and realism of the central figure heralded a completely new era. John Ruskin saw this leap not just in terms of technical skill but in Giotto's ability to reconcile spirituality with everyday life:

> Even Cimabue did not venture to leave the field of conventionally reverenced dignity. He still painted – though beautifully – only the Madonna, and the St Joseph, and the Christ . . . But Giotto came from the field; and saw with his simple eyes a lowlier worth. And he painted – the Madonna, and St Joseph, and the Christ, – yes, by all means, if you choose to call them so, but essentially, Mamma, Papa, and the Baby. And all Italy threw up its cap . . .

Through the Sienese Room with its lovely Simone Martini *Annunciation*, and the early Florentines and the fabulously decorative International Gothic paintings of Gentile da Fabriano and Lorenzo Monaco, pass on to **Room No.7**. Here is Masaccio and Masolino's *Madonna and Child* with St Anne, and Piero's portrait of Federigo di Montefeltro with his extraordinary profile, set against a wide Tuscan landscape. Uccello's marvellous *Battle of San Romano*, of which a counterpart is in London's National Gallery, was originally in Lorenzo il Magnifico's bedroom. After more 15th-century painters – Filippo Lippi, the Pollaiuolo brothers and Baldovinetti – you reach the rooms dedicated to the paintings of Sandro Filipepi, called Botticelli, and the most loved paintings in the Uffizi.

The Botticellis (by which I mean the two allegories of Spring and the *Birth of Venus*) are more popular than the Leonardos, the Raphaels or the powerful tondo of Michelangelo in **Room No.25**. Botticelli's Venus has an indescribable loveliness as she waits, shy and dreaming, to be blown ashore on her scallop shell. She was apparently modelled on Simonetta Vespucci, beloved of Lorenzo's brother Giuliano who was killed by the Pazzi in 1478. The *Primavera* epitomises the life in the young Lorenzo's court with its love of beauty and youth: classical mythology in a pastoral setting. Lorenzo himself was not a painter, but many of his poems show just the same quality of gaiety and romance. Botticelli, however, was soon to come under the austere influence of Savanarola; and many of his later pictures have an aura of pessimism completely alien to his early work. In *Calumny*, King Midas listens with ass's ears to his advisers Ignorance and Suspicion, while the innocent victim is dragged along by Envy, Deceit and Malice. The crone in black looking over her shoulder is Remorse.

Now to **Room No.15** and Leonardo da Vinci. In the *Baptism of Christ* (c.1470), done in collaboration with his teacher Andrea Verrocchio, we see Leonardo's earliest known work in oils. The two main figures of Christ and the Baptist are by Verrocchio as the established artist, but it is generally agreed that the kneeling angel on the far left, and most of the landscape, is the work of Leonardo, then in his teens. The sketch for the *Adoration of the Magi* was left unfinished when Leonardo was called to Milan in 1481; but even in its incomplete state it shows a great precocity. Its pyramidal composition ensures that, despite the number of figures depicted, there is no doubt as to the most important group. Leonardo's new technique of shading (*sfumato*) and the detail given to the figures, the horses and the setting show his amazing propensity for never-ending observation and research. The *Annunciation* was painted for the Convent at Monteoliveto, but its attribution as a Leonardo has been a constant source of debate.

Room No.18, the richly decorated Tribune Room, was designed by Buontalenti in 1584. It now houses the most famous sculpture in the gallery, the so-called *Medici Venus*. She was a Roman copy made in about the 1st century AD of a 4th-century BC Hellenic sculpture of Aphrodite of Cnidos. She has in the past held a particular magnetism for educated Europeans as a kind of up-market sex symbol. She was the only sculpture that Napoleon took from Florence. Today she seems overwhelmingly chaste and modest. On the walls of the tribune are some fine 16th-century portraits of the Medici, notably Pontormo's *Cosimo il Vecchio*, and Vasari's *Lorenzo il Magnifico*.

The next rooms are dedicated mainly to painters from other parts of Italy, (mainly Venetians), Germany and Flanders. But in **Room No.25** we find the amazing *Doni Tondo* of Michelangelo, his first known painting. This was commissioned by Agnolo Doni to celebrate his marriage to Maddalena Strozzi in 1504. The whole effect of the tondo is sculptural, emphasised by the frieze of naked figures in the background. It seems to echo Michelangelo's belief that sculpture, not painting, is the ultimate art form. Next we come to the work of Raphael, the perfect painter, whom even Vasari could hardly find words exalted enough to praise:

> One can claim without fear of contradiction that artists as outstandingly gifted as Raphael are not simply men, but, if it be allowed to say so, mortal gods . . .

Here also is del Sarto's *Madonna of the Harpies*, with a solemn Mary and a positively sniggering Christ.

The next room concentrates on del Sarto's pupil Pontormo, and then we leave the Tuscans for the Emilians, the Veronese and the Venetians. In **Room No.28** is another sex symbol, Titian's *Venus of Urbino*, painted for the Duke in 1538. If you have the stamina there are wonderful Canalettos and Tintorettos; fabulous Rubens and Dycks. Right at the end in **Room No.44** are three great Rembrandts: two self-portraits and a moving picture of an old man, hands folded, waiting with a look of profound resignation on his face.

If you wish, it is possible to visit the Vasari Corridor, built in 1565 to join the Uffizi to the Pitti Palace, when it became the official residence of the Medici Grand Dukes. The corridor runs over the Ponte Vecchio and as well as some interesting pictures has a fine view of the Ponte alle Grazie, rebuilt after the Second World War.

The Ponte Vecchio

The Ponte Vecchio is one of the most potent and widely recognised symbols of Florence. It was first erected in the Roman era, spanning the river at its narrowest point, when as well as being vital to the newly flourishing town it was also on the quickest route south from Venice to Rome. It became known as the Ponte Vecchio or Old Bridge when the Ponte alla Carraia was built in the 13th century. Initially the bridge had nine arches but in 1345, after one of Florence's disastrous floods, it was rebuilt as it now stands with only three arches and stone compartments for traders. At that time the shops were a motley collection of tanners, followed by butchers, greengrocers and other household merchants. In 1593 Grand Duke Ferdinand I decided that it was unfitting that the route between the two great Medici strongholds, the Uffizi and the Pitti, should be linked by such an undignified hotch-potch and decreed that the shops should belong only to goldsmiths and jewellers who would bring prestige to the area.

Unlike the other bridges which span the Arno, the Ponte Vecchio survived the repeated and often devastating floods which constantly threatened the city. Centuries later it was also the only bridge to survive the German bombardment in the Second World War. One account says that the Führer himself ordered the demolition of all the bridges 'except the artistic one', at the special request of the German Consul. Now the bridge is thronged day and night with tourists and hippies who cluster interminably around the statue of the great egocentric goldsmith, Benvenuto Cellini, with bottles of wine and

The Ponte Vecchio

cartons of cigarettes. Here too are pedlars and art students selling beads and watercolours of the city to anyone who will buy. One feels that despite Ferdinand's attempts the bridge has returned in spirit to the bazaar it always was. The Ponte Vecchio has a unique and wholly Florentine charm. From its cracking ochre parapet one can see the river and the old houses of the city stretching into the distance, while beyond lie the green hills, dotted with villas and cypresses.

Practical Information

Hotels and Restaurants

The area between the Duomo and the Piazza della Signoria is not the best place to stay, being incessantly busy and usually expensive. In the pedestrian Via Calzaiuoli is the comfortable *Hotel Calzaiuoli* (tel. 212456). For those who enjoy the efficiency of big hotels there are several in the large Piazza della Republicca of which the *Savoy* (tel. 283313) is the most popular.

One of the nicer central restaurants is the little trattoria known as the *Bucca dell' Orafo*, Via del Girolamo, in a cellar near the Ponte Vecchio, which is popular with Florentine businessmen. On the corner of the Piazza della Signoria is *Il Cavallino*, Via delle Farine 6, the best of the restaurants on the square, also very popular with the Florentines. Of the expensive cafés here the famous bar *Rivoire* retains a certain style out of season. Good food can be had in *Mario da Gianino* Piazza dei Cimatori 4, and in the *Antico Fattore* Via Lambertesca 1–3 near the Uffizi.

Museums

Museo del Bigallo   Piazza San Giovanni: usually closed.
Museo dell' Opera del Duomo   Piazza Duomo 9: open summer 09.00–19.30; winter 09.00–18.00; Sun and hols closed.
Casa di Dante   Via S. Margherita: open 09.30–12.30 and 15.30–18.30; Sun and hols 09.30–12.30; closed Wed.
Palazzo Vecchio   Piazza Signoria: open weekdays 09.00–19.00; Sun and hols 09.00–13.00; closed Sat.
Galleria degli Uffizi   Loggiato Uffizi 6: open Tues–Sun 09.00–18.45; Sun and hols 09.00–12.45.
Museo di Storia della Scienza (Science History)   Piazza Guidici 10: open 09.30–13.00 and 14.00–16.00; Sun 9.30–12.30.

7. WESTERN FLORENCE: from Santa Maria Novella to the Arno

Santa Maria Novella

To the west of the city, just a few minutes' walk from the vast Mussoliniesque railway station, is the great Dominican church of Santa Maria Novella. It overlooks a meagre fountain surrounded by pigeons and exhausted backpackers from the station, while all around are hotels, cheap one side, expensive the other. But despite this the square still has the charm of being one of the relatively few green areas in Florence and its outdoor cafés, though not exactly cheap, are pleasant for breakfast or a cool drink. At the far end of the square is a rather charming loggia, a close copy of the one designed by Brunelleschi for the Foundling hospital (see p.112). The two obelisks carried by tortoises are by Giambologna and mark the boundaries of the yearly chariot race which was instigated by Cosimo I in 1563 and continued until the last century.

But the main reason to come to the square is for the church itself. **Santa Maria Novella** was begun by the Dominicans in the mid 13th century just a few years before work started on its great Franciscan counterpart in the city, Santa Croce. The Dominicans and the Franciscans have long been involved in a rather unholy rivalry which is epitomised by the two churches – anything one had the other was compelled to better. It was partly this continual competition that led to the fabulous collection of treasures that each church still boasts. Now, with the relative decline of both orders, the rivalry has somewhat dimmed. If anything the Dominicans are still rather the grander of the two, bustling about in immaculate designer black-and-white gowns.

Santa Maria was mostly finished by the mid 14th century under the guidance of Fra Jacopo Talenti, who was probably also responsible for the lower part of the beautiful marble façade. Along the right-hand side are the arched *avelli*,

94

the vaults of well-to-do Florentine families – this was the old cemetery. About 100 years later the architect and theorist Leon Battista Alberti was commissioned by the powerful Rucellai family, for whom he built the palace in the Via Vigna Nuova, to put a second storey on the church façade and remodel the main door. He also designed the frieze, which combines the blown sails of the Rucellai crest with the ring and ostrich feathers of the Medici, the two families having recently been joined by marriage.

In 1565 Vasari was asked to update the interior of the church, which he did by whitewashing over all the original frescoes (Santa Croce received the same treatment) and shortening the windows to accommodate some new Renaissance side chapels. In the 19th century the windows were transformed back to their original shape and since then much of Vasari's whitewash has been removed to reveal the original 14th-century paintings.

The right-hand aisle contains various paintings of mixed interest, many of which are by G. Naldini, a rather dull pupil of Bronzino. In the second bay is Rosselino's fine tomb of the Dominican sister Villana delle Botti who died in 1451. Villana actually got married but then fled from the world because on looking in the mirror she saw a demon dressed in her riches. The cross before which she prayed has been moved from its original site in to the Cappella della Pura, between the fifth and sixth bays. In the transept is another good tomb, possibly carved by the 'Sweet-style' sculptor Tino da Camaino to house the body of Tedice Aliotti who died in 1336. Near the tomb of Paolo Rucellai is the Cappella Rucellai, where Duccio's *Madonna* used to hang before its removal to the Uffizi. It has been replaced by a statue of the Madonna and Child by Pisano and Ghiberti's tomb slab of Lionardo Dati. Passing the Bardi Chapel with some worn mural fragments, possibly by Cimabue, one comes to the chapel of Filippo Strozzi.

In 1486 the powerful banker Filippo Strozzi commissioned Filippino Lippi to decorate his new chapel with stories from the life of SS Philip and John the Evangelist. Filippino did not finally complete the work until 1502, and the result is a strange concoction of exaggerated, frenzied figures, extravagantly painted in a way which is seen by many as a direct forerunner of Mannerism. Strozzi actually died before they were completed and lies here in a delicately carved tomb by Benedetto da Maiano. It was in this chapel that the 'seven honest young girls of important lineage, dressed in sober clothes, together with three young men', supposedly assembled during the plague of 1348 to tell the tales of Boccaccio's *Decameron*.

The sanctuary is also frescoed, at the instigation of Giovanni Tornabuoni who commissioned Domenico Ghirlandaio and assistants to paint the lives of the Baptist and the Virgin. These are some of Ghirlandaio's best paintings, though their great charm lies more in the picture of life in 15th-century Florence than in religious sincerity. Many of the figures are actually representations of the donor's family and friends. On the back wall are the kneeling portraits of Giovanni and his wife, and in the vault, the four Evangelists. Like Lippi in the Strozzi chapel, Ghirlandaio also designed the stained glass.

On the left of the Sanctuary is the Gondi chapel, worked in marble by

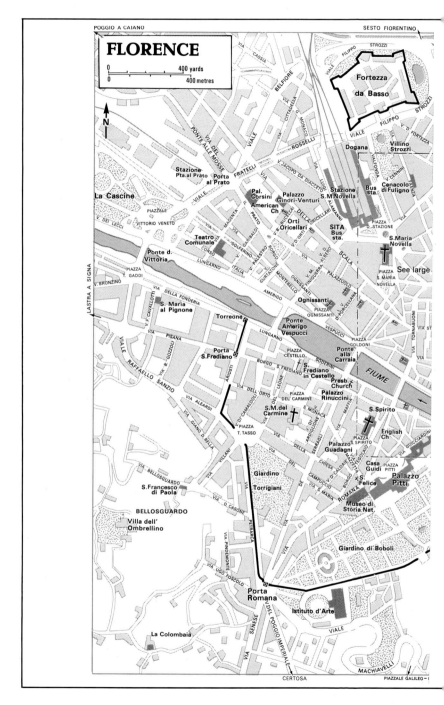

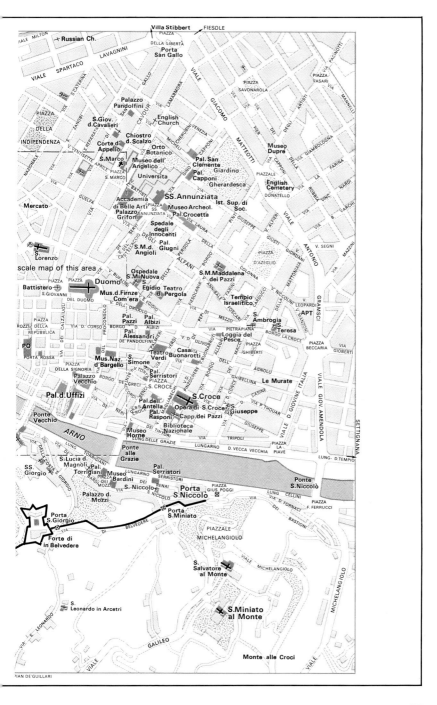

Giuliano da Sangallo. Here also is Brunelleschi's only surviving wooden sculpture – a fine crucifix which he made in answer to the one carved by Donatello in Santa Croce. Past the 14th-century Gaddi chapel is the other Strozzi chapel, frescoed by Nardo di Cione. It also contains an unusual polyptych, by Nardo's brother Orcagna, of Christ giving the keys to St Peter and the Book of Wisdom to Thomas Aquinas. The frescoes show the vision of life according to Dante; Purgatory, the circles of Hell, Paradise and the Last Judgement. At the top of the left aisle in the richly decorated sacristy is a marvellous early painted crucifix by Giotto and a pretty ornamental lavabo by Giovanni della Robbia.

The best painting in Santa Maria Novella is Masaccio's superb *Trinity* (c.1425) in the left aisle. It is a severe work set against a Brunelleschian architectural background, with a gaunt God behind the Cross and the Cardoni donors kneeling, life-size, at the edge. There is a strange, dry expression on the face of Mary, whose hand is raised towards the corpse as if to say 'Well, what did you expect from a boy like this?' On the nearby pillar is the pulpit, designed by Brunelleschi but probably executed by his son-in-law Buggiano.

The cloisters are reached through a door to the left of the façade. Built by Talenti in the middle of the 14th century, they are known as the Chiostri Verdi because of the green tint of the wonderful but faded frescoes by Paolo Uccello depicting scenes from Genesis. From the cloister go into the Spanish Chapel, which was also built by Talenti but gained its name later when Eleanor of Toledo made it over to her Spanish following. All over the vaulted interior is a complicated series of frescoes following the theme 'Christ, Saviour of Humanity, grants his Grace and his doctrine through the Church, in which and for which the Dominican order carries on its activity.' The dogs are hounds of God (Domini Cani) symbols of the Dominican order. On the right is the door leading to the Chiostrini dei Morti, the oldest part of the convent, with some more damaged Florentine paintings. The Chiostro Grande cannot be entered as it now belongs to the police, but it is possible to go into Talenti's refectory where there are various pictures by Alesso Allori and others.

Between Santa Maria and the Arno

Leaving the church of Santa Maria and wandering down towards the river, be sure to walk down the narrow **Via Vigna Nuova**. Here you will find the beautiful and innovative Renaissance **Palazzo Rucellai** which was designed for the wealthy and cultured merchant Giovanni Rucellai by the great architect and theorist Leon Battista Alberti. It was begun in c.1448, roughly the same time as the massive Medici palace, but it is very different in style; altogether lighter, smaller and with a Classical emphasis which was later much copied. It has three storeys, each with pillars of a different Classical order, separated by a frieze of the Rucellai blown sails and the Medici ring. Opposite is the rather less elegant **Rucellai Loggia** – one of the last family loggias to be built in the city because of the growing price of land. The loggias were used for many different public functions – Giovanni recorded that he arranged the marriage of three of his five daughters here all on one day to his 'great content'.

The area towards the Arno is dominated by the main road **Borgo Ognissanti** and is traditionally the working-class home of the wool trade. For many centuries this trade lay in the hands of the Umiliati, a practical and business-like religious order. The Italian historian Villari tells us, 'wherever a house of their order was established the wool-weaving trade immediately made advances'. The Order arrived in Florence in 1239 and by 1256 they had established a firm trade and built a small church in Borgo Ognissanti. Owing to Tuscany's poor sheep-rearing terrain, raw wool was bought in from abroad, mainly from England and Portugal, and it was then processed and woven in Florence before being sold around Europe and the Middle East. By the mid 14th century trade was booming under the Umiliati, who also owned a large number of properties which they rented out to the workers to live in; but by the late 15th century the wool trade was on the wane, and in 1547 Grand Duke Cosimo I expelled the too powerful Order across the river to the little church of San Jacopo sopr'Arno, giving the old church to the Franciscans. Like San Frediano across the river much of this area has retained its artisan character. It is also a good place to eat, with unpretentious *trattorie* like the busy and well-known Sostanza and, slightly more upmarket, the Fiaschetteria 'il Latini', with hams hanging from the ceiling and a lively Florentine clientèle.

The church of **Ognissanti** has been reconstructed and altered many times since its early founding by the Umiliati. One of the oldest parts still remaining is the slim 13th-century bell-tower, but most of the rest of the building has a distinctly 17th–18th-century flavour. The elegant façade is actually an exact copy of a 17th-century design by Nigetti. Inside is Ghirlandaio's *Madonna of Mercy protecting the Vespucci family*. The Vespucci were an extremely powerful local family who had made most of their huge fortune through the silk trade and banking. The explorer Amerigo was one of their clan. Another was the beautiful Simonetta, adored by Giuliano de Medici, whom Botticelli used as the model for his Venus. It is generally thought that Ghirlandaio also used her as his model for the Virgin, and that this painting is probably her best likeness. Also by Ghirlandaio is the picture of *St Jerome* in his study, near Botticelli's *St Augustine*. To the left of the church is the convent refectory which contains one of Ghirlandaio's masterpieces, an excellent Last Supper.

Following the Lungarno westwards, one eventually comes to the large and rather dismal park, the Cascine. In the 17th century the area was used as a hunting ground by the Medici Grand Dukes and later it was turned into a public garden by Napoleon's sister Elise Baciocchi. Now it is mainly frequented by a variety of unsavoury characters and is unsafe to visit at night. The Borgo Ognissanti meets the river at the Piazza Goldoni and the **Ponte alla Carraia**. This bridge, the first to be built after the Ponte Vecchio, was initially erected c.1219 for use by the wool workers from Ognissanti and San Frediano. It was named after the *carri*, the horse-drawn carts which carried the wool. Due to repeated flooding it had to be rebuilt several times. Its most recent collapse was due to bombing in the Second World War – since when it has been again rebuilt. Continuing along the Arno, one passes the big Palazzo Corsini with its amazing private collection of pictures. Next to the reconstructed 15th-century Palazzo Gianfiglizzi is the British Consulate, housed in the Palazzo Masetti. It was here that Louise of Stolberg lived with her lover, the poet Alfieri, after deserting her husband Charles Edward Stuart, the Young Pretender. (Bonnie Prince Charlie lived for many years in a palace on the Via Gino Capponi after his final departure from Britain – a pathetic and drunken figure).

The next bridge as you head eastwards along the river is the lovely **Ponte Santa Trinità**. First built in 1252 this bridge, like the Carraia, needed to be reconstructed several times following flood damage. In 1566 the bridge was completely rebuilt by Bartolomeo Ammanati, possibly using an idea by Michelangelo. He produced a beautifully proportioned three-arched structure with a gentle curve and openings wide enough to contain the Arno in full spate. Subsequently many studies were done on this bridge which, while looking elegant, proved sturdy enough to withstand the Arno for several centuries. But one thing it could not withstand was the Germans, who blew it up while retreating from the allies in 1944. After much local debate the bridge has been reinstated, using Ammannati's original plans and, where possible, the original stones gathered from the river. In 1954 the old quarries in the Boboli gardens were even briefly re-opened so that the new stone would exactly match the old.

Passing the large battlemented medieval palace of the Spini-Ferroni on your right, you reach the beginning of the smart shopping street, the **Via Tornabuoni**. Among the names to be found here are Gucci, Ferragamo, Giorgio Armani and Yves St-Laurent and the stylish bar, Doney, fashionable since the beginning of the century with the aristocracy and visiting *literati* of Florence.

Immediately before you stand the piazza and church of **Santa Trinità**. This was the parish church of the great local families of the Davizzi (and later the Davantzati), the Bartolini Salimbeni, the Strozzi and the Sassetti, all of whom had palaces nearby. It was founded in the early 11th century by the Florentine saint, Giovanni Gualberti, but the present church dates from around 1270. The façade was added towards the end of the 16th century by the Medici Grand Duke's architect Bernardo Buontalenti.

Inside are several family chapels containing various items of interest. On the right-hand side look particularly at the fourth chapel along, which belonged to the Bartolini-Salimbeni whose palace faces the church. It is a good example of a complete and undisturbed 15th-century chapel, with most of its contemporary fittings still intact and fresco decoration by Lorenzo Monaco (c.1425). Next door in the Ardinghelli chapel is a fine tabernacle carved by Benedetto da Rovezzano in 1510. The Sacristy, or Chapel of Onotrio Strozzi, may have been designed by Michelozzo and contains the tomb of Onotrio, father of the great humanist Pala Strozzi. Nearby is the Sassetti chapel, exquisitely frescoed by Domenico Ghirlandaio who also painted the altarpiece. The frescoes show the life of St Francis and the prophecies of Christ's birth. In the higher tier Ghirlandiao has painted the Sassetti family with Lorenzo de' Medici and his sons (on the steps) and their tutors Poliziano and Pulci. Past the chancel, which contains a *Trinity* by Mariotto di Nardo (1406), and the Cappella Usimbardi, is the Scali chapel which has an excellent tomb of Benozzo Federighi by Luca della Robbia (1405). More fine workmanship can be seen in Desiderio da Settignano and Benedetto da Maiano's wooden *Mary Magdalen*, although it has nothing of the power of Donatello's ravaged wooden figure in the Duomo museum.

Almost opposite the church is Baccio d'Agnolo's early 16th-century **Palazzo Bartolini-Salimbeni**, whose innovative qualities caused a stir amongst the conservative Florentines. Vasari describes it as

> the first edifice built with square windows having frontispieces and off which the columns of the door support the architrave, the frieze and the cornice. Therefore the Florentines derided these novelties with jibes and with sonnets, and they hung it about with garlands of boughs as is done in churches for the festivals, saying that it was more like a church than a palace; so that Baccio was well nigh losing his reason; however knowing that he had followed good examples and that the building was beautiful he took heart.

Vasari's only criticism was that

> In order to imitate Cronaca, he placed a huge antique cornice . . . on top of a small elegant façade, so that nothing could be worse, and all for lack of knowledge; it looks like a large hat on a small head.

Further along the Via Tornabuoni, on the same side, is the massive **Palazzo Strozzi** which was begun in 1489. The Strozzi were one of the oldest families in Florence, who got their name from an ancestor's infamous ability to strangle (*strozzare*) his enemies with one hand. In the middle ages they became one of the wealthiest families in the city and in 1427 Pala Strozzi's property was valued at around 25 per cent more than that of the Medici. However, it was not necessarily a good thing to advertise one's wealth, and Lorenzo Strozzi describes some of the problems his father Filippo had in building such a large palace.

> . . . he was confronted by the great difficulty that he who governed (Lorenzo de' Medici) might conceive that another's glory would outshine his; so fearing to do a thing that might arouse envy, he spread abroad the rumour that having so many children and so small a house, he was bound, having begotten them, to provide a dwelling for them, a thing better done during life than death.

Still further along is the 17th-century Baroque church of **San Gaetano**, designed by Gherardo Silvani. It contains a *Martyrdom of San Lorenzo* by Pietro di Cortona (c.1650) and, in the sacristy, a charming *Virgin and Child* by a follower of Botticelli. Across the road is the well-restored 15th-century Palazzo Antinori. It belongs to the successful wine-growing family who have opened a rather elegant but expensive *cantinetta* on the ground floor where you can eat Tuscan snacks from their *fattoria* and sample the Antinori wines.

Between Piazza S. Trinitá and Piazza della Signoria

Turning east off the Via Tornabuoni down the ancient Via Porta Rossa will take you to the 14th-century **Palazzo Davantzati** which has been well restored and equipped to show the style of life of a Florentine noble family in the 14th –16th centuries. The palace is a good example of the change in building styles between the Middle Ages, when defence was the main priority, and the Renaissance when there was a new emphasis on elegance and comfort. As in most palaces, the ground floor was a loggia rented out by the Davizzi family for use as shops – the commodity was in this case wool. This arrangement generally suited the owners of palaces for, as well as bringing in a small revenue, it enabled them to keep tabs on the workers and the atmosphere of the city. The Palazzo Davantzati was one of the first palaces to have a court-yard which, while not of the graceful proportions of the Renaissance, was a great step in the direction of improved light and ventilation. The solid stairs are the only remaining ones of this date in the city. The palace was also unusual in having its own well.

Another feature in which this palace was grander than many of its neigh-bours was in having two *piani nobili*, on the first and second floors, both with large halls for entertaining and business functions. In the 15th century the building was also used by the tax officials before the Uffizi was built.

The bedchambers are also to be found on these floors. Some of these are beautifully decorated – most notably one of the second-floor apartments which is charmingly frescoed with the story from the popular French courtly verse, the *Châtelaine de Vergi*. Typically, for both medieval and Renaissance palaces, the kitchen is on the top floor. The roof loggia was added in the 16th century by the Bernardo Davantzati, who bought the palace from the Davizzi family in 1578. The palace no longer belongs to the family as the last Davantzati threw himself out of a top floor window in 1838, following in the footsteps of his gloomy ancestor Bernardo whose death by defenestration is also recorded in the family annals.

Leaving the palace and continuing eastwards down the Via Porta Rossa, one comes to the **Mercato Nuovo**, mainly housed in a large loggia built by Cosimo I and originally intended to be used for the sale of precious commodi-ties such as gold and silk. Traditionally it was here that large sums of money changed hands – in the 1420s it was recorded that there were as many as 72 banks operating in the immediate area. Now it is home mainly to the sellers of fancy straw- and leatherwork goods, as well as lace articles and souvenirs; the clientèle is largely composed of the wealthier tourists. To the south of the loggia is the small early 17th-century fountain known as the *Porcellino*, with Pietro Tacca's bronze copy of a Roman boar. The boar has always been considered a symbol of luck and is still usually surrounded by people, rubbing its rather worn nose, and throwing a few lire into the water. Nearby, towards the river, is the 13th-century **Palazzo di Parte Guelfa** which was modified in the 15th century under the guidance of Brunelleschi. Inside the hall which he designed is a charming lunette of the Madonna and Child by Luca della Robbia. The outside stairs and loggia were added by Vasari in c.1590.

Heading back towards the river, turn down the narrow Via SS Apostoli to the tiny medieval **Piazza del Limbo**, which got its name from being the ancient burial ground of unbaptised infants. The square is guarded by the lovely old church of SS Apostoli, still with its 11th-century façade (though the door is by Rovezzano and dates from around 1512). The church has one of the loveliest early interiors in Florence. According to Vasari it was a great influence on Filippo Brunelleschi. Like most churches, SS Apostoli underwent many improvements – the ceiling is 13th-century, the aisles are 15th-century and the chancel was added by Dosio in the 16th. The church contains two 14th-century Madonnas, one by Jacopo di Cione and the other by followers of Orcagna. The tomb of Oddo Aldoviti (d.1507), the patron of the church who lived on the south side of the square, is also by Rovezzano.

Practical Information

Hotels and Restaurants

Centrally located just off the Via Tornabuoni is the ancient *Hotel Porta Rossa* (tel. 287551) Via Porta Rossa 19, which retains an old-world atmosphere and has large rooms for families. Nearby, tucked behind the river at Borgo SS Apostoli 25 is the minute medieval *Cestelli* pensione with only six bedrooms. There is an abundance of hotels near the station, many of which are situated in or around the Piazza Santa Maria Novella. The more expensive of these include the *Hotel Minerva* (tel. 284555) Piazza S Maria Novella 16, which has a swimming pool, and the slightly cheaper *Hotel Roma* (tel. 2703660) at Piazza Santa Maria Novella 8. Right at the other end of the scale in the square is the eccentric *La Mia Casa*, (tel. 213061) incredibly cheap and with a definite character of its own.

There are plenty of restaurants to suit all pockets in this part of town. A friendly reliable trattoria near the centre is *Nella* in the Via delle Terme of Via Tornabuoni. At the top of the Via Tornabuoni the graceful Antinori palace houses a rather expensive wine bar where you can taste the family's wines and farm produce. Popular with Florentines is the *Fiaschetteria 'Il Latini'* Via dei Palchetti 6, (near the Rucellai palace) with dried hams hanging from the ceiling and good food. Another eating-house popular with locals is the tiny white-tiled *Coco Lezzone*, Via del Parioncino 26, which gets extremely crowded but serves very good food. One of the most popular Florentine trattorias of all, *Sostanza*, is also near here in the Via Porcellana 25 in the Ognissanti quarter. *Sostanza* has been going since 1869 and has built up a strong reputation as an authentic working man's trattoria with hearty local cooking.

Museums

Palazzo Davanzati   Via Porta Rossa: open Tues–Sat 09.00–14.00; Sun and hols 09.00–13.00.

Santa Maria Novella Cloisters   Piazza Santa Maria Novella: open Mon–Thurs and Sat 09.00–14.00; Sun and hols 09.00–13.00; closed Fri.

Cenacolo Ognissanti   Borgo Ognissanti 42: open Mon, Tues and Sat 09.00–12.00.

8. NORTHERN AND EASTERN FLORENCE:
from San Lorenzo to Santa Croce

San Lorenzo

A few minutes' walk to the north of the Duomo stands the great church of **San Lorenzo**. Around three sides of it runs the busy street market – stall upon stall selling jumpers, ties and scarves, leather bags and jackets, jeans and junk jewellery – just the place to buy cheap presents. For food, the massive 19th-century, cast-iron Mercato Centrale nearby is a paradise for serious food shoppers – with fruit and vegetables, meat and fish, cheese and oil and endless other delights spread out over two gigantic floors (now with a car park in the basement). Behind it is the old market square which was partly destroyed to make room for the covered market.

The present church of San Lorenzo, on the site of a much earlier basilica, was commissioned in around 1420 by the Medici from the great Renaissance architect Filippo Brunelleschi. As the rough-hewn exterior testifies, it was never completely finished, although nearly 100 years after it was begun a competition was held for the design of a façade. Michelangelo won the award, but after much to-ing and fro-ing the project was abandoned in favour of his working on a new sacristy for the church.

By contrast the inside of the building feels extremely complete, with an aura of harmonious unity and well-considered design. Wherever you enter the church, it is important to go and stand by the main door looking down the aisle to get the best feeling of the architect's intentions and skill in carrying them out. Gazing down the uncluttered aisle at the characteristic white plaster and elegantly named *pietra serena* stone, it becomes easy to understand

and appreciate Brunelleschi's breakaway from the Gothic style of the earlier great churches of Florence. Here we do not feel that man is insignificant in the presence of God. Rather, it seems as if this building was actually created more for man than for God – its proportions complement rather than diminish the human race. Everything has been determined logically, using the Classical elements of circle and square, the legacy of the great theorist Vitruvius. The main unit of measurement is the square of the crossing under the cupola, and every measurement keeps a fixed proportion with that one element. Even Brunelleschi's decorative use of plaster and stone encourages us to appreciate the proportions which he had measured out with such care.

In the nave are two bronze pulpits, begun by Donatello in 1460 and eventually finished by his pupils Bertaldo and Bartolomeo Bellano. These were his last works, and forcefully illustrate his later style. The scenes on the side panels are claustrophobically chaotic and crowded. There is an acceleration of emotion, and the figures themselves seem brittle and uncomfortable. In complete contrast is the gentle, almost whimsical tabernacle by Desiderio di Settignano in the right aisle – perhaps equally influential in its time. Also in this aisle is a 16th-century *Marriage of the Virgin* by Rosso Fiorentino and a tomb slab (1388) of the organist Fra Landini. The right transept houses a wooden crucifix by Pollaiuolo. In the left aisle is a vast *Martyrdom of St Lawrence* by Bronzino and, in the last chapel, an interesting modern painting by Pietro Annigoni of Christ in the carpenter's workshop. The transept houses a gentle *Annunciation* by Filippino Lippi which, unfortunately, has been rather crudely restored.

On the left flank of the transept is the **Old Sacristy** – a beautifully proportioned square, domed chamber and an early masterpiece of Brunelleschi, who finished it in 1429, well before the rest of the church was completed. It was commissioned by Giovanni de Medici, who is buried here with his wife in a tomb by Buggiano. The exquisite sculptural decoration – four scenes from the life of St John the Evangelist and four Evangelists in the lunettes – is by Donatello, who was also responsible for the fine bronze doors and the painted stucco reliefs above. Nearby is a splendid monument of Piero the Gouty by Verrocchia (1477).

One hundred years after the building of the old sacristy, Michelangelo was asked to build a **library** to house part of the growing collection of Humanist and Classical manuscripts accumulated by the Medici since the days of Cosimo il Vecchio. The library is dominated by a huge daring curved flight of stairs based on a clay model by the master but, as with so many of his ventures, left to be finished by someone else – in this case Vasari and Ammanati.

Off the main church, reached by a separate entrance, are the **Medici Chapels**; the Chapel of the Princes, and Michelangelo's New Sacristy. The Princes' Chapel is a pompous multi-coloured *pietradura*-and-marble affair built, by the sweat of the Turkish slaves, under the direction of Nigetti and many others between 1606 and 1738. It was based on a design by Vasari, Ammanati and the extravagant Don Giovanni de Medici. In it are some oversized bronze sculptures by Tacca of Ferdinand I and Cosimo II. More

San Lorenzo – street market and church

attractive are the fine inlaid marble coats of arms of the various cities of the Grand Duchy.

The so-called New Sacristy was designed and sculpted by Michelangelo. On the entrance wall are buried Lorenzo il Magnifico and his assassinated brother Giuliano. The exquisite *Madonna and Child* by Michelangelo was rudely dismissed by Augustus Hare as a 'mere sketch in marble'. But it is the far grander monuments to the later Medici – Lorenzo, Duke of Urbino, and Giuliano of Nemours – that really catch our attention. Michelangelo's Giuliano, seated above the allegorical figures of Night and Day, and Lorenzo, poised thinking above Dawn and Dusk, have been the subject of admiration for centuries and have been praised particularly by the poets. In the last century Walter Swinburne wrote this truly appalling verse:

> *Is not thine hour come to wake, o slumbering Night?*
> *Hath not the Dawn a message in thine ear?*
> *Though thou be stone and sleep, yet shalt thou hear*
> *When the word falls from Heaven – Let there be light.*
> *Thou knowest we would not do thee despite*
> *To wake thee while the old sorrow and shame were near;*

I prefer Elizabeth Barrett Browning:

> *. . . Michel's Night and Day*
> *And Dawn and Twilight wait in marble scorn.*
> *Like dogs upon a dunghill, couched on clay.*

And, of course, the sculptor's own words:

> *Caro m' e l sonno, e piu l'esser di sasso,*
> *mentre che'l danno e la vergogna dura:*
> *non veder, non sentir, m' e gran ventura:*
> *pero non mi destar, deh! parla basso.*

> *Dear to me is sleep; still more, being made of stone.*
> *While pain and guilt still linger here below,*
> *Blindness and numbness – these please me alone;*
> *Then do not wake me, keep your voices low.*

The Medici Palace, Castagno museum, and San Marco

Almost opposite the church of San Lorenzo rises the solid biscuit-coloured stone **palace of the Medici**, built in the 15th century by Cosimo il Vecchio. The story goes that Cosimo asked Brunelleschi to design him a palace, but when he saw the grandiose drawings that the architect had prepared he cancelled the commission, opting for a simpler design by his old friend Michelozzo. This was typical – despite his enormous power Cosimo was little given to displays of grandeur and he was always sensibly reluctant to deliberately arouse envy in the breasts of his enemies.

The palace, which finally got underway in about 1445, was built in tough brown mascagni stone. Its graded rustication, growing finer towards the top, was much copied throughout the city. Later the palace was modified by Michelangelo, who introduced his famous 'kneeling windows' on the ground floor. The building was changed again by the Riccardi family, who substantially enlarged it after they acquired it in the mid 17th century.

The palace is now used by the Prefecture and is worth visiting both for its fine decorated courtyards and, especially, for the exquisite frescoes in the chapel. This small, rather dark, room with its fine inlaid door is one of the few parts of the palace that has remained more or less as Michelozzo designed it. The paintings are the masterpiece of the decorative International Gothic artist Benozzo Gozzoli. Ostensibly a picture of the Journey of the Magi, the splendid procession is in fact an extremely complimentary portrait of the Medici family, winding their way through a rocky Tuscan landscape. A young Lorenzo sits resplendent on a grey charger, followed by other members of the clan. In the crowd behind, the painter himself appears – his name written in gold on his red cap. Gozzoli was a pupil of the holy painter Fra Angelico, whom Vasari said he always copied. But although the landscape shows Angelico's influence, Benozzo's treatment of a religious subject as a Florentine carnival with portraits of the nobility could not be more different from the simple austere approach of the devout and deliberately simple Angelico.

Outside, the Via Ginori reveals a series of fine 15th- and 16th-century palaces before turning into the Via San Gallo. If you are going up to the Angelico Museum in San Marco, then this is a more interesting route than the Via Cavour. Where you would turn right for San Marco, turn left into the Via XXVII Aprile, where you will immediately come to the Cenacolo di Sant' Appolonaia and the small but fascinating **Castagno museum**. The museum contains the rather sinister, dark *Last Supper* (c.1445) and some beautiful but fragmented scenes from the Passion of Christ. Castagno's *Resurrection* is strikingly similar in composition to Piero della Francesca's universally praised version painted a few years later in Borgo Sansepolcro. Vasari had a peculiar hatred for Castagno, saying that he resembled Judas Iscariot and even that he murdered his fellow-painter Domenico Veneziano because he was jealous of his superior skill. Actually Veneziano outlived Castagno by several years, but Vasari's smear campaign was enough to cause the ruling bodies at SS Annunziata to paint out all Castagno's frescoes in the church. This little museum shows that, demonic or not, Castagno was a superb painter and it is a great pity that so much of his work has not survived.

Crossing back over the Via San Gallo, one reaches the Piazza San Marco which runs along the busy Via Cavour. In this square, which hums with students from the University and tourists clutching cameras who wait hotly by the much used bus stop for Fiesole, is the **Convent of San Marco**, home of one of the quietest and most beloved of Florentine painters, Fra Angelico.

In 1436 a dilapidated Sylvestran monastery in the square was made over, at the behest of Cosimo il Vecchio, to the Dominicans. Cosimo then hired his friend, the architect Michelozzo, to improve and enlarge the complex, which he did by pulling down the old cloister but leaving the shell of the church and the refectory and rebuilding the new convent around them. At its reconsecration in 1444 Antonino Pierozzi, later Saint Antonino, became prior, but there also moved in the monk known as Fra Giovanni of Fiesole. Fra Giovanni was a painter and manuscript illuminator much admired by Cosimo, both for his skill and for his pious and gentle spirit. Vasari described Fra Angelico – as he came to be called – as a man 'whose whole life was devoted to the service of God and the benefit of the world and his neighbour'. Some years later, in 1481, the convent also became home to a rather less gentle though equally Godfearing character – the 'passionate pessimist' Girolamo

Savonarola from Ferrara. Savonarola shook the city to its core with his tirades and dreadful fanatical prophecies until he too fell out of favour and was burned as a heretic. Fortunately, through the tireless work of Fra Angelico, San Marco retains more of his tranquil spirit than that of Girolamo's.

To the right of the entrance to San Marco is the old **Ospizio dei Pellegrini**, where pilgrims were sheltered and fed. In it are now housed some 20 panel paintings by Angelico and his school, perhaps the finest being a *Deposition*, the *Virgin Enthroned* and 35 scenes from Christ's life which were finished by Baldovinetti. In Michelozzo's elegant cloisters the frescoes are mainly 16th-century, but the *Crucifixion with St Dominic* is by Angelico. Vasari tells us that 'Fra Angelico would never take up his brushes without a prayer, and whenever he painted a Crucifixion the tears would stream down his face . . .'. The Chapter House contains another large *Crucifixion*, and in the small refectory nearby is a *Last Supper* by Domenico Ghirlandaio and his studio.

The first floor of the convent is mainly given over to the monks' cells and the *Library*. The Library is a graceful hall built by Michelozzo to house the religious books which Cosimo de' Medici loved to come and read. The double-vaulted cell at the end was Cosimo's own, kept for his use on his frequent retreats from society. The other cells belonged to the monks, and each has its own mural painted by Fra Angelico and his school. The paintings repeatedly depict the same religious subjects – it should be remembered that they were painted to encourage contemplation and religious devotion rather than worldly excitement or amusement. Henry James gave this interpretation of Angelico's work:

> On reflection you may see that the painter's design, so far as coherent, has been simply to offer an immense representation of pity, and all with such concentrated truth that his colours here seem dissolved in tears that drop and drop, however softly, through all time . . . No other painter learned to render with deeper force than Fra Angelico the one state of the spirit he could conceive – a passionate pious tenderness.

The Galleria dell' Accademia and Piazza SS Annunziata

In the south corner of the Piazza San Marco, next to the University, is the **Galleria dell' Accademia** (entrance in Via Ricasoli). Despite its obvious importance, housing both Michelangelo's *David* and paintings by Botticelli and other talented Florentines, I find this museum curiously uninspiring. The best bit by far, and more interesting than the great white David who is perpetually surrounded by clicking cameras, are the magnificent *Quattro Prigioni* (c.1522) – four unfinished prisoners fighting their way out of great blocks of marble – a must for devotees of Michelangelo. Here is the most potent evidence of Michelangelo's belief that the sculpture is already there within the stone and that man's job is simply to remove what is unnecessary and release it from its claustrophobic confines. Among his other sculptures here are the *Palestrina Pietà* from Rome and a serious *St Matthew*. Of the many paintings in the *Sale Fiorentine*, look particularly at the celebrated panel from the Adimari wedding chest, painted in the 14th century when decorated wedding chests were the height of fashion.

Just a few minutes' walk away is one of the loveliest squares in the city – the **Piazza Santissima Annunziata**. The amazing thing about this square is the fact that, despite its harmonious appearance, it was actually assembled over a period of roughly 200 years. The equestrian statue of Cosimo I was begun by Giambologna when he was nearly 80, and finished after his death by Tacca who was also responsible for the two green fountains.

Standing to the north of the Piazza is the church of **SS Annunziata**, also mainly built by Michelozzo in around 1444. Previously it had briefly been a Franciscan convent, but the brown brothers abandoned it when the great church of Santa Croce was completed. In 1234 it was refounded by a group of seven Florentine families in the Order of the Servants of Mary (*Servi di Maria*). Later it became a popular pilgrimage centre because of a miraculous image of the Virgin housed there. In front of the church is the *Chiostrino dei Voti* designed by Michelozzo, the walls of which are covered by a series of 15th–16th century murals. Perhaps the loveliest of these is Alesso Baldovinetti's badly faded *Nativity*. The other pictures include a *Journey of the Magi* and *Birth of the Virgin* by Andrea del Sarto; *The Marriage of the Virgin* by Franciabigio; *The Visitation* by Pontormo; *The Assumption* by Rosso and Cosimo Rosselli and the young del Sarto's *Life of San Filippo Benizzo*.

Entering the church, one is struck by its richly-decorated but gloomy Baroque interior which is slightly relieved by the fine 17th-century ceiling by Pietro Gambelli. The *Tempietto* which houses the heavily repainted Miraculous Virgin was also designed by Michelozzo, but the canopy is 17th-century. In the nearby chapel are five fine inlaid panels and a small painting by del Sarto. The chapels on the north side contain two good works by Andrea del Castagno. The ornate Baroque Feroni chapel houses his *St Julian and the Saviour* while his *Trinity with St Jerome* is next door. In the next Chapel is a Perugino *Crucifixion*.

The best works in the right aisle are Bernardo Rossellino's monument to Orlando de Medici and a 16th-century marble *Pietà* by Baccio Bandinelli, who is interred here with his wife.

Michelozzo's Rotonda, or Tribune, was later modified by Alberti; in the chapels can be found a *Madonna* by followers of Perugino, a *Resurrection* by Bronzino and one of Giambologna's many crucifixes.

Next to the church is a beautiful light cloister with paintings by Mascagni, Pocetti, Roselli and Salimbeni; but to my mind, by far the most beautiful painting is Andrea del Sarto's small masterpiece, the exquisite *Madonna del Sacco*, painted in a lunette opposite the entrance. Off the cloister is the Cappella di San Luca, which contains a crucifix by Sangallo, the tombs of various artists and more 16th-century paintings.

Running along the east side of the square is one of the loveliest buildings of the Renaissance. Brunelleschi's **Spedale degli Innocenti**, named after Herod's slaughtered babes, was one of the first foundling hospitals in Europe. Commissioned by the important *Arte della Seta* (silk-workers guild) as a charitable enterprise in about 1419, it has remained in use (though now it is state funded) and, on sunny days children can still be seen playing in the gardens at the back. On the left of the portico is the old wheel on which desperate mothers could deposit their offspring while remaining anonymous – a tradition that continued until 1875.

To design the hospital Brunelleschi probably took as his prototype a slightly older building at Lastra a Signa near Florence. Aided by the Roman theorist Vitruvius, whose writings had been rediscovered some 10 years earlier, Brunelleschi proves the beauty of mathematical proportion and symmetry in his use of the two elements that were to become his favourite working units – the circle and the square. He created a loggia of perfect Classical proportions. The height of each slender column corresponds exactly to the depth of the loggia as well as to the space between the columns, creating cubes of space. The importance of the circle is emphasised by the half circular arches, so light that they hardly seem to touch down at all. (Only the middle nine arches are original, the outer ones having been added later.) The Roman influence can also be traced to the small, beautifully spaced windows on the first floor with their low pediments. Between the arches are charming blue and white terracotta medallions of the Innocenti by Andrea della Robbia.

It is possible to enter the Spedale to visit the small gallery and Pinacoteca, which contains some good Florentine paintings, including works by Lorenzo Monaco and Domenico Ghirlandaio, and an early Botticelli. Brunelleschi's two cloisters, the main Chiostro degli Uomini and the lovely Chiostro delle Donne where the women of the institution work, are also worth looking at. To the west, opposite Brunelleschi's loggia, is Antonio Sangallo's loggia dei Servi, built a hundred years after the Foundling hospital, and now housing an extremely elegant, tasteful and expensive hotel.

Just south of the square is the Rotunda di Santa Maria degli Angeli, which was begun by Brunelleschi in 1434. Three years later work was halted because of the war with Lucca, and it was not finally completed until 1959 when it was opened as a lecture hall. Another interesting church in the vicinity is the 17th-century church of **Santa Maria Maddelena dei Pazzi**, built on to an earlier church by Giuliano da Sangallo. His fine cloisters are worth a visit, as is Perugino's marvellous fresco of the *Crucifixion* (c.1495) which completely covers one wall of the chapter house.

Bargello

Returning into town, one enters the Bargello–Santa Croce neighbourhood to the east of Florence. The area around the Bargello was for centuries the most heavily populated in Florence, and many of its inhabitants worked in the law

The Bargello

courts. Even when the criminal courts finally moved out of the Bargello they remained in the area, and today prisoners are still held in the nearby Via delle Stinche. Along with lawyers and jailors, this was (and still is) an area for stationers and copyists who, as well as providing the wealthy with ornate and beautiful manuscripts, also worked for the lawyers and magistrates.

Just by the Bargello is the old **Badia**, founded in 978 by Willa, wife of the Margrave Uberto and mother of Ugo who is buried here. It is thought that Arnolfo di Cambio renovated the building in the 13th century, but the interior was completely remodelled in the 17th. Dante mentions that the church bell was the townspeople's clock and that his beloved Beatrice Portinari attended Mass here. Inside the church is a lovely painting by Filippino Lippi (c.1484) of the Virgin appearing to St Bernard. The monument to Ugo and the tomb of Bernardo Guinigi are both by Mino da Fiesole, as is the Madonna and Saints (c.1467). The tomb of Gianozzo Pandolfini is from the workshop of Rossellino. In the chapel are some badly damaged frescoes by Nardo di Cione which recount the Passion, unusually including the suicide of Judas. In Rossellino's *Chiostri degli Aranciare* are some 15th-century murals, certain of which are, needless to say, *in restauro*.

The great battlemented **Bargello** was begun in c.1255, probably by Ser Lapo who was Arnolfo di Cambio's teacher. Although it was not finally finished until the mid-14th century, from the end of the 13th it was the seat of the Podestà, the chief magistrate of the city. The Podestà was imported from another city, not less than 80km distant, for the term of one year, in an effort to make sure that the justice system was as fair and unbiased as possible. It was in the beautiful courtyard of the Bargello that many of the city's hangings and other punishments took place. Further disgrace was inflicted by the practice of painting pictures of the accused, often accompanied by an insulting poem, on the walls of the building for the public to enjoy. After the infamous Pazzi conspiracy when Giuliano de' Medici was killed, Botticelli painted members of the Pazzi clan on the tower wall while Leonardo made a detailed sketch of Bernardo Baroncelli who was hung outside a window.

At the beginning of the 16th century the great building was made over to the Chief of Police and became a prison, its elegant halls divided up into small cells. When the death sentence was abolished in 1786 there was a symbolic burning of the instruments of death and torture in the courtyard. The building remained a prison until the 1850s, when it was dismantled and restored to its original state.

Entering the Bargello, you find yourself in one of the finest courtyards in Tuscany. All over the walls are terracotta and stone *stemme* – the carved coats of arms of the 204 podestà of Florence. The great stone staircase leads up to a beautiful vaulted upper loggia, probably designed by Orcagna. The lower part of the courtyard contains various 16th-century sculptures by Ammanati, Giambologna and others, as well as a fine 17th-century cannon. To the right of the entrance is the small *Sala del Trecento* with works by Arnoldi and others. Room No.1 on the right is dedicated to Michelangelo and his followers. Here is Michelangelo's early *Bacchus* (1497) as well as his exquisite Tondo, the *Virgin and Child with St John*, an unfinished *David* and a bust of *Brutus* (1540). Also to be found here are works by Cellini, Sansovino, Giambologna, Tribolo and Vincenzo Danti. Cellini's bust of *Cosimo I*, made between 1546– 57, has an intense, neurotic expression and is among the most compelling of his sculptures.

Returning to the courtyard, one climbs the stone stairs to the loggia where Giambologna's *Mercury* is waiting, together with his splendid giant birds, made for the Medici villa at Castello. To the right is the Great Hall, with some marvellous Renaissance sculptures by Donatello, Michelozzo Benedetto da Maiano, Desiderio da Settignano and others. Donatello's wonderful bronze *David* is here – sensual, dreaming and abstracted – completely different in character to the brittle, alert *David* that Verrocchio made in reply (housed upstairs). Donatello's David was the first free-standing figure of the Renaissance deliberately made to be viewed from every angle. His other works here include the *Marzocco* lion (the Florentine symbol of justice), an early, slightly frowning *St George*, and *St John*. Also of great interest are the two competition bronze panels of 1402, produced by Brunelleschi and Ghiberti in an attempt to win the commission for the Baptistery doors. The competition was very close, and opinion still varies on the merits of each panel. Brunelleschi's is certainly the more dramatic, with the angel physically restraining Abraham from killing his son; but Ghiberti's is perhaps more perfectly composed around the strong diagonal line of the rock.

The second floor houses the Sala di Giovanni della Robbia and the Sala di

Verrocchio with his fine bronze *David* (c.1475) and charming *Madonna and Child*. Also here is the vibrantly energetic small work by Pollaiuolo of *Hercules and Anteus*. In the Sala dei Bronzetti is the best display of bronzes in Italy. To do justice to the whole of the Bargello, with its staggeringly rich collection of Italian sculpture, takes a long time, but for anyone with even the mildest interest in sculpture, it is essential viewing. Nowhere else can one find such a broad overview of Italian Renaissance sculpture.

Immediately south of the Bargello is the Piazza San Firenze with the late 15th-century Gondi Palace designed by Giuliano da Sangallo. Facing it is the Baroque church of San Firenze, created in the 18th century from three separate buildings.

Santa Croce

In the extreme eastern quarter of Florence, in a low-lying area that has traditionally been the ghetto of the poorer working classes, is the large square of **Santa Croce**. Already by the Middle Ages the square had become a sort of equivalent of a Roman Forum. It was here that public meetings were held, where the underpaid and overworked masses gathered to hear of their salvation and listen to the Gospel which proclaimed that, though beggarly in the eyes of men, they were blessed in the eyes of God. It was here too, at the beginning of the 13th century, that the first Franciscans were sent to do good works and set up a small church. As the Franciscan following grew, the crowd became too large for the building and the preachers would move into the increasingly packed square to deliver their message. Later the square was filled with crowds watching the famous 'bonfires of vanities' encouraged by both San Bernardino of Siena and Girolamo Savanarola (see p.85). The square had secular uses as well and was the natural centre for carnivals and competitions. In Florence's hey-day, the great jousts took place here, and the Medici and other nobles would show off their skills dressed in costumes decorated by Botticelli and Verrocchio. Also popular was the rather less elite *Calcio* – a football match played amid much festivity between local teams.

At the end of the square stands the church, resplendent with its new and not altogether beautiful 19th-century façade. The present massive building was begun in the middle of the 13th century when the old church became too small, but was not finally consecrated until 1443. The bell-tower was added in 1847. Inside is one of the richest concentrations of art in the city. One cannot help wondering what St Francis himself would have felt about this fabulous accumulation of wealth in his name, begun after his death.

The interior is vast and conveys the Gothic notion of man's insignificance compared to God. Even for the irreligious tourist, the huge space is as daunting now as it was for E. M. Forster's heroine in *A Room with a View* when she stumbled into the church without her Baedeker:

Piazza Santa Croce

> Of course, it must be a wonderful building. But how like a barn! And
> how very cold! Of course it contained frescoes by Giotto, in the pres-
> ence of whose tactile value she was capable of feeling what was proper.
> But who was to tell her which they were?

Originally the frescoes would have been even harder to locate, as Santa Croce
would have been completely covered in 13th–14th century frescoes. But, like
Santa Maria Novella, it was subjected to one of Vasari's 'improvement'
schemes and most of the early pictures (including the Giottos) were white-
washed over and refrescoed by various 16th–17th century artists. In the last
century these later paintings were removed with varying degrees of care and
skill to reveal what lay beneath. Also visible along parts of the nave, at a
height sometimes reaching 4m, are the water marks from the last disastrous
flood of 1966, which did untold damage, particularly to Cimabue's tremendous crucifix in the museum.

Santa Croce is known as the great mausoleum of Florence. In it are many
of the tombs and monuments of the city's foremost sons. The French 19th-
century writer Stendhal was so overwhelmed by being in the same building
as this 'fantastic gathering' that he was seized by palpitations and walked in
'constant fear of falling to the ground'. Predictably, fifty years on, Mark Twain
showed rather less reverence and got a good deal nearer the truth:

> We went to the Church of Santa Croce, from time to time, to weep over
> the tombs of Michelangelo, Raphael and Machiavelli (I suppose they

are buried there, but it may be that they reside elsewhere and rent their tombs to other parties – such being the fashion in Italy) . . .

His cynicism was not altogether misplaced – many of these great men are not actually buried here, and with a few notable exceptions the monuments are clumsy, pompous works of the 18th and 19th centuries. Vasari's monument to Michelangelo in the right aisle is perhaps a slight improvement on the others, but it is not until we reach Rossellino's marvellous tomb of the Humanist Leonardo Bruni (d.1444) that we begin to be really impressed. According to Vespasiano di Bisticci, Bruni was buried in Classical Roman style, swathed in a purple silk robe and holding a copy, not of the Bible, but of his own work: The History of Florence. All of this was faithfully reproduced by Rossellino, right down to the laurel wreath on his brow. This is a true tomb of the Renaissance: there is a sculptural balance between the perfect architecture of the tomb and its inhabitant, who is watched over by the Madonna but holds the key to success in his own hands. Another fine work by Rossellino is the delicate *Madonna del Latte* on the first pillar of the right aisle. Next to Bruni's tomb is another lovely work – Donatello's gilded *Annunciation* carved in *pietra serena* at the beginning of the 14th century.

From the right transept one enters the Castellani Chapel, frescoed by Agnolo Gaddi and containing a crucifix by Pietro Gerini dated 1380. The next chapel, the Baroncelli, is decorated by Taddeo Gaddi (Agnolo's father), who also designed the window, with scenes from the life of the Virgin. On the altar is a *Coronation of the Virgin*, signed by Giotto but actually painted by his followers. The picture of the Virgin giving her girdle to St Thomas is by Mainardi (c.1490), a pupil of Domenico Ghirlandaio. Just outside the chapel is a 14th-century tomb attributed to the Sienese Balduccio. The corridor leading to the Sacristy is designed by Michelozzo, as is the Noviziata.

In the Sacristy are more frescoes by T. Gaddi, Gerini and followers; the fine inlaid wooden furniture was built by Giovanni di Michele in the 15th century. Off the sacristy the Rinuccini Chapel has yet more 14th-century paintings, including the Lives of the Virgin and Mary Magdalen by Giovanni da Milano (c.1336), and an altarpiece by Giovanni di Biondi. At the end of the corridor the Noviziata or Medici Chapel was commissioned by Cosimo il Vecchio in 1445. It contains one of the loveliest della Robbia terracottas, Andrea's *Madonna and Child with Saints*, made in around 1480. The paintings are probably by Spinello Aretino (John the Baptist) and Paolo Schiavo (*Madonna with Saints*).

Along the eastern end of the church is a row of small chapels named after wealthy donor families and dedicated to the family's patron saint. Starting from the right is the Velluti Chapel, housing some badly damaged traces of frescoes by a follower of Cimabue. Next to it is the Cappella Calderini with more, heavily restored works by T. Gaddi. Passing the Cappella Bonaparte, one comes to the two most important of the chapels – Peruzzi and Bardi – containing the great fresco cycles of Giotto and his school. Giotto di Bondone, born in 1266 in the Mugello countryside outside Florence, was raised as a shepherd and, according to Vasari, was found drawing in the road by Cimabue who immediately made him his pupil. Ruskin describes Giotto's huge contribution to art in terms of reconciling the dreamlike stylised spiritualism of the Byzantines with a realistic human tenderness:

> Domestic and Monastic. He was the first of Italians – the first of Christians – who knew equally the power of both lives, and who was able to show it in the sight of men of all ranks, – from the prince to the shepherd; and of all powers, – from the wisest philosopher to the simplest child . . . He makes the simplest household duties sacred; and the highest religious passions, serviceable and just.

In the Peruzzi chapel Giotto's subjects are, on the left, the *Life of the Baptist* and, on the right, *St John the Evangelist*. In the Bardi Chapel is the marvellous *Life and Death of St Francis*. Also in the chapel is a 13th-century altarpiece of St Francis – an excellent example of early panel painting – devised like a comic strip to spread the stories of the Gospel to the illiterate masses.

In the large main chapel is Agnolo Gaddi's fine interpretation of the Legend of the True Cross. It is interesting to compare this, painted in c.1380, with Pierro della Francesca's masterpiece on the same subject begun in Arezzo in 1452. Many of the compositions, most notably the Dream of Constantine, are remarkably similar in composition. The altarpiece has been reconstructed from fragments by various 14th-century artists. The painted crucifixion dates back to 1340 and is possibly by the Master of the Fogg *Pietà*. The next chapel (Tosinghi) has another fine altarpiece by del Biondo and Neri di Bicci, and the one after that has more 14th-century paintings by Bernardo Daddi. The end chapel, decorated by Giotto's favourite pupil Maso di Banco with the life of San Silvestro, has retained its lively humour despite overzealous restoration.

In the 2nd Bardi chapel at the end of the left transept is Donatello's wooden *Crucifix*, upon which Brunelleschi poured scorn by saying that Christ had the body of a *contadino*. Brunelleschi then produced his own version for the church of Santa Maria Novella, to show Donatello how it should have been done. Despite Donatello's generous assertion that the other artist had indeed produced the better work, I prefer this simple peasant Christ to almost any other in Florence.

At the beginning of the left aisle is the beautiful Renaissance tomb of the humanist Carlo Marsuppini, carved by Desiderio di Settignano ten years after Rossellino's tomb of Bruni directly opposite. The main paintings in the left aisle are a *Pietà* by Bronzino, Santi di Tito's *Resurrection* and Vasari's *Doubting Thomas*. By now you will probably be exhausted, so before going through the entrance to the right of the church to see Santa Croce's other treasures, sit for a while in one of the square's various bars and get your breath back over a long cool drink.

On re-entering, cross the 14th-century cloister to explore one of the true gems of Italian Renaissance architecture, the little **chapel** built by Brunelleschi for the powerful Pazzi clan. It was built on the same basic design as the Old Sacristy at San Lorenzo, a cube topped by a hemispheric dome, but modified into an even more pleasing and harmonious shape. For most of the decoration Brunelleschi chose the della Robbia workshop, whose simple terracottas perfectly suit the cool white and grey of the plaster and *pietra serena*. Notice the small decorated dome in the porch and the delicately carved frieze by Desiderio, as well as the fine carved doors by Giuliano da Maiano. But most of all enjoy the proportions and harmony of the small but perfect interior.

The second cloister is another Renaissance jewel, although the architect has remained unknown. From these joyous sights we now come to one of the saddest – the great destroyed *Crucifix* of Cimabue in the refectory museum. During the flood of 1966 Cimabue's triumphal Cross floated out through the door of the museum where it had just been hung and disappeared down the street to where it was eventually rescued in a state of almost total ruin. Despite painstaking restoration, most of the damage has been irreparable. Now the crucifix hangs on a pulley ready to be lifted out of danger if necessary. On the other wall is Donatello's gilded *St Louis*, a young boy swamped in too-big bishop's clothing. He was made for the Guelph party niche in Orsanmichele but later decried as being too grand by the Ghibellines and consequently removed. Also here is Taddeo Gaddi's massive *Last Supper*, as well as Orcagna's *Triumph of Death* and Veneziano's *St Francis and John the Baptist*.

After you have left Santa Croce behind you there is one more important visit to make before abandoning the rest of the day to reading, eating and drinking. Five minutes' walk from the church up the Via Pinzochere is the Michelangelo museum at Casa Buonarroti. The house was actually built after Michelangelo's death by his nephew (though possibly to the master's design) incorporating two earlier houses belonging to the family. The small museum contains a few of Michelangelo's earliest works including the exquisite *Madonna della Scala*, as well as facsimiles of some of his drawings and tributes by other artists. Leaving the museum, make sure you return to town by the Via Ghibelline so that you can stop off at Vivoli's in the Via delle Stinche and buy yourself the most delicious ice-cream in Italy. You deserve it.

Practical Information

Hotels and Restaurants

One of the nicest *pensioni* in Florence is the charming, gently old fashioned *Rigatti* (tel. 213022), Lungarno Generale Diaz 2. It is simple, very reasonably priced, with a small loggia overlooking the Arno and public rooms that epitomise what a Florentine *pensione* should be. Far more expensive and sophisticated, in a lovely setting in the Piazza SS Anunziata, is the recently revamped *Hotel Loggiato dei Servi* (tel. 219165) in a fine Renaissance building which echoes Brunelleschi's foundling hospital across the square. A less elegant but pleasant pensione to the east of town is the *Liana* (tel. 587608) on the Via Alfieri, with rooms looking on to the large garden.

Around Santa Croce, which is traditionally a working class area, there are many simple *casalingha* trattorie, often serving good basic Tuscan food. In Via Verdi (16) is *La Maremma da Giuliano* with excellent food, though often very crowded as is another good restaurant, *I Che C'e C'e* at Via dei Magalotti. At the other end of the scale is one of the most highly acclaimed and expensive restaurants in Italy, the *Enoteca Pinchiorri* (tel. 242757) in the Via Ghibellina near the Bargello. This is a superb and serious restaurant with a truly excellent wine list – a real treat for even the most serious gormet. A spin-off from the Enoteca is another good new restaurant on the Via Fiesolana – *Da Noi* (tel. 242917) – run by ex-employees of Giorgio Pinchiorri.

If you just want an ice-cream, it is absolutely imperative that you go to the justly renowned *Vivoli* at Via Isola delle Stinche 7 where you can buy the most delicious ices in Tuscany, if not Italy.

Museums

Medici Chapels   Piazza Madonna degli Aldobrandini: open Tues–Sat 09.00–14.00; Sun and hols 09.00–13.00.
Palazzo Medici-Riccardi   Via Cavour 1: open 09.00–12.30 and 15.00–17.00; Sun and hols 09.00–12.00; closed Wed.
Cenacolo di Sant' Apollononaia (Castagno Museum)   Via XXVII Aprile: open weekdays 09.00–14.00; Sun and hols 09.00–13.00; closed Mon.
Galleria dell' Academia   Via Ricasoli 60: open weekdays 09.00–14.00; Sun and hols 09.00–13.00; closed Mon.
Museo di San Marco   Piazza San Marco 1: open weekdays 09.00–14.00; Sun and hols 09.00–13.00; closed Mon.
Spedale degli Innocenti   Piazza SS Annunziata: 09.00–13.00; closed Wed.
Museo Archeologico   Via della Colonna 36: open 09.00–14.00; Sun and hols 09.00–13.00; closed Mon.
Museo di Firenze com'era   Via Oriuolo 4: open weekdays 09.00–14.00; Sun and hols 09.00–13.00; closed Thurs.
Casa Buonarroti   Via Ghibellina 70: open 09.30–13.30; closed Tues.
Bargello   Via del Proconsolo 4: open weekdays 09.00–14.00; Sun and hols 09.00–13.00; closed Mon.
Santa Croce Museum and Pazzi Chapel   Piazza Santa Croce 16: open summer 10.00–12.30 and 14.30–18.30; winter 15.00–17.00; closed Wed.

9. FLORENCE:
The Oltrarno

The Oltrarno, the area that lies over the river, is my favourite part of Florence. Within the walls there are green hills to climb into the suburbs of Arcetri and Bellosguardo, with majestic views and olive groves, while nearer the river lie the less picturesque but more fascinating areas of San Niccolo, Santo Spirito and San Frediano. These are traditionally the artisan quarters of the city, and they have retained much of their medieval character groundfloor workshops (*botteghe*) opening on to the busy narrow streets. Most of these *botteghe* now deal in carpentry and furniture repairs, whereas previously they were associated with the wool trade: carding, dyeing and weaving. The wool workers were generally paid subsistence wages and worked at the discretion of the Greater Guilds, the *Calimala*, *Seta*, and *Lana*, owned by the wealthy merchants and bankers.

As well as workshops there are palaces here. As early as 1200 the nobles began to move over the river, partly for the fresher air and, more importantly, to keep an eye on business. It is here we find the ancestral homes of the great families of Frescobaldi, Ridolfi, Ricasoli, Guadagni, Nerli and Bardi. As in the rest of Florence, the attitude of the *popolo minuto* to the nobility was, to say the least, changeable. The 14th-century historian Giovanni Villani reported that, by the middle of the century, relationships between them had become so bad that eventually civil war almost erupted.

> On 24 of September, 1343, the people rose against the Bardi, Rossi, Frescobaldi, Mannelli and Nerli, *Grandi* of the Oltrarno, who at once seized and held the bridges. The palace of the sons of Messer Vieri de' Bardi was strong and the tower was well fortified, as was the house of the Manelli at the head of the Ponte Vecchio, then built of wood. The people could not pass over it, nor could they cross the Ponte Rubaconte [now the Ponte alle Grazie], on account of the strength of the palaces of the Bardi of Saint Gregorio; so they left a guard under the houses of the Alberti and also at the Ponte Vecchio, and then with many soldiers on horseback they went to the Ponte alla Carraja which was guarded by the Nerli. The people of San Frediano, Cuculia and the Fondaccio were however so numerous that before the others arrived they had stormed the bridgehead and the houses of the Nerli, who were put to

flight. And thus the victorious people passed over the bridge, and joined those of the Oltrarno and furiously attacked the Frescobaldi . . . Twenty-two rich and splendid palaces and houses were burnt and it is estimated that the loss was more than 60,000 golden florins.

It was also on the Oltrarno that Michele di Lando finally gave the signal in 1378 for the workers to riot against their masters in a bid for better conditions and their own unions. The success of what was known as the Ciompi uprising was, however, short-lived: conditions returned to what they had been and di Lando was banished from Florence in 1382.

Despite these repeated lootings and burnings the area kept its medieval appearance until the Second World War, when many of the old tower houses round the Ponte Vecchio were razed by the Germans in an attempt to stop access to the bridge. Now it has mainly been rebuilt, including the busy Borgo San Jacopo with its expensive restaurants frequented mainly by tourists. For those who do not wish to pay the high prices of Camillo's it is better to walk over to the area immediately round Santo Spirito, where there are various cheap family-run *trattorie* and bars with simple food and rough wine. At lunchtime and early evening these are mainly frequented by working men in overalls with plaster and furniture polish on their hands. Later, families and students of all nationalities arrive as well and the noise level rises dramatically as people argue enthusiastically above the clatter of plates and children. The most popular of these *trattorie* is perhaps the Casalinga in Via del Presto di San Martino. Between the two extremes are the restaurants in the Piazza Santo Spirito itself and the popular Carmine in Carmine square, both with outside tables in summer. But, before eating, there is sightseeing . . .

From the Porta San Niccolò, to the east, the road winds steeply up to the famous Piazzale Michelangelo, now just a huge and crowded car park with a wide view of the city. Here, in the summer, the parapets heave with tourists being photographed against the spectacular backdrop, and vans sell over-priced fizzy drinks and souvenirs. Just above the Piazzale is the elegant, late 15th-century church San Salvatore al Monte, designed by Cronaca. This was a favourite with Michelangelo who referred to it as *mia bella villanella* (my pretty country girl).

San Miniato

Almost at the top of the steep cypress avenue perches one of the most perfect of Florentine churches, the small Romanesque basilica of **San Miniato al Monte**. One of the rare early Christian martyrs in Florence, San Miniato was probably an Armenian merchant killed for his beliefs by the Emperor Decius in about 254AD. As with most of the Tuscan saints, the details of his life and death are obscured by legend. The most popular version is that he was fed to wild beasts in Florence's amphitheatre, where he fought valiantly with a panther. He then suffered the usual torments of the boiling cauldron, the

The beautiful Romanesque façade of San Miniato

gallows, stoning and, finally, beheading, whereupon he picked up his head and fled across the Arno and up the hill, eventually collapsing where the church now stands. His bodily remains were, for some reason, apparently taken to Metz, but more were found in the hillside by the resourceful Bishop Hildebrand when he decided to rebuild the church in c.1015. The church took nearly 200 years to complete and was initially made over to the Black Benedictines of Cluny. It has since changed hands and is now part of the Olivetan Order.

San Miniato's façade is a beautiful example of Tuscan Romanesque although its compositional clarity and proportion led to the belief, held right through the Renaissance, that it was actually a Roman building. In his *Outline of European Architecture*, Nikolaus Pevsner describes it as 'a first synthesis of Tuscan intellect with Roman simplicity and poise'. Built in two tiers, it is decorated in white and dark-greenish marble from Prato, using geometric designs that reinforce the architectural form, growing more intricate towards the top. Unlike the northern architecture of the time, the façade is basically flat with no niches or room for sculptural decoration. The restored 13th-century mosaic shows Christ between the Virgin and St Miniato, and on top stands the eagle, symbol of the *Calimala* (cloth guild), patrons of the church.

The interior is also unusual. There is no transept, and the choir is raised above a large hall-crypt supported on slender Classical columns, some of which have Roman capitals. The pavement is of inlaid marble, and on the first panel one can see the date it was created – 1207. The intricate marble transenna and pulpit, with its charming, squat, Romanesque figure supporting the lectern, are also from this period. Many of the medieval-looking inlaid sprites and creatures have an eastern feel about them (perhaps a result of the Crusades?) which accords strangely with the Classical columns and ornamentation. The large mosaic in the apse is late 13th-century but has been repeatedly restored.

In 1448 Piero the Gouty commissioned Michelozzo to build a chapel to house the miraculous crucifix that had spoken to St John Gualberto. The chapel was designed to fit in with the rest of the building in the same dark and white inlaid marble. The ceiling was made by Luca della Robbia and at the back were placed some panels painted previously by Agnolo Gaddi and left unfinished at his death in 1396. The two main figures are San Miniato and St John. The crucifix itself has long since been removed.

Another treasure is the fine Renaissance **Chapel of the Cardinal of Portugal** where architecture, sculpture and painting are, unusually, given equal importance. The chapel was built for the young Cardinal Jacopo di Lusitania, who died in Florence in 1461 aged 25. It was designed by Brunelleschi's pupil Antonio Manetti. The beautifully carved tomb is by Antonio Rossellino (younger brother of Bernardo) and the terracotta vault is by Luca della Robbia. The painted altarpiece is by the Pollaiuolo brothers, and there is a rather worn but lovely *Annunciation* by Alesso Baldovinetti, with a childlike Virgin who raises her right hand in the traditional gesture of inquiry.

In the sacristy is a series of restored frescoes by Spinello Aretino (1385–7) showing the life of St Benedict. They are interesting mainly because they show a halfway point between the simple figurative style of Giotto and the increasingly popular Gothic tradition with its emphasis on elegance and decoration. Outside again, you will see on the right the early 14th-century **Episcopal Palace** which was used as a barracks for the Spanish soldiers during the reign of Grand Duke Cosimo I.

There are also some cloisters dating back to the 15th century. The unfinished but solid campanile was built in the 16th century replacing an earlier one destroyed in 1499.

If you are feeling strong, walk further along the Viale Galilei towards Arcetri, where Gallileo lived, until you come to Via Leonardo on the right. This is one of the prettiest lanes in Florence, with olive groves and high stone walls. At the Porta San Giorgio is the star-shaped Forte di Belvedere, built by Buontalenti in 1590 for Ferdinando I. The building is now open only for exhibitions, but a 19th-century gazetteer records it as a 'small, but not inelegant, Casino'. The garden, set at different levels, has one of the best views over the domes and towers, bridges and palaces of the city.

The Pitti Palace

Just below is Florence's lagest and most grandiose palace of all; the massive **Palazzo Pitti**. Strangely, for such an important building, nobody is quite sure who actually designed it. Vasari attributes it to Brunelleschi, but there is little evidence to support this theory and the building was actually started some time after his death. It is more or less certain that the architect Luca Fancelli (1430–95) did some work on it but it is not clear how much.

Luca Pitti, who commissioned the palace, was a wealthy Florentine merchant who planned to eclipse the Medici and to this end set about building a palace of unsurpassed grandeur. Macchiavelli described the lengths to which the vain old nobleman went to outdo his rivals, and reported that, as well as the aid he received from the corporations and citizens, 'all those who were under ban, and whosoever committed murder or theft or anything else for which he feared public punishment, provided that he were a person useful for the work, found secure refuge within these buildings'. At this stage the palace comprised only the central section, with seven first-floor windows, but it was still considered magnificent to a degree. Soon afterwards, however, the fortunes of the Pitti collapsed and a century later it was sold to the very rivals it was meant to outshine.

Eleanor of Toledo and her husband Duke Cosimo de Medici entrusted the improvement and enlargement of the building to the popular architect and sculptor Ammannati, who remodelled the façade and built the classic 16th-century courtyard at the back. The two wings, by Guiseppe Ruggieri, were not added until the second half of the 18th century. In 1860 the Pitti had become the property of the ruling House of Savoy, and was briefly the residence of Victor Emmanuel during Florence's short spell as the country's capital.

The Pitti Palace now contains six separate museums. The traveller with limited time will not want to go to all of them. The **Museo degli Argenti**, in the summer apartments of the Grand Dukes, has a fine collection of silver, jewellery, ivory and other treasures from the Medici palaces. It also includes Lorenzo il Magnifico's collection of antique vases from Rome, Byzantium and Venice. A visit might also be made to the **Galleria d'Arte Moderna** which has mainly Tuscan paintings of the 19th and 20th centuries. For those interested in the impressionistic Macchiaioli school of painters, there are some good rural scenes by the movement's leader Giovanni Fattori. There is also the coach museum, the former Royal Apartments and the small Contini-Bonacossi collection of Italian and Spanish paintings and furniture.

The largest, and easily the most important, of the Pitti galleries is the extensive **Galleria Palatina** which was first opened to the public in 1833. The pictures, many of exceptional quality, crowd together in a daunting show of magnificence. The collection was started in the 17th century by the Grand Dukes, growing rapidly in content and scope. Many of the Flemish and Venetian pictures were acquired by Grand Duke Cosimo III and his son, Crown Prince Ferdinand, at the beginning of the 18th century; the Tuscan ones, rather earlier. In a single room one can find Titian, Van Dyck, Rubens, Andrea del Sarto and Tintoretto. There are also some of the finest Raphaels. Of the 11 of his paintings shown, I think that the tondo of the *Madonna della Seggiola* is the most perfect, with its compact composition and exquisite detail. Of the dozen pictures by Rubens I would choose the magnificent *Four Philosophers* in the Hall of Mars. Earlier this century many pictures were moved over to the Uffizi, but the Palatine collection remains immensely impressive for anyone with the stamina to do it full justice.

Outside lie the Bóboli Gardens, pleasant in spring when a few roses bloom and the grass is still green, but dismally hot and dusty in high summer – unless one goes first thing in the morning or as late as possible before closing time. The gardens were built by the Medici when they acquired the Pitti. Eleanor of Toledo had hated the cramped city life in the Palazzo Vecchio and was determined that her new home should have as much space and greenery as possible. With this in mind, she bought up the surrounding land as far as the Porta Romana. She then employed the designer Tribolo, but he died in 1550 and the work was handed over to the inventive Buontalenti and later to Ammannati's nephew Giulio Parigi. The result was an extravaganza of Mannerist playfulness; with strange comic statues, grottoes and fountains, epitomised by the extraordinary rustic *Grotticina di Madonna*, by Giovanni Fancelli and Bacio Bandinelli, where bizarre goats frolic among the stalactites. Another joke is the famous star of innumerable postcards – the obese dwarf *Morgante*, riding on a sea-turtle in a gross parody of Neptune. Vasari and Buontalenti's richly decorated Grotto Grande houses casts of Michelangelo's Prisoners (see p.110), which were briefly displayed here, among statues by Rossi and Giam bologna. Throughout the rest of the park, with its amphitheatre, *Kaffeehaus* and cypress walks, one comes across more statues, some antique, some Mannerist: hiding in hedges, perched on stones, and rising out of fishponds.

From the Pitti to Santo Spirito

Almost opposite the Pitti at number 21 is the house where Dostoyevsky stayed while he was writing *The Idiot*. Nearby, on the corner of Via Maggio, is **Casa Guidi** where the Brownings lived after their secret marriage, and where Elizabeth Barrett Browning wrote her epic poem about the unification of Italy:

> I heard last night a little child go singing
> 'Neath Casa Guidi windows, by the church
> O bella libertà, O bella! – *stringing*
> The same words still on notes he went in search
> So high for, you concluded the upspringing
> Of such a nimble bird from sky to perch
> Must leave the whole bush in a tremble green,
> And that the heart of Italy must beat.
> While such a voice had leave to rise serene
> 'Twixt church and palace of a Florence street.

Piazza Santo Spirito

The Via Maggio is the main road into the city from the south and is correspondingly busy. Towards the river it is lined with palaces, most of which were built after the Medici came to the Pitti and the Oltrarno became a fashionable address.

For the visitor, one of the nice, cheaper places to stay in Florence is the Pensione Sorelle Bandini in the **Piazza Santo Spirito**. The pensione is housed in the top of the Palazzo Guadagni, built in the early 16th century, probably by Cronaca. The Guadagni were an ancient Guelph family who made their money in banking in the 13th century. Rarely can there have been such a hell-bent tribe; their history is repeatedly stained with the blood of their assassinations, beheadings and poisonings. Their palace, however, is charming (apart from a temperamental and scruffy lift) with pleasant rooms and a magnificent loggia where one can sit and look at the city's red rooftops or follow the goings-on in the square below.

The square itself never feels quite as hot as the rest of the city. It has the atmosphere of a provincial market town, with trees shading the benches where old women sit round a sluggish fountain. In the mornings the market takes over, selling fruit and vegetables, household goods and underwear. If it rains great green canopies are erected. In the summer the restaurants and bars put up their sunshades and drunks doze and gossip on the church steps. In past centuries the square was used as a football pitch for the ever popular *Calcio* between the locals and neighbouring teams. Another tradition, which still continues, is the Festa of Santa Rita on 22 May, when yellow roses are blessed and then sold in the church and carried out in a bright stream at the end of the service.

The Renaissance church of **Santo Spirito** stands at the end of the square. The land was originally bought in the middle of the 12th century by the Augustinians for use as a vineyard. Soon afterwards they built a convent on the site, which became established as one of the most renowned seats of learning in the city. Boccaccio bequeathed his library to the school after his death. By the end of the 14th century there was a growing feeling among the monks that a new church was needed. For fifty years they gave up a meal every day and put the money towards building costs, which, combined with other donations, paid for the new building. The now elderly Brunelleschi was commissioned to produce a design. It was his last and, many say, his greatest work, although built mainly after his death in 1446. In 1471 work was set back by a fierce fire which destroyed all the medieval parts except the refectory, and the building was not finally finished until the 1490s.

The church was designed on the traditional Greek Cross plan, with a flat ceiling and a cupola over the crossing. It is initially rather like Brunelleschi's earlier church of San Lorenzo, but the proportions are if anything even more regular. The nave is twice as high as it is wide, as are the square bays in the aisles. These bays run right the way around the cross of the church and were apparently meant by the architect to go across the entrance wall as well. The church is exactly four bays wide and there would have been four main entrances instead of three: one into each bay. As Vasari characteristically points out, it was a pity that the master's plans were not adhered to.

> Certainly, if it had not been for the malevolence of those whose claims to superior understanding are always leading them to spoil the lovely works which have been begun by others, it would today rank as the most perfect church in the Christian world.

It is also a pity that the ornate Baroque high altar was placed right in the middle of the crossing, disturbing the serene flow of space that otherwise characterises the church.

In the south transept is the altarpiece of the Nerli Family, one of Filippino Lippi's best paintings. It depicts the Virgin and Child with Saints and the donors, with a view of the Porta San Frediano in the background. Also of note is the fine marble sarcophagus of Count Neri Capponi by the Sweet-style sculptor Antonio Rossellino. The Renaissance vestibule and sacristy were designed by Sangallo at the commission of Lorenzo il Magnifico. After only a few weeks its cupola collapsed and had to be rebuilt, to the mortification of everyone involved. In the medieval refectory, now the Fondazione Salvatore Romano, are the damaged remains of some fine monumental frescoes attributed to followers of Orcagna and his brother Nardo di Cione.

Behind the church, the Via Santo Spirito runs parallel with the river from the Piazza Frescobaldi, with its large palace, past the Capponi, Manetti and Rinuccini palaces on the left and the Frescobaldi on the right. In the 18th century the Palazzo Manetti (No.23) was the home of the British envoy to

Florence, the great correspondent and friend of Horace Walpole, Sir Horace Mann. Most of his guests, however, stayed in his private guest house, the Casa Ambrogi, since destroyed in the war. The road ends at the Via de' Serragli, the main road out of the city towards Siena. Its northern end has various 17th- and 18th-century palaces but, turning towards the Porta Romana, it becomes lower and narrower with medieval houses and ordinary shops. In Florence shops seems to specialise as much as possible: there are tripe shops selling nothing else at all; pigmeat shops; pasta shops; and chocolate shops.

San Frediano and the Carmine church

To the west of Via de' Serragli is the area known generally as **San Frediano**, with bustling alleys, workshops, and dangerously narrow pavements, perpetually blocked by motorbikes and people passing the time of day together so satisfactorily that they won't be shifted by a polite *'permesso'* . . . The modern writer Vasco Pratolino is familiar with the type:

> The people of San Frediano, the toughest and liveliest of the Florentines, are the only ones who retain authentically the spirit of a people that has been able to make something graceful even out of clumsiness, and whose ingenuity is a perpetual effrontery. The Sanfredianini are sentimental and pitiless at once: their idea of justice is symbolised by the enemy's remains hung to a lamp-post; and their idea of Paradise, summed up in a proverb, is poetic and vulgar: a Utopian place where there is an abundance of millet and a shortage of birds.

In this area, dedicated to the working man, at the back of the big car park which is the Piazza del Carmine, rises the rough-hewn façade of one of Florence's greatest treasure troves; the **Carmine church**. In 1268 a church was built here by the Carmelite Order on the site of an earlier convent. In 1771 it was virtually destroyed by fire although, miraculously, two chapels (including Masaccio's Brancacci chapel) and the sacristy survived. Rebuilt at the end of the 18th century and decorated with some rather disastrous frescoes by Domenico Staggi, it was described in a guidebook written at the beginning of this century as, 'one of the most meretricious and worthless buildings of the 18th century, full of every sort of flamboyant ornament and insincere, uncalled-for decoration'.

Tommaso di Ser Giovanni was born in the Val d'Arno in 1401. Commonly known as Masaccio, (which roughly translated means Ugly Tom) for his rough and ready appearance, he joined the painters' guild in 1422. He was almost immediately commissioned to work under the more established painter Masolino (dear little Tom) on a family chapel belonging to the Brancacci. Felice Brancacci was a wealthy silk trader who had recently returned from Cairo, where he had been ambassador and had accumulated much wealth for which the decoration of his chapel would atone. For its decoration he chose the rather unusual theme of the life of St Peter, with two panels of Adam and Eve at the entrance. Some of these panels were painted by Masaccio, some by Masolino and some by the two in collaboration. The work was finally finished by Filippino Lippi some fifty years later.

Looking at the two pictures of Adam and Eve – the Expulsion on the left by Masaccio, the Temptation on the right by Masolino – one quickly becomes aware of the difference in quality of the two painters. In the naked grief and shame of the exposed couple, Masaccio shows a force of narrative which the lesser painter can only imitate; his Adam and Eve are pallid and bland by comparison. In the most famous picture of the series, the Tribute Money, we see all Masaccio's genius in his group of sturdy Disciples. The face of Christ was probably painted by Masolino, as the more senior artist; again it is bland when compared to the rugged, monumental portraits of the others who achieve the immense dignity of Donatello's Prophets.

Strangely, Masaccio was not a particularly popular painter during his life-time. The people generally preferred the highly decorative Gothic style, epit-omised by Gentile da Fabriano, which was then in fashion and to which school Masolino really belonged. Only the artists flocked to see his work and learn new skills of perspective, through his use of light, and the clarity with which he placed his figures in the landscape. These students included Fra Angelico, Castagno, Ghirlandaio, Botticelli, Michelangelo and Leonardo da Vinci who later wrote:

> After Giotto the art of painting declined again, because everybody imi-tated the paintings that were already done; thus it went on from century to century until Tommaso of Florence, nicknamed Masaccio, showed by his perfect works how those who take for their standards anyone but Nature – the mistress of all masters – weary themselves in vain.

Masaccio died in 1428 in Rome, aged 27, having set Renaissance painting truly on its way. Though not a native of the area he epitomised the Sanfredian-ini, with his bluntness, his strength, and his amazing skill. He was buried, appropriately, in the Carmine church and Annibale Caro wrote this short but apt epitaph.

> I painted, and my picture was like life;
> I gave my figures movement, passion, soul:
> They breathed. Thus, all others
> Buonarroti taught; he learnt from me.

Practical Information

Hotels and Restaurants

Annalena Via Romana 34, 50125 Firenze (tel. (055) 222402). A pleasant pensione overlooking a garden in an old palace.
Sorelle Bandini (tel. 275308) Piazza Santo Spirito 9. One of my first choices

in Florence, situated in a charming square with cool rooms and a delightful loggia overlooking the red roofs of the Oltrarno. Very reasonaly priced. More expensive and luxurious, also on this side of the river is the *Hotel Silla* Via dei Renai 5, 50125 Firenze (tel. (055) 284810), which has a nice terrace.

The Oltrarno still has many good cheap *casalinga* restaurants and cafés frequented by students, artisans and tourists. One of the best of these is the extremely cheap *Ristorante Casalinga* just behind the Piazza Santo Spirito. The Borgo San Jacopo has many (in my view rather disappointing and overpriced) touristy restaurants of which the most popular is *Camillo*. More fun is the *Carmine* on the corner of the Carmine square with tables outside. You can also eat outside in the various restaurants in the leafy Piazza Santo Spirito.

Museums

Palazzo Pitti   Piazza Pitti: main galleries open weekdays 09.00–14.00; Sun and hols 09.00–13.00; closed Mon.
Museo Bardini   Piazza dei Mozzi: open weekdays 09.00–14.00; Sun and Hols 09.00–13.00; closed Wed.
Forte di Belvedere   Costa San Giorgio: open daily 09.00–20.00 (gardens only).

10. THE PROVINCE OF FLORENCE

If you have tired, temporarily, of the hot dusty city and long for something more peaceful, there are plenty of beautiful and interesting places to visit nearby. For those who really wish to escape, there are parts of the Florentine countryside as lovely as any in Tuscany: the north in particular is surprisingly unspoilt. Many short excursions outside the city can be made fairly easily by bus, but you really need a car to do justice to the Mugello and Chianti.

North and East of Florence

On the edge of Florence, in the north of the city, are the Medici villas of Careggi, Petraia and Castello. They are situated fairly close together on the edge of the seemingly interminable northern suburb of Florence in what must once have been a fine situation. **Careggi**, one of the earliest, was bought by Cosimo il Vecchio's brother Lorenzo in 1417. Some years later it was enlarged by Michelozzo, but the side *loggie* were added in Lorenzo il Magnifico's day by Giuliano da Sangallo. Cosimo in particular always loved Careggi, and it was here that he would retreat to his library with a few friends when the stress of city life became too onerous. He was also a keen farmer and, to unwind, would work for days at his vines, almonds and olives. His grandson Lorenzo inherited his love both of study and of the countryside, and often came here with his 'Platonic Academy' to read and listen to music, talk and write poetry. Much of Lorenzo's poetry is thoughtful and charming – a characteristic mixture of gaiety, love of nature and beauty and an increasing preoccupation with the transience of life.

> Quant' è bella giovinezza
> Che si fugge tuttavia!
> Chi vuol esser lieto, sia;
> Di doman non c'è certezza.

> How fair is youth and how fast it flies away.
> Let him who will be happy;
> of tomorrow nothing is certain.

Careggi has fairly recently been turned into a nurses' home, and permission to visit must be sought from the Ospedale di Santa Maria Nuova in Florence.

About a couple of kilometres away in Castello are the villas of Petraia and Castello, roughly half a mile apart. **Petraia** was a fairly late acquisition of the family, bought by Cardinal Francesco de' Medici from the Salutati family in 1595. It is set in a fine, well-kept garden with terraces and ornamental ponds. The courtyard, which has been glassed over, is extravagantly frescoed by il Volteranno with the exploits of the Medici. After the Risorgimento the villa became the property of Victor Emmanuel II, who added most of the present lavish decor. Along the road is the villa of **Castello**, acquired by the family in 1477. Originally Botticelli's *Primavera* and *Birth of Venus* both hung here. The ornate gardens were laid out by Tribolo and his successor Buontalenti at the behest of Cosimo I, who spent much of his childhood at the villa. Statues were also added by Pierino da Vinci, while the strange animals in the grotto are the work of Giambologna.

Another short bus ride north from the centre of the city takes you up the Via Bolognese to the **Museo Stibbert**, with its amazingly eclectic contents collected by the fanatical Italo-Scot Frederick Stibbert at the end of the 19th century. A few minutes' walk away is Harold Acton's villa **La Pietra**. Its Italianate garden, one of the loveliest in Tuscany, was mainly recreated by the present owner's father, Sir Arthur Acton.

Further away, in the hills some 8km to the north of Florence, is the charming little town of **FIÉSOLE**, renowned for its staggering view, its Roman amphitheatre and its delightful villas. Fiésole is substantially older than Florence and was once far more successful. As early as the 7th or 8th century BC it was an Etruscan settlement. In the beginning of the 1st century BC, as the Roman colony of Faesulae, it had a forum, baths and temples as well as the great amphitheatre which is still standing, partly protected by massive Etruscan walls. During the Dark Ages Fièsole began to decline, while the small straggling town of Florence in the valley started to grow. In the early Middle Ages Florence was determined to subdue the hill town which was increasingly becoming a refuge for highwaymen and bandits. In the 11th century Florence began a series of raids on Fiesole as well as offering inducements to the Fièsolans to move down to the city; in 1125, after a long siege, Fiésole was finally subdued.

By 1125 little was left of Fièsole except the old cathedral, the **Badia Fièsolana**, in a beautiful remote position with a fine view, just outside the tiny hamlet of San Domenico about 1km from the town. The Badia was probably built on the site of the martyrdom of St Romulus and was the cathedral of Fièsole until the 11th century. In 1464 Cosimo de' Medici had the little church rebuilt, incorporating the remains of a charming Romanesque inlaid marble façade. The lovely cruciform interior was also redesigned at this time, possibly by a follower of Brunelleschi.

In the hamlet is the parish church of San Domenico, a 15th-century building containing some marvellous pictures, including a *Baptism* by Lorenzo di Credi and a gentle *Madonna with Angels and Saints* by Fra Angelico, who first took orders here in the convent. In the Chapter House are other beautiful paintings by him – a frescoed *Crucifixion* and a *Madonna and Child* (c.1430). Nearby, on the road up to Fiésole proper, is one of the finest villas of the Renaissance – the Medici villa of **Belcanto** which is unfortunately closed to the public. Belcanto was designed by Michelozzo for Giovanni de' Medici but paid for by his father Cosimo il Vecchio. Giovanni chose the site because of its spectacular view over Florence but Cosimo, then in his seventies, was annoyed by the choice both because of the poor quality of the steep stony land and because he always maintained that the best view was looking over one's own property.

The walk up to the town is short but steep; fortunately there are many bars in the main square where you can quench your thirst. The large Piazza Mino da Fiésole (named after the sculptor who lived here) is on the site of the Roman forum. At the southern end, near the monument of Victor Emmanuel and Garibaldi, is the 14th–15th century **Palazzo Pretorio** next to the little **Oratorio di Santa Maria Primerana** with its handsome 17th-century porch. At the opposite end, facing the much restored **Bishop's Palace**, is the **Cathedral of San Romolo**.

The Cathedral was first consecrated in c.1030, but was enlarged in the 14th and 15th centuries and restored, rather crudely, in the 19th. The interior resembles that of San Miniato al Monte, with its unusual raised choir and Roman pillars. In the Cappella Salutati is the exquisite tomb of Bishop Leonardo Salutati who died in 1465. It was carved by Mino da Fiésole, who was also responsible for the fine altar front. The four Evangelists are by Cosimo Rosselli. On the High Altar is a painted altarpiece by Neri di Bicci, and in a nearby chapel is a late 15th-century marble one by Andrea Ferrucci. Over the main west door is a statue of the Cathedral's patron saint, Romulus, in a decorated niche by Giovanni della Robbia. Behind the Cathedral is the **Museo Bandini**, which has a good collection of Florentine paintings including works by Taddo Gaddi, Neri di Bicci and Bernardo Daddi as well as two pictures uncertainly attributed to Fra Angelico and Filippino Lippi.

From the Cathedral a steep road with stunning views leads up through the public gardens. To the west is the restored 14th-century church of **San Francesco**, housing some Florentine paintings, a choir arch by Benedetto da Maiano and a quirky little Missionary Museum. Below it is the older, more interesting church of **San Alessandro**, which is thought to have been founded in the 6th century on the site of an Etruscan temple. In the simple interior are some original Roman columns.

SETTIGNANO is another elegant suburb and, like Fiésole, has long been a popular place to build a villa. In the Renaissance the area was renowned as the home of several sculptors including Desiderio, the Rossellino brothers, and Benedetto da Maiano. Michelangelo also spent some of his youth in the area, probably at what is now known as the Villa Michelangelo. The attraction of this area for sculptors consisted mainly in its proximity to the *pietra serena* stone quarries at nearby Monte Cerceri.

In 1829 the eccentric English poet Walter Savage Landor moved to the 15th-century **Villa Gherardesca** near Settignano. He had previously lived in Florence but had found the city hot and dirty and the Florentines 'beyond all others a treacherous, tricking, mercenary race'. In Settignano he had an earthly paradise with 'the best water, the best air and the best oil in the world'. Actually Landor left the villa seven years later after the break-up of his marriage, but he still saw Tuscany as his spiritual home and was buried in the English cemetery in Florence along with several of his compatriots including his friend Elizabeth Barrett Browning.

Some sixty years later, the young American art-critic Bernard Berenson moved into a villa called **I Tatti**, just north of Settignano. Here, over his long lifetime, he collected together a formidable collection of Tuscan art and books. Even during the dangerous days of the Second World War Berenson remained in or near his beloved home overlooking Florence, grumbling gently to his diary at each new inconvenience.

> The pine-clad, cypress-studded hills above me, cobwebbed over with innumerable paths, my favourite haunts for over half a century, must now be untrodden ground. They have been sown by the Germans with mines, and wayfarers have lost their lives. Walks must be limited to the highroad winding steeply past Vincigliata to the hill-top above – a little arduous for my eighty years.

Berenson's villa with its lovely garden is now owned by the Harvard School of Renaissance Studies, and access must be sought from them to see the house and pictures. Another fine villa in the area is the Villa Gamberai, a kilometre or so to the south-east of the village, with a really superb Italianate garden which is occasionally opened to the public.

In the main square at Settignano is the much-reconstructed 16th-century church of **Santa Maria**, containing a terracotta from the studio of Andrea della Robbia and a pulpit by Buontalenti. A few kilometres away, off the Florence road at Ponte a Mensola, is the 9th-century Benedictine church of **San Martino a Mensola**, supposedly founded by Scotland's patron saint, Andrew. In the elegant 15th-century interior are pictures by Cosimo Roselli, Neri di Bicci and Taddeo Gaddi, as well as an *Annunciation* by a follower of Fra Angelico. In the sacristy is a small museum.

Travelling further into the country towards the north-east one reaches the fertile **MUGELLO VALLEY**. An interesting route out of Florence is through Pratolino, where the remains of one of the most fantastic gardens in Italy – the **Parco Demidoff** – is sometimes open to the public. The first villa at Pratolino was built by Buontalenti for Francesco de' Medici, a vast Mannerist extravaganza surrounded by a park full of grottoes, fountains, moving statues and a series of Mannerist tricks. The villa was destroyed in 1822 because it

The countryside of the Mugello

was too expensive to maintain, and later the new Villa Demidoff was built. The garden is rather depleted but some things remain as they were, for example Giambologna's colossal statue, *L'Appenino*. A few kilometres further out, through twisting hilly roads, is the aptly-named convent of **Monte Senario**, with a huge sweeping view. The convent was begun in 1241 but underwent heavy restoration in the 16th century under the direction of Cosimo I. A few kilometres on, the ground drops away and you enter the Mugello valley with its gently rolling countryside, undiscovered churches and grand villas of the nobility.

Just east of the Bologna Autostrada (A1), on the western edge of the Mugello, is the Medici villa of **Caffaggiolo**, built by Michelozzo for Cosimo il Vecchio in 1451. The site was chosen, in an area where the Medici owned a lot of land, with a view to strengthening the local peoples' allegiance to the family. As well as this the Mugello was a suitably remote retreat from Florence in times of strife or plague. Michelozzo constructed Caffaggiolo more like a fortress than a pleasure villa, with a moat and high, battlemented tower, both of which were demolished by Napoleon's brother-in-law Prince Borghese who acquired the villa in 1864. Now the property, which Vasari described as possessing 'all the requisites of a distinguished country house', has fallen into disrepair. Peering through the gates, one can see that the once fine garden is covered with weeds and has become a pleasure-ground for hens.

A kilometre or two up the hill, in a much lovelier position, is another Medici villa, **Il Trebbio**. This was originally a medieval fortress which was restyled, probably by Michelozzo, into an elegant country house. Like Caffaggiolo, il Trebbio was a popular retreat from city life for generations of Medici. Cosimo il Vecchio would come to the area to read and study, Lorenzo il Magnifico to discuss philosophy and art with his many friends. Other popular diversions were hunting, and fishing in the river Sieve – a particular hobby of Grand Duke Cosimo I. Cabriana, a contemporary of Cosimo's, described these expeditions which would take place throughout the summer:

> In the little stream of the Sieve, which flows into the valley of the Mugello, the Duke would catch various fish, such as trout, and would divide his haul among his courtiers and watch them with great delight as they ate the fish which they had cooked in the neighbouring meadows, he himself lying on the grass.

Throughout the Mugello are many other villas of the wealthy Florentines. Look out particularly for the 15th-century Villa Pozzolino near Bivigliano, and the massive fortress-like Castello del Trebbio a few kilometres north of Pontassi-eve, which belonged to the treacherous Pazzi family.

The principal town of the Mugello, **Borgo San Lorenzo**, is a disappointing place – a spreading industrial new town which has grown up to replace the old one destroyed in an earthquake in 1919. A few kilometres to the north is the more attractive town of **Scarperia** which has a fine 13th-century Palazzo Pretorio, decorated with a stemme of the town governors. Opposite, in the oratory of the Madonna di Piazza, is a *Madonna and Child* by Benedetto da Maiano and some interesting 14th-century paintings on the walls. A few kilometres to the north-east, in the village of **Sant' Agata**, is a beautiful 13th-century Romanesque *pieve* with a wonderful simple interior containing a couple of fine pictures. A couple of kilometres away in Mollinuccio is a restaurant of the same name with a relaxed family atmosphere and good *casalinga* cooking. To the north-west of Scarperia the country becomes so mountainous, with twisting roads and steep valleys, as to be known locally as 'little Switzerland'. Between Scarperia and Caffaggiolo is the ancient convent of Bosco ai Frati, supposedly founded c.600AD but rebuilt in the 13th, 15th and 17th centuries. In the church is a fine Renaissance crucifix of uncertain attribution.

Travelling east from Borgo san Lorenzo towards Dicomano, one passes through the hamlet of Vespignano, the birthplace of Giotto, followed closely by the small town of **Vicchio**, birthplace of Fra Angelico. It is easy to imagine these two gentle painters coming from this area of quiet hills and pleasant climate, where the traditional white Chiantigiana oxen are still used on some farms. Like many other local towns, Vicchio suffered in the earthquake of 1919 and much of it has been rebuilt. In the Piazza Giotto is a small Museo del Beato Angelico which contains works taken from nearby churches. At Dicomano, you are in the wine growing region of Chianti Putto and there are plenty of local wines to taste and buy. In the 13th century Dicomano belonged to the fierce Conti Guidi of Poppi in the Casentino. Later it fell under the sway of the Bardi, joining the *Commune* of Florence in 1375. At Dicomano you have two choices – to turn south to Florence via Rufina and Pontassieve or to take the road north to San Godenzo. In **San Godenzo**, an attractive hill village, is a wonderful Romanesque abbey, begun in the 11th century, and – like San Miniato al Monte – with a raised choir. On the lovely main altar is a 14th-century polyptych by Bernardo Daddi. The southern route to Florence is less picturesque but good for buying Chianti – passing through Rufina, where some of the best wine is to be had, and the sprawling untidy town of Pontassieve with its strange high bridge.

West and South of Florence

Leaving Florence to the west, on the road leading towards the unlovely town of Émpoli, is the walled village of Artimino with its exuberant Mannerist villa. The villa, a hunting lodge for Ferdinando I, was virtually rebuilt for him by the prolific Bernardo Buontalenti in the late 16th century. It is possible to buy wine from the *fattoria* here, and there is also a restaurant. The area around Artimino is famous throughout Tuscany for its wines, which are recorded as being popular with the Medici. Nearby in the parish church of Carmignano is the exquisite *Visitation* by Pontormo. **Émpoli** itself, though not beautiful, does have an excellent picture gallery in the Collegiata, with paintings by Bicci di Lorenzo, Lorenzo Monaco, Botticini and Pontormo.

The area to the south of Florence is equally rich territory. Near the city is the fine old Charterhouse (*Certosa*) of Val d'Ema (sometimes called the Certosa di Galluzzo) and the pilgrimage church of Santa Maria dell' Impruneta, while further away the hills of Chianti stretch temptingly into the distance. If you are staying in Florence, any of these areas can easily be managed as a day trip. The Charterhouse is only a few kilometres out of town, up a steep hill off the Via Senese just past the sprawling village of Galluzzo. It was founded in 1338 by the wealthy Florentine banker Nicola Acciaioli, and he and his family are buried here in an underground chapel in the church of San Lorenzo. In the old Palazzo degli Studi is a good museum, with an extraordinary series of pictures by Pontormo depicting the Passion. Here too are pictures by Mariotto di Nardo, Lucas Cranach and Bronzino.

A few kilometres to the south is the agricultural village of **Impruneta**, where the fine church of **Santa Maria** with its 16th-century façade overlooks the main square. The story is that in the 11th century the Buondelmonte family who owned the land were uncertain as to where to build their new church. After some debate they set loose a riderless cart full of stones, and where the bullocks pulling it stopped they immediately unloaded and began to build. The church was much rebuilt in the 15th century, but more recently underwent total renovation to repair the ravages of the Second World War. The 14th-century polyptych by Pietro Nelli had been virtually destroyed, but was put back together and is now on the altar. Luckily the two terracotta tabernacles by Michelozzo, decorated by Luca della Robbia, remained largely unharmed. Also of interest is the marble predella, the *Miraculous Madonna* which is thought to be by a follower of Donatello. In the sacristy is an early 15th-century *Trinity* attributed to Mariotto di Nardo.

Back on the main Siena road one quickly reaches the market town of **San Casciano in Val di Pesa**. San Casciano is famous mainly for its church of the Misericordia in which there are several fine Sienese paintings, including Simone Martini's *Crucifixion* painted on wood. A few miles away, at the strangely named *Sant' Andrea in Percussina*, is the villa where Niccolò Machiavelli spent many years in exile from Florence and where he wrote some of his best works. In a letter to one of the Medici he describes how he spends his days on the farm, trapping thrushes, berating his employees and spending the afternoons at the local inn.

> . . . I act the rustic for the rest of the day, playing at *cricca* and *tric-trac* which lead to a thousand squabbles and countless slanging matches – our fights are usually over a farthing, but we can be heard shouting nonetheless from San Casciano. So, trapped among this vermin, I rub the mould from my wits and work off the sense of being so cruelly treated by Fate – content to be driven along this road if only to watch for her [Fate] to show some sign of shame.

But his evenings were spent rather differently:

> When evening comes I strip off and go into my study. On the threshold I take off my muddy, sweaty, workday clothes and put on the robes of court and palace, in this graver dress I enter the antique court of the ancients and am welcomed by them, and there I taste the food that alone is mine, and for which I was born. And there I make bold to speak to them and ask the motives of their actions, and they in their humanity reply to me . . . I have written down what I have gained from their conversation, and composed a small work, *De Principatibus* . . . And if you have ever been pleased by any of my fancies this should not displease you.

Continuing into the countryside towards the old towns of Montespertoli and Castelfiorentino, one eventually joins the route No.429 on the way to **Certaldo**. This is another fine old town, built like Siena of rose-coloured brick on a hill above the new suburb. Certaldo, as any local will tell you, has a special place in history as the home of another great writer, Giovanni Boccaccio, author of the *Decameron*. The house where he died in 1375 has been totally rebuilt since the Second World War, but the lovely 15th-century town hall is still standing and has some fine cloisters decorated by Pietro Fiorentino in the 15th century. In the chapel next door are some fragments of pictures by Benozzo Gozzoli and Giusto d'Andrea.

To the east of the Florence–Siena autostrada is the area traditionally known as Chianti. Here are the great sweeping hills covered with vineyards, producing Chianti Classico from the Sangiovese grape. Only the wine from a strictly defined area is allowed to boast the black cockerel seen on the Chianti Classico label. Most of the other Chianti growers, which are in general as good as the others, are grouped together under the Chianti Putto label. Among the vineyards are olive groves, chestnut woods and large, untidy, honey-coloured *fattorie* insufficiently sheltered by tall black cypresses. As well as the bigger vineyards, many of the smaller farms also offer wine for sale. If you have time it can be fun to follow vague signs up seemingly interminable dusty tracks that apparently (and often actually) lead nowhere in search of the perfect vintage. In fact the quality is often as good in the small as in the larger vineyards, and of course it is always important to taste before you buy. If you are coming from Florence the traditional route into Chianti is the Via Chiantigiana (No.222) which passes through Strada, Greve and Castellina. No doubt partly owing to its abundance of good wine, this area has become extremely popular with the English and Germans, and it is not unusual to walk into what you think is a remote village bar and discover your local MP sipping Sambuca.

In general the small towns and villages of Chianti are sleepy and attractive although also with an increasingly touristy feel about them. **Greve** is the principal wine-selling town of the region and has a good *Enoteca Gallo Nero* which sells a large selection of Chianti Classico wines. Every September Greve has a Chianti wine fair – a paradise for wine-bibbers. The best part of the town itself is the elegant porticoed main square surrounded by 17th-century buildings. Nearby is the village of Panzano with a 12th-century Oratorio di SS Annuziata which has interesting modern doors. Outside Panzano on the Via San Leoncino is one of the very nicest hotels of the region, the Villa le Barone, for which you need to book well in advance.

Further south is the lovely medieval village of Volpaia in fine countryside near the tiny town of **Radda-in-Chianti**. Small though it was, Radda became the seat of the Chianti league in 1415 and it is still round here that some of the best Chiantis are to be found. There is a pretty restored medieval town hall and in the parish church is an interesting wooden crucifix of the 15th century with hinged wooden arms. Outside the town, past the growing modern suburb, is the popular restaurant La Villa Miranda run by an awesome matriarchy who offer a good but rather expensive array of local produce. Alternatively you can buy their delicious hams and cheeses in their shop and eat them elsewhere.

Castellina, another pleasant small town, is a few kilometres away off the spectacularly lovely road from Poggibonsi in the heart of Chianti. Castellina was the head of the Chianti league for a while in the Middle Ages and is still dominated by the restored medieval grey stone castello from which it got its name. In the square is an elegant restaurant. A few miles to the east is another wine town, **Gaiole**, with a 13th-century Pieve di Spaltenna which still has its cloister and its original tower. Within walking distance to the east is the charming medieval village of **Barbischio**, and also nearby is the little settlement of **Badia a Coltibuono** where the old monastery has become a successful *fattoria* with its own restaurant and shop.

Spread out in the countryside among the villages and *fattorie* are the con-

Radda-in-Chianti

verted villas of the holidaymakers – old farms discreetly hidden up long tracks beside cool swimming pools where glasses clink and lizards dart. This is the 'Chiantishire' of modern writers who come back again and again and each time complain that it is a little worse than before. Perhaps it is, but it is still undeniably lovely and, depending on where you go, relatively peaceful. In terms of the complainers, my preference is for Dylan Thomas's (rather less subtle) view of villa life, written over forty years ago before it was fashionable to complain:

> In a shuttered room I roast
> Like a pumpkin in a serra
> And the sun like buttered toast
> Drips upon the classic terra,
> Upon swimming pool and pillar.
> Loggia, lemon, pineclad pico,
> And this quite enchanting villa
> That isn't worth a fico,
> Upon terrace and frutteto
> Of this almost a palazzo
> Where the people talk potato
> And the weather drives me pazzo.

Practical Information

Hotels and Restaurants

FIÉSOLE *Villa Bonelli* (tel. (055) 59513) Via F. Poeti 1–3. A reasonable, pleasant, modern hotel with good service and lovely views from the top-floor restaurant.
In the Mugello valley to the north of the city is the rather run-down and eccentric, but extremely charming, *Hotel Villa Ebe* (tel. 848019) in a remote position off the small road between Scarperia and Grezzano. Near the Medici villas at Castello is another nice hotel housed in the 16th-century Villa le Rondini (tel. (055) 400081) on the Via Bolognese Vecchia (224). Not far away is the hearty country restaurant *Lo Strettoio* at Serpiolle.
South of Florence on the Via Grevignana between San Casciano and Mercatale is another excellent country restaurant, *La Biscondola* (tel. (055) 821328).

CERTALDO In the top part of town are the charming *Hotel Il Castello* (tel. (0571) 668250) Via B, della Rena, and the family run *Hotel Osteria del Vicario* (tel. (055) 668228) with another good restaurant.

CHIANTI REGION There are many hotels and restaurants in the Chianti hills and villages but while many have quite high culinary standards they tend to be expensive and full in the summer.
In **Castellina in Chianti** is the *Pensione Belvedere di San Leonino* (tel. (0577)

740887) 53011 Siena – one of the better value and more charming pensione converted out of an old farm. A few kilometres away on the San Donato Road is the expensive but charming *Tenuta di Ricavo* another tastefully converted cluster of old buildings also boasting two swimming pools. Also with a pool is the lovely *Villa Le Barone* near Panzano (tel. (055) 852215) 50020 Firenze – again rather expensive but undoubtedly charming. Outside **Radda-in-Chianti** is the small pensione *Podere Terreno* (tel. (0577) 738312) 53017 Siena, in lovely countryside near the pretty village of Volpaia. Outside **Gaiole** is a 12th-century converted monastery known as the *Castello di Spaltenna* (tel. (0577) 749483) 53013 Siena, which has a few simple bedrooms and a wonderful vaulted restaurant.

Museums

Certosa di Galluzzo   Via Senese: open 09.00–12.00 and 15.00–18.00 (winter 14.30–17.00); closed Mon.
Villa Medicea della Petraia   Bus 28 from the station towards Sesto Fiorentino: open 09.00–sunset; closed Mon.
Villa Medicea di Castello   Bus 28 from station: garden only open 09.00–18.30 or sunset, closed Mon.
Villa Demidoff   open May–Sept, Fri–Sun and hols 10.00–20.00, gardens only.
Museo Stibber   Via Federico Stibbert (Florence): open weekdays 09.00–12.45; Sun and hols 09.00–12.30; closed Thurs.

FIÉSOLE
Museo Bandini   Via Dupre: open 10.00–12.00 and 14.00–17.00, 14.00–18.00 summer.
Anfiteatro Romano   open 09.00–19.00 summer, 09.00–16.00 winter.

EMPOLI
Museo della Collegiata   Piazzetta San Giovanni: open 09.00–12.00, Thurs–Sat also 16.00–19.00, closed Mon.

CERTALDO
Palazzo Pretorio   Piazzetta del Vicariato: open summer 08.00–12.00 and 16.30–19.00 (closes at 15.00 or 18.00 in winter).

POGGIO A CAIANO
Villa Medicea   gardens only open 09.00–18.30 or sunset.

11. AREZZO, CORTONA AND THE CASENTINO

Arezzo

The lovely old city of **AREZZO** rises on a hill above a sprawling modern town some 80 kilometres to the south-east of Florence. Arezzo first became successful in Etruscan times when it was mainly dependent on its growing manufacture of pottery, metal utensils and weapons, becoming one of the 12 city states of Etruria. Later the Romans arrived and quickly began to exploit the town's strategic position as the meeting place of the three valleys – the Casentino, the Val d'Arno and the Val di Chiana – which even at that stage were important trade routes. Later, under the domination of the powerful and warlike feudal families of the Conti Guidi from Poppi, the Pazzi Ubertini and the Tarlati, Arezzo became a growing threat to Florence. Over the years, as the problem got worse, the bigger town became increasingly determined to do something about her small but troublesome neighbour. In 1262 the great and bloody battle of Campaldino took place in the valley below Arezzo and the home armies were demolished by the Guelphs of Florence. Arezzo did briefly win back independence, but in 1335 the town was attacked and besieged by Perugia and a year later, in a seriously weakened state, she finally fell to Florence for good.

As any Aretine will tell you, Arezzo has a long list of distinguished inhabitants. In Roman times the town was the home of the great patron of arts and literature Maecenas who supported and encouraged such greats as Horace and Virgil. Less well-known but perhaps the most influential citizen was Guido Monaco who was born at the end of the 10th century and invented today's standard musical notation. Some 300 years later the great poet Petrarch was born here, although he left the city as a young boy, exiled to France. During the Renaissance Arezzo produced the writer Pietro Aretino, the painters Spinello Aretino and his son Parri and, most prominent of all in the city, the painter, architect and splendid biographer Giorgio Vasari (1511–74).

Arriving by train, there are two main routes up from the station to the old town. Directly ahead of you as you come out is the Via Guido Monaco which goes through the leafy piazza of the same name, past the Palazzo del Popolo, and ends up near the church of San Francesco which contains Piero della Francesca's magnificent paintings of the legend of the True Cross. Turning right out of the station towards the Roman amphitheatre you soon come to the Corso Italia – a smart pedestrian zone filled with expensive shops where the evening ritual of the *passeggiata* is performed. Antiquarians may prefer to continue past the Corso to the **amphitheatre** itself before toiling up the hill to the old town. There are differing opinions about when this Roman structure was actually built but it was probably between the 1st century BC and the 2nd AD. Despite having suffered repeated raids by medieval builders (look at some of the stones of church of San Bernardino for example) enough of it has remained intact for us to know that it seated up to 10,000 spectators, indicating just how important a place Arretium must have been. In 1547 San Bernardino of Siena founded an Olivetan monastery within its walls and it is here that the town's archeological collection is kept on display, despite serious damage in the last war. The **Museo Archeológico Mecenate** has exhibits dating back as far as the Stone Age as well as various Etruscan and Roman objects. Its pride and joy however is in its finely decorated local *coralline* vases, which were made in and around Arezzo as early as the 1st century BC.

At the top of the increasingly steep Corso Italia stands what is undoubtedly the loveliest church in the city – the parish church, **Santa Maria della Pieve**. Although it is recognised as being one of the oldest churches in Arezzo, no-one is sure when it was actually begun. Indications are that it is basically a 12th-century structure, perhaps built on to an even older church. It has a wonderful 13th-century Pisan-style façade with layer upon layer of Romanesque arches which diminish in size as they increase in number towards the top. Under the church is a tiny dressmaker's shop and, if you look in the window at night, the yellow light illuminates a black-clad lady bending over her sewing. Above her, rising to about 200 feet, is the campanile with forty double windows, known inaccurately as the tower of 100 holes. Above the church's main door are some 13th-century carvings (c.1215) of the Virgin and the months of the year. Almost as lovely as the outside is the austere interior with a raised choir, wooden dome and an ancient crypt. In the Baptistery chapel is an early 14th-century font with three panels of the life of the Baptist by Agostino di Giovanni.

The rounded apse of Santa Maria protrudes into the **Piazza Grande**, the historical centre of the old city. The Piazza Grande is one of the most charming squares in Tuscany, sloping and irregular, surrounded by old houses and palaces of different periods, no two of which are the same. Next to the apse of Santa Maria to the west of the square, a flight of steps leads up to the 17th –18th century law-courts. Next to the law-courts is Vasari's handsome **Palazzo delle Logge**, begun in 1573 and named after its grand arcaded loggia which runs along the edge of the square. The loggia and the surrounding area are

Arezzo – Piazza Grande

used to house part of the large antiques market which is held on the first Sunday of every month. Standing in front of the loggia is the old *petrone* where criminals were exposed to public shame. The fine **Palazzo della Fraternità dei Laici** is a mixture of different styles. The ground floor is Gothic, designed by Baldino di Cino in 1376. The first floor and the sculptural decorations date back to 1433 and were the work of the Renaissance architect Bernardo Rossellino. The top of the building, including the loggia and balustrade, were completed some thirty years later by Giuliano and Aligozzo da Settignano. Finally the belfry was added in the 16th century by the indefatigable Aretine Giorgio Vasari.

Traditionally the Piazza Grande is the meeting point of the four main *contrade* or districts of the town. As in most Italian towns these *contrade* are fiercely competitive and each year this rivalry reaches its zenith in a medieval jousting match known as the *Giostra del Saracino*. Like the *Palio* in Siena, the *Giostra* is performed in full medieval regalia and more or less the whole day (the first Sunday in September) is given over to processions, drum beating and flag twirling. If anything the costumes are even more varied and splendid than the Sienese. Horsemen, dignitaries and damsels, protected by miniature armies of foot-soldiers, parade, sweating in ermine, velvet and steel, through the steep streets.

The competition itself involves a horseman from each *contrada* galloping across the Piazza Grande with a lance and striking hard against a shield which hangs from the left arm of a life-size wooden puppet. On the shield are numbered squares which decide the score. The puppet is fixed on a pivot and

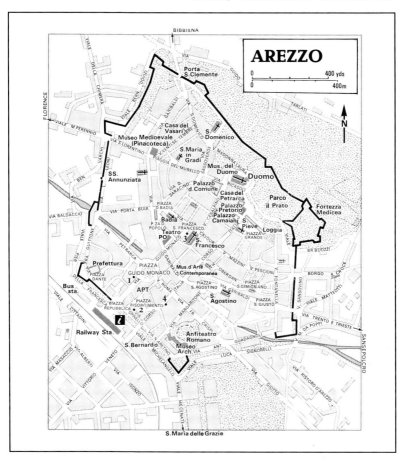

in his other hand hang three leather balls which swing round viciously at the 'knight' when he hits the shield. Unlike the *Palio* the *Giostra* usually goes on for a few hours while the sweltering foot-soldiers become more and more fractious until scuffles start to break out – a sort of fancy dress football hooliganism. To watch this whole magnificent scene you must buy tickets, which you can normally do on the day of the Corso Italia near the entrance to the square.

At the top of the Corso on the left is the **Palazzo Pretorio**, initially built in 1320 but completely re-vamped in the 17th century. The coats of arms that decorate the front belong to the governing families of the city. Just around the corner is the Casa del Petrarca built in the 17th century on the spot where the poet was supposedly born, but substantially rebuilt after suffering terrible damage in the second World War. Now it is the seat of the Académia Petrarca di Léttere, Arti e Scienze.

At the highest point of the hill stands the **Cathedral**, in front of the pleasant shady park known as the **Passeggio del Prato**, which continues right down to the solid 16th-century Medici fortress. The cathedral was begun in 1277 on the site of an earlier Benedictine church. In the centuries that followed the building was repeatedly altered and enlarged: the portico is 14th-century, the campanile dates from 1860 and the façade was not added until the beginning of the 20th century.

The inside is notable mainly for the fine series of early 16th-century stained-glass windows along the right-hand aisle. They were made by Guillaume de Marcillat (1477–1529) who left France in a hurry after a murder and spent most of the rest of his working life in Italy. His windows have a narrative approach unusual in Italian windows of that time, although the idea was taken up soon after by the local artists. They show the Calling of Matthew, the Woman taken in Adultery, the Purifying of the Temple, and the Raising of Lazarus. Nearby is the tomb of Pope Gregory X who died while on a visit to Arezzo in 1276.

At the end of the left aisle is a rather static but statuesque *Mary Magdalen*, standing majestically in a red cloak, by the great Piero della Francesca. To her left is the magnificent tomb of the warlike bishop of Arezzo, Guido Tarlati. Guido became Bishop and Lord of the city in the early 1300s, some few years after the terrible defeat at Campaldino, and for the next few years he waged war on the neighbouring towns, winning back the losses of the previous years. Eventually he was excommunicated by the Pope and, after a quarrel with his single, immensely powerful ally, Castruccio Castracani of Lucca, he died of fever in the Pisan Maremma, having reconciled himself with the church. His tomb, which is said to have been designed by Giotto, has sixteen panels showing episodes of his life which, for a bishop, involved rather a lot of fighting. The organ gallery is by Vasari. Behind the altar is another great tomb, the marble Arco di San Donato, which is carved by a collection of local and Sienese artists. Donato, patron saint of Arezzo, was martyred in the ancient Rome probably under the Emperor Diocletian. The large 18th–19th century Cappella della Madonna di Conforto contains some terracottas of the family of della Robbia. In the Sacristy, among other works, is an interesting detached fresco, *Saint Jerome in Penitence*, by the little-known artist Bartolmeo della Gata.

In terms of artistic importance, however, the cathedral is far from being the most important church in Arezzo. That honour goes without any doubt to the simple, 13th-century church of **San Francesco**, with its plain unadorned façade and barn-like, aisleless interior. Above the entrance is another window by Guillaume de Marcillat, this time of Pope Honorius III honouring the rule of St Francis, probably done in the early 16th century. There are also two portraits of saints by the talented Florentine, Andrea del Castagno, as well as pictures by the local painter Spinello Aretino. In the Tarlati chapel, which contains a Crucifix by Spinello, there is also a fine *Annunciation* which has been attributed to Luca Signorelli. But none of these things are the real reason why lovers of painting come to this church and quite possibly why they have come to Arezzo in the first place. In the main choir chapel are some of the most beautiful and important paintings of the Italian Renaissance – the cycle of frescoes by Piero della Francesca depicting the sacred Legend of the True Cross.

Piero began painting in San Francesco in the early to mid 1450s. He was called in after the death of Lorenzo di Bicci who had been commissioned to decorate the chapel by the Bacci family but died having painted only the vaulted ceiling. Apart from the *Annunciation* on the bottom left-hand side of the altar, Piero's subject matter was taken from a popular legend written by Jacopo de Voragine and tells the story of the origin and discovery of the True Cross. Because of Piero's love of symmetry and order the story is not pictured in sequence, so it is important to know the complicated chain of events to make sense of the narrative.

The story starts when the old dying Adam sends his son Seth to the Archangel Michael who gives him some seeds from the Tree of Original Sin to plant in the old man's mouth at his death. The tree which grows is later chopped down by Solomon and finally used as a bridge. When the Queen of Sheba visits Solomon she is about to cross the river when she miraculously realises that the Messiah will die on this wood and kneels before it in homage. Solomon is perturbed and buries the tree, which he now considers as a symbol of the end of the kingdom of his people the Jews. But the wood is later retrieved and fulfils its destiny as the Cross on which Christ dies. Three centuries pass and, on the eve of a great battle against Maxentius, the Emperor Constantine hears in a dream that to win the battle he must fight in the name of the Holy Cross. He does this, and wins, and then asks his mother Helena to go to Jerusalem to find the sacred object. But the only person who knows its whereabouts is a Jew named Judas, who refuses to tell the secret until he is tortured and put down a well. Eventually he admits that the three crosses from Calvary are hidden in a pagan temple, which is then destroyed and the crosses found. Out of the three, the identity of True Cross is established when it performs a miracle, reviving a dead boy. But the story is not over yet. In 615 the Persian king Chosroes steals the Cross, which is then taken from him in battle by the Emperor Heraclius who returns with it to Jerusalem. But on his arrival he is prevented from entering the city in glory by a divine power which persuades him to set aside false grandeur, and enter bearing the Cross in a gesture of humility as Christ would have done.

Piero's *Legend of the True Cross* is undoubtedly one of the greatest masterpieces of Italian art. Although some of the work was obviously done by assistants, the whole series gives a quite stunning picture of his power and innovatory skill as an artist. Particularly noticeable is his advanced perspective technique (he later gave up painting altogether to become a mathematician) and his clear use of colour and form. His pictures have a potent charm – with an attention to detail and design that in no way reduces the powerful simplicity of the narrative action. Look particularly at his splendid array of clothing and different headdresses. Above all there is a stillness about his figures, even in the midst of battle, that enhances their dreamlike quality.

To the north of the old city is the 13th-century church of **San Domenico**, another simple aisleless structure, commissioned by the powerful Tarlati family in 1275. Vasari mentions this church as being designed by the Pisan sculptor Nicola Pisano, but there is no other evidence to substantiate this. At the top of the campanile hang two 14th-century bells. Inside is a powerful wooden crucifix painted in around 1275 by the early Florentine master Cimabue. There are also some interesting though faded pictures by two local painters, Spinello Aretino and his son Parri di Spinello. The Gothic tabernacle is attributed to Giovanni Francesco.

Nearby on **Via XX Settembre** is the home of Giorgio Vasari, one of Arezzo's most famous sons. Vasari's greatest contribution to posterity lies less in his prolific output of painting and architecture than in his splendid biographies of Italian painters which, if not always accurate, are always amusing. Vasari bought this house in 1540 and proceeded to decorate it in his most extravagant style. It is now a museum and *Archivo Vasariano* and one can visit by appointment the sumptuously frescoed rooms, most notable of which is the Camera d'Apollo.

A few minutes' walk away in the Via San Lorentino is the graceful 15th-century Palazzo Bruni-Ciocchi which houses the main picture gallery, containing some fine Aretine and Tuscan paintings, and a collection of Majolica (glazed pottery) dating from the 13th–18th centuries.

Directly south, on the Via Garibaldi, is another lovely Renaissance building, the church of **SS Annunziata**, which was designed by Bartolomeo della Gata and Antonio da Sangallo. It contains some more stained glass by the Frenchman Guillaume de Marcillat who was responsible for many of the windows in the cathedral. Another fine church in this area is Santa Maria in Gradi, named after the flight of steps leading up to the main door. It was built mainly by the flamboyant Florentine architect Bernardo Ammannati who did a lot of work for the Medici Grand Dukes. The bell-tower was added in the mid 17th century. Inside is a characteristic terracotta – the *Madonna del Soccorso* by Andrea della Robbia.

If you have more than a day in the province of Arezzo, and you enjoyed the Pieros in San Francesco, you should spend a morning at the little town of **Borgo Sansepolcro**. There, some twenty miles to the east of Arezzo nestling on the Umbrian border, you will find perhaps the single greatest Renaissance treasure in all Tuscany.

Sansepolcro is a pleasant town with a 16th-century Medici fortress and some fine old houses. Its 11th-century cathedral has been much altered but contains a few objects of interest, a della Robbia tabernacle and an *Ascension* possibly by Perugino. Next door, the Palazzo delle Laudi was built at the turn of the 16th century and has an attractive arcaded courtyard.

But the town's claim to fame is housed in the Museo Civico – the *Resurrection* of Piero della Francesca. Piero's Christ faces you squarely, weary but defiant above the sleeping soldiers. Initially unsurprising, this Christ has a face that you keep glancing back to and which holds you each time with a greater intensity. There have been many critical interpretations of this masterpiece. I rather like this one by James Elroy Flecker:

Sleep holds you sons of war; you may not see
(You whose charmed heads sink heavy in your hands)
How 'twixt the budding and the barren tree
With glory in his staring eyes, he stands.
There's a sharp movement in this shivering morn
That blinds your senses while it breaks your power:
The Phoenix grips the eagle: Christ reborn
Bears high the standard. Sleep a little hour:
Sleep: it were best ye saw not those bright eyes
Prepared to wreck your world with errant flame,
And drive strong men to follow mysteries,
Voices, and winds, and things that have no name.
Dare you leave strength half-proved, duty half-done?
Awake! This God will hunt you from the sun!

The other Pieros in the room are marvellous too. Opposite the *Resurrection* there is a solemn but gentle *Madonna*, also standing absolutely face-on, shielding the lesser mortals under her cloak. On another wall is a fragment of *St Julian*, the only thing to survive from the church of San Francesco, a few minutes walk away. The young St Louis in his bishop's mitre has a worried frown of responsibility on his adolescent face.

A few kilometres away in a tiny chapel in the cemetery of **Monterchi** is another of Piero's Madonnas, this time standing, heavily pregnant, between two angels. The *Madonna del Parto* was painted while Piero was working on the True Cross cycle in Arezzo. As well as being extremely beautiful she is, in her condition, a very unusual subject for a painter to choose, and has become honoured locally as the protector of pregnant women. Her thoughtful, almost mournful stillness is emphasised by the exact symmetry of the two angels caught in the same pose drawing back the curtains.

Near Monterchi is the pretty walled town of **Anghiari** which has a good rustic *casalinga* restaurant, the Locanda al Castello di Sorci. Anghiari is linked to Sansepolcro by what must be one of the straightest roads in Italy.

Cortona

About thirty kilometres south of Arezzo lies the ancient city of Cortona. Leaving Arezzo on the Cortona road, one passes first through the walled market town of **Castiglion Fiorentino** on a hill overlooking the edge of the wide Val di Chiana. In the main square are some fine civic buildings, notably the elegant 16th-century Loggia di Vasari and the much restored, early 16th-century Palazzo Comunale which now houses the Pinacoteca, a small but interesting collection of paintings and sculptures. Five kilometres south, high up the hill, is the impressively fortified 12th-century **Castello di Montecchio** Vesponi which, in the late 14th century, was given to the English *Condottiere* Sir John Hawkwood by the Florentines in return for his military services. The

Val di Chiana is traditionally a cattle-raising area and produces the best beef in Tuscany.

A few kilometres south is **CORTONA**, believed to be one of the oldest cities in Italy. It was probably founded by the ancient Umbrian tribes, but it first rose to fame as one of the most powerful of the renowned 'League of Twelve' Etruscan lucomonies (city states). By the 4th century BC the Romans had arrived, but in the 2nd century they were temporarily routed by the great Carthaginian general Hannibal. Hannibal turned the area into a battlefield, luring the people of Arezzo down on to the Cortona plain, where he demolished their army and killed their leader. The Romans revived, however, and held sway over the town for the following centuries until, in around 450AD, the Barbarian invasions plunged Cortona into a chaos that she shared with the rest of Tuscany throughout the Dark Ages. In the Middle Ages the town began to flourish again and rose up as an independent *commune*. Again like her neighbours, she was racked not only by external raids from Arezzo and Perugia but also by internal strife as the town split into the factions of Guelph and Ghibelline. The situation stabilised for some years under the rule of the powerful Casali family in the 14th century, but eventually in 1411 Cortona fell to Florence and joined the growing territory under Florentine domination.

The town's Etruscan origins can first be recognised in parts of the great wall that still surrounds the old town. Equally impressive is the **Tanella di Pitagora** (Cave of Pythagoras) lying south of the walls – a cruciform Etruscan tomb built with massive wedge-shaped stones. Other ancient tombs can also be found at Il Sodo and Camucia in the plain that stretches away below the city. Once inside the walls, the best Etruscan remains can be seen at the 13th-century **Palazzo Pretorio** (sometimes called Casali) which was substantially remodelled in the Renaissance manner by Filippo Berretini. One of the few remaining parts of the medieval structure is the fine inside courtyard, later covered with *stemmae*, the coats of arms of the town governors. Inside, the Accadémia Etrusca (founded in 1726) houses a collection of Etruscan, Roman and Egyptian objects. One of the most charming exhibits is a wooden Egyptian funeral boat the size of a child's toy, dating back, staggeringly, to about 2000BC. Less appealing but also fascinating is a large bronze Etruscan lamp (c.500BC) and a strange votive hand covered in different symbols.

Despite Cortona's strong link with ancient days, the town's appearance is mainly medieval. The streets are mainly steep and narrow, some with worn steps and others with old overhanging houses crossed by crumbling arches. In the main square is the sturdy 13th-century **Palazzo Communale** with a wide flight of steps, where tourists sit down to take the weight off their aching feet and local boys and girls eye up eligible visitors. Above their heads are the squat bell-tower and the town clock, added in the 16th century. Originally the square was graced by a fountain, but this was removed in 1250 to make more room, even though the square was probably larger then anyway. Raised above the square is the little Piazza Pescherina, now covered in restaurant tables, but originally the fish market. The small 14th-century **Palazzo Passerini** (or **del Popolo**) was traditionally the home of the Capitano del Popolo. It was much restored in 1514, perhaps in preparation for the impending visit of Pope Leo X which took place in the following year.

To reach the **Cathedral** it is necessary to walk through the Piazza Signorelli and up the narrow alley that leads between the theatre and the Palazzo Casali to the Piazza del Duomo. The Piazza del Duomo, situated on the edge of the old town above the walls, is really little more than a car park from which there is a fine view. The Cathedral, on the right of the square, is basically a Romanesque building which some say was redesigned by the great Nicola Pisano in 1260. It was remodelled again during the Renaissance, possibly by Giuliano da Sangallo. The aisled interior contains some carved altars by Francesco Mazzuoli (c.1650) and a series of paintings by followers of Cortona's most famous native painter, Luca Signorelli.

For real artistic excitements it is better to go to the **Museo Diocesano** opposite the Cathedral. This has been constructed out of two churches, one on top of the other, joined with a flight of steps by Vasari. The bottom church, the oratory, is frescoed by Cristoforo Gherardi on Vasari's design. The best of the paintings are to be seen upstairs in the former Baptistery, which still has its 15th-century font made by an artist with the lovely name of Cuccio di Nuccio. Possibly the most exquisite of the gallery's treasures is the wonderful rosy *Annunciation* by Fra Angelico, who lived in Cortona for ten years. In the background of the picture it is possible to make out Lake Trasimeno and Castiglione del Lago. There is a fine tryptych, also by Fra Angelico, a *Crucifixion* by Pietro Lorenzetti and a winsome *Madonna and Child* of the Sienese School of Duccio. All in all, it is a really excellent small collection.

Tucked away throughout the town are other fine things to see. A few minutes walk to the south-east from the Piazza della Repubblica is the old church of **San Francesco**, which was founded by Frate Elia Coppi in 1245 (not many years after the Saint's death in 1228). It was a Frate Elia who also gave the church its most precious object, a reliquary of the True Cross: a 10th-century Byzantine ivory tablet which he brought from Constantinople and which is now housed in a 16th-century gilt frame. Frate Elia is buried here under the choir. It is possible that the local painter Luca Signorelli also rests in this church, although it is not clear where.

Walking eastwards up the hill one reaches another charming church enclosed behind iron gates, the little *pieve* of **San Niccolò**. In 1440 the church became an oratory for the newly established order of San Niccolò which was founded by the peace-loving San Bernardino of Siena. In the Baroque interior are frescoes by Luca Signorelli: *Madonna with Saints* (the emblem of the Order), a *Deposition* and a *Virgin and Child*.

Just outside the town walls to the south is the plain, early 15th-century church of San Domenico, containing more works by Signorelli and his pupil Bartolomeo della Gatta, as well as a tryptych by Lorenzo Gherini (c.1400). It was here that the great but humble painter-monk Fra Angelico worshipped when, for over a decade, he made Cortona his home.

Following the Via Santa Margherita past the medieval Porta Berarda and up towards the Medici Fortress, one passes a rather different sort of religious painting: along the wall at intervals are the *Stations of the Cross* by a modern painter from the city called Gino Severini. The series was commissioned by the townspeople in thanks to God for saving their city from bombardment in the Second World War. The Via Santa Margherita has long been a sacred road to the Cortona people because it was along this route that their patron Saint Margherita re-entered the city when she returned after long absence in 1272. The beautiful Santa Margherita lived much of her early life in sin with her lover in Montepulciano, but after his death she repented of her immoral ways and returned to Cortona with her son to lead a life of poverty and penance, devoting herself to self-abasement and the welfare of the poor. At one stage she decided to return to Montepulciano and walk around the streets, wearing nothing but a rope around her neck to proclaim her guilt; she was, however, dissuaded from this plan by her friend and biographer Fra Giunta. Her other achievements were to open a hospital and use her increasing influence to promote peace among the fractious neighbouring towns. At the top of her road is a pilgrims' church in her name, which houses her tomb and some relics in a 17th-century silver shrine on the altar. High above the church rises the Medici Fortezza di Giralfalco, built mainly in 1556 by Cosimo I, from which there are more magnificent views.

Not far outside the walls of Cortona are two remarkable Renaissance churches. Leaving the town by the Porta Agostino and following the road to Camucia you will find the lovely church of **Santa Maria delle Grazie al Calcinaio**, designed on the plan of a Latin cross by Francesco di Giorgio Martini between 1485 and 1518. The church's name refers to the nearby lime quarry and a miraculous image of the Virgin that was found on its walls – it is now on the altar of the church. The beautifully proportioned interior of the church is decorated with white plaster and the grey *pietra serena* stone that was so popular with Renaissance architects. On the other side of the city is the church of **Santa Maria Nuova**, in the shape of a Greek cross, which was designed by Giovanni Battista Infregliata but taken over and re-vamped by the tireless Vasari who is responsible for much of its present appearance.

Three kilometres further out in the same direction is the Franciscan convent known as **Le Celle** (the Cells), which was founded by St Francis himself on a hill by the river Cingone. For a fairly humble complex, Le Celle has had an awesome ecclesiastical guest-list, including Fra Elia of Umbria, the Blessed Guido, St Bonaventura and St Anthony of Padua.

Today the most elegant place for visitors to stay is another religious house – a 14th-century monastery known as the Contesse after its founder, a local noblewoman. Today it is a fairly stylish hotel conveniently situated just outside Cortona on the via Contesse. Attached to the main buildings is a little 18th-century church. Also worth a visit, although unfortunately it is not possible to stay there, is the fine Renaissance **Palazzone Passerini**, set in an elegant garden and boasting a huge fortified tower. The palace was built by Giovanni Battista Caporali of Perugia (c.1476–1560) for Cardinal Passerini. Tradition has it that it was here that the painter Luca Signorelli fell off some scaffolding to his death while decorating the chapel in 1532. In 1969 the building became a school.

If, instead of taking the Cortona road out of Arezzo, you choose the more westerly route towards Siena it is worth branching off into the lovely tree-clad and agricultural hills to the east of Chianti. Just off the main road about 24 kilometres from Arezzo is the little town of **Monte San Savino**. It is notable mainly as the birthplace of the sculptor Andrea Sansovino, who is thought to have designed the Loggia dei Mercato. The Loggia is situated on the town's main street, the Corso Sangallo, presumably named after the town hall which was built by Antonio da Sangallo the Elder. In the Piazza Gamurrini is the church of Santa Chiara which has some terracottas by Sansovino and others. A few kilometres away in lovely countryside is the picturesque hill village of **Gargonza**, which has been turned into a tasteful and up-market resort run by the Count Roberto Guiccardini. The region has other charming villages, one of the most attractive being the small hill-town of **Civitella**, which has a bar near the walls of the village on which you can sit and sip your drinks while enjoying a fabulous view over the valley.

Not far from Civitella, running along the route of the old Roman Via Cassia, is the great A1 motorway which roars ceaselessly southwards to Rome and northwards to Florence and Bologna. Before reaching the border with Florence it passes by the small town of **Montevarchi** which holds a large market every Thursday. A few kilometres on is the rather larger town of **San Giovanni Valdarno** where the great painter Masaccio was born in 1401. Nowadays it is a rather dull industrial town, though still retaining some fine old buildings in the centre. Perhaps the most interesting of these is the 13th-century Palazzo Pretorio which may have been built by Arnolfo di Cambio. On the front are numerous coats of arms belonging to the families of the town officials in the 15th and 16th centuries. It also has a couple of fine churches: the 14th-century San Giovanni Battista with a lovely portico, and, also 14th-century, the oratory of San Lorenzo which houses a large polyptych of the same period by Giovanni di Biondo. There is also a small Pinacoteca which joins on to the mainly 15th-century Church of Santa Maria delle Grazie, named after a miraculous image of the Virgin housed there. Just a couple of kilometres away is the 15th-century **Convent of Montecarlo** which has a very beautiful *Annunciation* by Fra Angelico. A few kilometres further north in the village of **Gropina** is the lovely Romanesque church of San Pietro with a fascinating ancient carved pulpit.

The Casentino

To the north of here lies the area known as the **CASENTINO**, the fertile valley of the upper Arno which is surrounded by the densely wooded mountains of the Pratomagno to the west and Alpe della Luna to the south east. In the Middle Ages this area was ruled by the immensely powerful Guidi Counts.

Members of one of the most awesome of all Tuscan feudal families who also owned vast areas around Pistoia. Their strongly fortified 13th-century castle (possibly worked on by Arnolfo di Cambio) still dominates the little town of **Poppi** rising on a small but steep hill above the Casentino valley. Poppi, as well as being the seat of the Guidi lords, is also worth visiting for its charming arcaded streets and little 13th-century monastic church of San Fedele, built for the local Vallombrosan order and containing a bronze gilt bust of San Vittoriello.

A few kilometres away is another fine old hill town – **Bibbiena** – which because of its strategic position became the most important town of the region. It still has a few rather elegant town houses which testify to its former power. Easily the grandest of these is the late 15th-century Palazzo Dovizi which was built for Cardinal Bernardo Dovizi in 1497. Cardinal Dovizi, the friend and secretary of Pope Leo X, was a native of Bibbiena and eventually adopted the town's name as his own. Opposite the palace in the church of San Lorenzo are some terracottas by the della Robbia family. San Ippolito, further up the hill, is another church worth seeing, though less for its Baroque re-vamp than its lovely window by Biggeri and some 14th- and 15th-century pictures.

The Casentino has two main claims to fame throughout Italy. The first is its food – delicious smoked ham and salami from the pigs that rootle under its beech trees, and its profusion of the wonderful *funghi porcini*, the large, deliciously rich, wild mushrooms of the Italian hills. The other aspect of its importance lies in its religious houses, particularly Camáldoli and La Verna. Nearby is the fine 17th-century monastery of Vallombrosa, which was founded in the 11th century by the Tuscan saint, Giovanni Gualberto.

Perched on a forbidding rock some 1000m up is the monastery of **La Verna**, the most visited of the Casentino's religious sanctuaries. The reason for its importance as a centre of pilgrimage is that it was here that St Francis received the Stigmata of Christ. Francis travelled to La Verna (sometimes called Alvernia) in 1213 at the invitation of Count Orlando of Chiusi, who owned the mountain. Protected from wild beasts by fifty armed men, the earliest Franciscans climbed up the cliff face to the top where they made their sanctuary. Ten years later, on 17 September 1224, Francis received the wounds of Christ. The day is still commmemorated by pilgrims along with the Saint's name day, 4 October.

Near the entrance to the friary is the little church of Santa Maria degli Angeli or Chiesina, which Orlando built for Francis in 1216 but which has been much enlarged since. It was here that Orlando wished to be buried. The chapel also contains two of the 15 della Robbia terracottas to be found throughout the complex. Adjoining the Chiesina is the aisleless Chiesa Maggiore, which was begun in the mid 14th century but not finished until the 16th. There are several more della Robbias here, including a lovely *Adoration*. Off the long Corridor of the Stigmata, which is covered with 17th-century frescoes of the life of Francis, is the dank and dripping cave where the Saint used to sleep and pray. At the end of the corridor, through the Chapel of the Cross, is the Chapel of the Stigmata built on the spot where he received Christ's

La Verna

wounds, with a large Crucifixion scene by Andrea della Robbia. Pilgrims may also walk down the steep steps to the precipice off which the Devil tried to push Francis and kill him. The story goes that when Francis landed on the rocks they became soft 'like liquid wax' and he remained unhurt.

A few kilometres away to the north-west in the little town of **Camáldoli** is the mother house of the religious order of the Camáldolese, a branch of the Benedictines. This monastery was founded in 1012 by Saint Romuald, a nobleman from Lombardy, whose aim was to revitalise flagging monastic life in Italy. To this end he founded over a hundred monasteries and religious houses. Camáldoli is another remote site, some 90m up amid dense fir forests. It was given to Saint Romuald by the Maldoli family from Arezzo and became known as Campo (field) Maldoli. The monastery church, SS Donato and

157

Ilariano, was completely rebuilt in the 16th century and given a Baroque re-vamping in the 18th century. Inside are various paintings by Vasari, including one of the patron saints of the church. More interesting is the lovely mid 16th-century cloister and the pharmacy, still with its original fittings of 1643.

A few kilometres up the mountain, right on the Tuscan border at a height of about 120m, is the **Eremo**, the hermitage of Camáldoli. Near the church, stand twenty little single dwellings, each with its own enclosed vegetable garden to the front. Many of these cells are very ancient: some are even thought to have been built by Romuald himself (possibly Nos.5, 10 and 15). As well as a number each cell has a name, there are the cells of St Francis and St Martin and the cell of the True Cross. The little church was founded in 1027 but has been repeatedly altered since. On the façade are carvings of Romuald and St Benedict, fathers of the Order. Inside are two rather fine 16th-century tabernacles by Gino da Settignano and a series of 17th-century paintings showing Romuald's life and work. The French glass-worker Guillaume de Marcillat (1477–1529), whose windows can be found in many of the churches in Arezzo, is buried in the small chapel of the Rosary. Try to visit the Eremo early in the morning if you wish to glimpse the tranquillity and peace of the lives of the remote, white-clad brotherhood in bygone days.

Another place of pilgrimage, although for very different reasons, is the small village of **Caprese Michelángelo** – birthplace of the great painter, sculptor and architect. Although Caprese has always insisted on its connection with Michelangelo, it was proved conclusively only in 1875 (to the chagrin of nearby Chiusi della Verna who had also been claiming the honour) when a copy of the birth certificate was found. He was born in 1475, probably in the 14th-century Casa Communale, as his father was town Podestà. The building is open to the public and the friendly old keeper of the keys will show you around the rather empty house and the small museum which contains casts of some of Michelangelo's work.

Caprese is in the heart of the wild mushroom country and no-one should leave the area without trying the delicious local *funghi porcini* if they are in season. If you are a mushroom fanatic you should book a meal at the chalet-style hotel Fonte della Galletta a few kilometres to the west of Caprese amid forests of beech and fir. Here you can have what can only be described as a *porcini* pig-out – a gourmet mushroom feast with mushrooms in each of the courses. There is soup, risotto, pasta, pork – all *ai funghi porcini*, all delicious – but I can guarantee that even the most avid *funghi porcini* enthusiast will not want to see, smell or taste a mushroom for some time afterwards.

Practical Information

Hotels and Restaurants

AREZZO   One of the most central hotels in the town is *Cecco* on the Corso Italia 215 (tel. (0575) 20986)
Bibbiena   *Amorosi Bei*, Via Dovizi 18 (tel. (0575) 593646). A reasonably simple, if slightly poky, hotel with a restaurant, run by an old lady in the old part of town. Further up the Via Dovizi is an unpretentious *casalinga* restaurant where the locals eat.
In **MOGGIANA**, near Camáldoli is another good restaurant, *Il Cedro*, high up in the hills.

CAPRESE MICHELANGELO   A few kms west of the painter's birthplace is the *Fonte della Galletta*, a chalet-style haven for mushroom fanatics with a large restaurant where the delicious *funghi porcini* of the region are served in every way imaginable. There are also rooms (tel. (0575) 793925).

CORTONA   *L'Oasi G Neumann* (or *Le Contesse*) Via Contesse, 52044 Cortona (tel. (0575) 603188). This hotel, elegantly housed in an old convent on the edge of town, is one of the nicest places to stay in the area.
A few km south west of Arezzo near **Monte San Savino** is the *Castello of Gargonza*, a cluster of charming old buildings tastefully converted into upmarket holiday accommodation by the present Count Guiccardini (tel. (0575) 847021). On the edge of the complex is a terrace restaurant.

Museums

AREZZO
Museo Statale d'Arte Medioevele   Via San Lorentino 8: open weekdays 09.00–19.00; Sun and hols 09.00–13.00.
Museo Archeologico Mecenate   Via Margaritone 10: open weekdays 09.00–14.00; Sun and hols 09.00–13.00; closed Mon.
Casa di Giorgio Vasari   Via XX Settembre 55: open weekdays 09.00–19.00; Sun and hols 09.00—13.00.

CORTONA
Museo Diocesano   Piazza Trento Trieste: open daily summer 09.00–13.00 and 15.00–18.30; winter 09.00–13.00 and 15.00–17.00; closed Mon.
Museo dell' Academia Etrusca   Palazzo Pretorio: open summer 10.00–13.00 and 16.00–19.00; winter 09.00–13.00 and 15.00–17.00; closed Mon.

SANSEPOLCRO
Museo Civico   Via Aggiunti 65: open 09.30–13.00 and 14.30–18.00, daily except 1 Jan, 1 May, 15 Aug, Christmas Day.

EREMO DI CAMÁLDOLI   approx 50km north of Arezzo: open weekdays
08.30–11.15 and 15.00–18.00; Sun and hols 08.30–10.45, 12.00–12.30
and 15.00–18.00.

12. SIENA

According to legend Siena was founded by Senus and Aeschius, sons of Remus, who was suckled with Romulus by the she-wolf that is the emblem of both Rome and Siena. Aside from legend, it is known that there was definitely an Etruscan colony on the hills where the town now stands, and later a Roman settlement bearing the name Sena Julia. Whether this name is related to Senus, son of Romulus, no-one really knows. The town, which was never large, shrank away throughout Dark Ages, but started to flourish again under the domination of the Lombards in the later Middle Ages. Like Florence, Siena's wealth lay mainly in the cloth trade and banking. Also like Florence, the city evolved a wealthy and powerful merchant class dominated by a few rich and predictably quarrelsome families. There were the Piccolomini (who claimed to be descended from the great Etruscan Lucomo Lars Porsenna), the Buonsignori, the Chigi and the Cacciaconti. Also prominent were the Salimbeni, running a constant feud with the even grander family of Tolomei who claimed to be direct descendants of the Ptolemies of ancient Egypt. The bickering between the two families lasted literally hundreds of years, and was stopped only at the order of Grand Duke Cosimo I when the town finally lost its independence in 1559.

But by far the most bitter rivalry was between Siena and the Guelph city of Florence. Siena, staunchly Ghibelline, had managed to capture and dominate most of the towns of southern Tuscany, but was powerless to move northwards. Florence had subdued, or won the allegiance of, many of the northern cities and obviously wanted to control the whole state. At base, however much of the rivalry between the towns was economic; Siena had the advantage of being situated on the old Via Francigena (now the Via Cassia), the only direct route to Rome. In their repeated battles Florence, being substantially the larger town, was usually the victor. But, on a day in 1260 that the Sienese still talk about, the Florentines suffered a colossal and humiliating thrashing at Montaperti. Sienese reports put the Florentine deaths at 10,000, with 12,000 taken prisoner. The Florentine flag was tied to a donkey's tail and ignominiously dragged around town. But the triumph was short-lived; nine years later in Colle val d' Elsa the Sienese Ghibellines were totally crushed, never to rise again.

Throughout the Middle Ages Siena's governments had been notoriously unstable and chaotic. But in 1287 a new oligarchy was established under what came to be known as the *Nove*, the 'Nine Good Men', merchants chosen

Siena

to represent the three areas of the town (the *terzi*): Città, San Martino and Camollia. For once Siena had a stable and sensible government, and the town flourished accordingly, in commerce and, above all, in the arts. This was the time of the great Sienese painter Duccio and his pupil Simone Martini. It was also the time of the Lorenzetti brothers, Pietro and Ambrogio, whose picture of the Good Government in the town hall shows what life in early 14th-century Siena was like. Disastrously, in 1348, the Black Death laid the town almost to waste, killing three quarters of the population. The *Nove* were overthrown by the nobles, and for the next two centuries the town spent much of its time in confusion and chaos. The brightest lights in these years were the two Sienese saints: Catherine (1347–80), who helped to bring the Pope back from Avignon to Rome, and Bernardino (1380–1444) who fought unceasingly to purify the lives and morals of his countrymen. In 1531 a Spanish garrison was set up in the city but was soon expelled by the Sienese. A few years later the joint forces of Charles V and Grand Duke Cosimo I of Florence attacked the town. A long and terrible siege followed, with the Sienese reduced to eating dogs, leaves from the scant trees and even grass. Finally the city capitulated in a state of total collapse. Banks were closed for more than sixty years as a result. Soon after, the battered and exhausted republic became part of the Grand Duchy of Tuscany.

The centre of Siena, like that of many other Tuscan towns, has remained largely untouched since those times. The streets are still narrow, jumbled and steep, with shrines on corners and lined by ancient redbrick houses with washing hanging out. To get to the main square it is easiest, and most enjoyable, to walk. Cars are for those in a hurry who know exactly where they are going: which streets are one-way, and which streets are too narrow or likely to be blocked. It is better by far on foot, with time to study the carvings above old doorways and count the brick bridges in ancient alleys. Perhaps the most impressive of these is the via della Galluza, which Virginia Woolf must have had in mind when she wrote in her diary, 'Here we are in the noise of Siena – the vast tunnelled arched town, swarmed over by chatting shrieking children.' It is essential to have enough leisure to peer into the lovely shady courtyards of old palaces, where you may find ancient wells, coats of arms, and time-worn statues. Most importantly, the Campo itself must be approached on foot, because otherwise you might fail to appreciate fully the way in which the great shell-shaped space opens up before you after the dark, sombre streets.

Built at the point where the three hills of Siena meet, the **Campo** is the true centre of the town. Near the top is a copy of Jacopo della Quercia's lovely fountain, where pigeons drink greedily out of the mouths of marble wolves. Around the edge tourists sit outside cafés, drinking in the ambience with their wine or cold beer. The drinks are expensive but generally pronounced worth it. The food, on the other hand, is usually not. By day the Campo has a lazy feel. Visitors write postcards and have long lunches, while groups meander slowly in and out of the Palazzo Pubblico, guide books in hand. In the evening it livens up briefly for the *passeggiata*, when Italians meet to walk and talk.

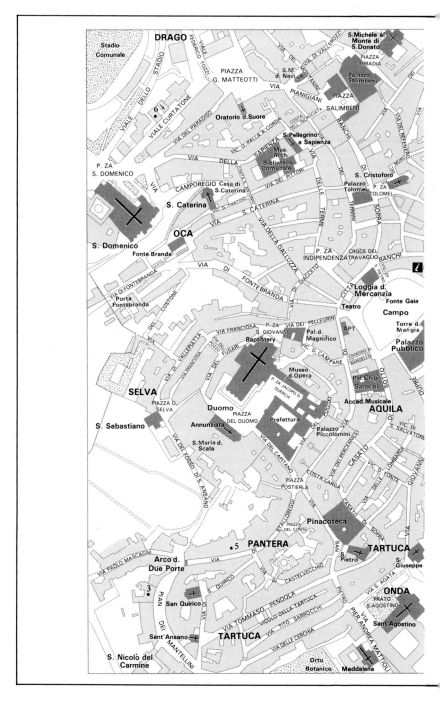

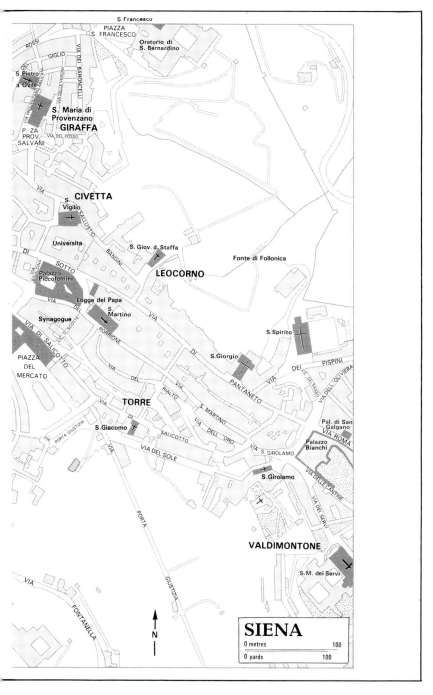

Siena's scallop-shaped Campo

Here, while the young men circle in on potential partners, proud fathers watch their immaculately dressed offspring running backwards and forwards over the gently sloping stones, oblivious of the lengthening shadows. Soon the souvenir stalls start to pack away their guidebooks and trinkets, while their reproduction Palio banners still flutter gaudily in the dying light.

The Palio

Anyone who has been in Siena at the beginning of July or the middle of August will find their pictures and memories hopelessly dominated by **Palio** madness. Photographs will show every building alight with the bright flags of the Sienese *contrade*, and boys made beautiful by medieval dress. The haunting Palio chant (there is really only one song, which is repeatedly sung in a minor key) will echo round the brain as it did through the narrow streets of the town. To the beat of a single drum the tune rises and dies all through the night, so that sleep in the small hotels is slow in coming and dreams are constantly interrupted. It does not matter if you are not in town for the actual race, when hotels are hard to come by; the practices begin days before and the aftermath of celebration and defeat end days after. Before the six trial races start the great Campo is turned into a race-track; the stones are covered with mustard-coloured sand and the most dangerous corners hung with mattresses. The cafés are hidden behind scaffolding with tiers of benches, and the waiters spend even more time than usual dragging tables and chairs out, and in, and back out again.

From the arched windows of the town hall hang the seventeen silk flags of the Sienese *contrade*, each bearing a different symbol. When Siena was an independent republic there were around sixty *contrade*, each based, like a parish, round its church, and dominating the life of the neighbourhood. Now there are only 17, and they function more as social and recreational bodies, although the allegiance given to them is no less strong. Each area has a main church, a hall, sometimes a small museum where trophies and historical items are displayed, and elected leaders or *priori*. Baptisms and weddings are always a part of *contrada* life, and the death of a good *contrada* member is mourned on posters around the town. The areas are divided under the following symbols: the Goose, the Tortoise, the Forest, the Wave, the Ram, the Unicorn, the Caterpillar, the Giraffe, the Owl, the She-wolf, the Porcupine, the Dragon, the Panther, the Tower, and the Snail. Only ten can take part in each race; the rest must wait until next time.

On the eve of the race each *contrada* will hold a banquet in its main square or street. The next morning the horse is solemnly taken into the church to be blessed. If it performs what in any other situation would be thought a disgrace, it is considered extremely good luck. The horses are allocated to the *contrade* by lot, but the jockeys are professionals who have been hired at great expense for the occasion. While any good Sienese would blanch at the word 'corruption', one can't help suspecting that a few lire change hands over the result. It does not really matter. The trial races, the *prove*, are usually chaotic; horses seem unable to line up facing the right way, pistols go off with deafening results at surprising times and only half the horses seem to be trying. But for those who cannot face standing in a furnace of crammed bodies for two hours the *prove* are the best option. Apparently it is possible to buy sitting tickets for the main event but they are few and far between, expensive, and must be bought long in advance. The *prove* are also better for young children, who have a chance of being able to see and spend less time squashed into inactivity in the stifling August heat.

For the brave, however, itself the race is an unforgettable sight. It begins with nearly two hours of processions in medieval dress. First come the six mace-bearers of the city, then the standard-bearer of the *commune*, musicians, more flag-bearers and other dignitaries, guards and pages. Then come the competing *contrade*, one by one, led by drum and flag. Part of the reason why the procession takes so long is because of the *sbandierata*, flag throwing, with which the *alfieri* of each *contrada* honour the Archbishop, the leader and the people of the city. These displays culminate in the breathtaking *alzata* when the flags fly like flaming comets into the sky and are miraculously caught in their descent. Much of this can be seen just as well in the surrounding streets, although the town hall makes a stunning backdrop to the pageantry. At the end of each group is the *barbero*, the racehorse following the jockey on another horse. The non-competing *contrade* come next, and then finally the prize banner, *il Palio*, hoisted above a chariot pulled by the old white oxen of Tuscany.

The race itself (once it has finally begun – there are usually a couple of false starts) lasts about two minutes and is simply a frantic dash three times around the Campo. Most of the spectator seats have been taken in bulk by one *contrada* or another and are occupied mainly by young men and girls, the team scarves round necks and waists, trying to out-sing each other. Inevitably when the excitement becomes too much, or the defeat too bitter, scuffles break out and the police move in. When it is over there is a profound feeling of anticlimax until the evening, when the winners have another feast, and once again sing the night away. A few days later costumes and flags are carefully returned to store and the great scallop-shaped square returns to its normal self; sleepy by day and lively at evening.

The Palazzo Pubblico

Dominating the Campo is the fabulous Palazzo Pubblico, built to accommodate the *Nove*, the Council of Siena, at the end of the 13th and beginning of the 14th centuries. This must be one of the loveliest buildings in Italy. Built in the soft red brick of Siena, and decorated with silver grey Travertine, it has fine, triple-mullioned, Sienese windows and a slender tower soaring optimistically skywards. Here there is nothing of the feeling of extravagant boast that characterises the cathedral – the Palazzo Pubblico is everything it should be: graceful but proud, gently curving in order exactly to fit its position in the square. In the spandrel of each window hangs the black-and-white shield of the *Balzana*, the symbol of the city. The round sun-like emblem on the top storey was designed by San Bernardino during his attempt to purify Italy. The letters stand for Jesus Hominum Salvator – Jesus, Saviour of Mankind. Copies of this monogram became widely used by the saint, who apparently commissioned them from a man whose living as a card- and dice-maker had been ruined by Bernardino's insistence on a higher morality.

The slim **bell-tower** rises 111m above the Campo. It was begun in 1338, but work was interrupted by the Plague and it was not finished for many years. It has always been known as the Mangia, after the first bell-ringer, who was nicknamed Mangiaguadagni (wastrel, literally Eat-up-your-wages). When the mechanical chimer was installed in 1780 it too immediately took on the name Mangia. The bell itself was dedicated to Santa Maria Assunta. There are 503 steps for the energetic to climb, with a fine view at the top over the city and surrounding hills. At the base of the tower, looking like a large portico, is the **Cappella di Piazza**, a chapel built in thanksgiving for the end of the Plague, which claimed the lives of 80,000 of the 120,000 townspeople. Begun in 1352 by Domenico d'Agostino, it was completed in 1376, but re-vamped over a hundred years later by Antonio Federighi who added the frieze of owls and the cornice.

Inside the Palazzo, the Gothic courtyard of the Podestà was built in 1325. Its walls are decorated with the heraldic emblems of various town dignitaries. Upstairs are the great civic rooms where the government once met. Now it is the **Museo Civico**, housing some of the best Sienese paintings of the 14th century. Less important are the 19th-century Sienese pictures in the Sala di Risorgimento which depict scenes from the life of Victor Emanuel II. Most of the paintings in the town hall are Sienese, with the notable exception of the Sala di Balia which was frescoed in 1407 by Spinello Aretino (from Arrezzo) and his son Parri. The frescoes show episodes from the life of the Sienese Pope Alexander III and his victory over the Emperor Frederick Barbarossa, recognisable by his red beard.

Off the Sala del Mappamondo is the chapel holding Sodoma's painting, the *Holy Family with St Leonard.* The **Cappella** itself is frescoed by the Sienese painter Taddeo di Bartolo (c.1407) and depicts stories from the Virgin's life and various saints and prophets. The iron gate is thought to have been designed by Jacopo della Quercia and the wooden choir stall is early 15th-century too. The paintings in the anti-chapel are also the work of Taddeo di Bartolo, with a huge St Christopher emphasising the duty of those in power to look after the poor and weak. The **Sala del Mappamondo** is named after Ambrogio Lorenzetti's huge map of the world which was here but is now lost. On one wall is the vast *Maestà* by Simone Martini, painted in 1315. This was probably his first important commission and established him as a top Sienese painter. Much of the loveliness of this painting lies in its colours – now faded to a series of glowing golds, roses and russets against a midnight dark sky.

On the opposite wall is the now controversial equestrian portrait of Guidoriccio da Fogliano which was traditionally thought to have been painted by Martini in 1328. Guidoriccio, a rather ugly little man, magnificently decked out in gold, patterned with black diamonds and trailing leaves, rides on his grey charger across a barren Sienese landscape. Recent scholars claim that this painting is a fake and say that the camp fortifications are Renaissance and not Gothic. Another factor in this argument is that there is, apparently, another fresco underneath by Sodoma who lived over a hundred years later than Martini.

The door beneath the Guidoriccio is the entrance to the Hall of the Nine, sometimes known as the Hall of Peace, where the Nove sat in government over the city. Here are the great secular frescoes of the mid 14th century by the Sienese master Ambrogio Lorenzetti. They illustrate Good and Bad Governments and their effects on the Sienese town and countryside. The Good King, dressed in the white-and-black of Siena is surrounded by the Virtues who sit in judgement beside him. Peace, lolling at the end of the seat, tapping her knee with an olive branch, looks positively bored with all this harmonious living. On the wall to the right of the King we are shown the effects of his wife and stable reign on the town and countryside of Siena. All is order and calm as the merchants and farmers of Siena go peacefully about their business. Young girls can be seen dancing with a cheerful decorum to the beat of a tambourine. Over the whole scene floats the angel of Security keeping the peace with scroll and gallows.

The frescoes showing the effects of a bad government are worn and badly damaged. But it can still be seen that Tyranny, the leader, is a demonic figure with horns and ghastly fangs. He is advised by the Vices; Avarice bends his right ear, Vainglory his left. The results of his corrupt labours are mayhem and misery. Over the scene hovers the semi-naked figure of Fear, sword in hand. While Siena obviously aspired to the first image, all too often the town bore a closer resemblance to the second. In the 15th century the French historian Philippe de Commines commented, 'There is always strife in this city, which rules itself less steadily than any other town in Italy.' Up the stairs is the large south-facing loggia, where much of the town business was carried out in the hot weather.

Via di Città and the Cathedral

Back outside, before leaving the square, look across at another lovely palace, the gothic **Palazzo Sansedoni**, which was built in the 13th century and later enlarged. Leaving the Campo at the top western corner one joins the Via di Citta, one of the main streets of the town. To the left, just past one of Siena's rare trees, is the grey stone tower of the **Palazzo Chigi-Saracini**, begun in the 12th century. It was from this tower that the drummer boy Ceccolini apparently watched the battle of Monteaperti, reporting back the results to the anxious townsfolk. In the fine courtyard there is an old well and a statue of Pope Julius II by Fulvio Signorini (1610). The strange emblem of the owners – a negro's head accompanied by what looks like a blancmange – can be seen all round the building. In 1932 Conte Guido Saracini turned the palace into a music school. Now music can be heard wafting down the Via di Città and there are free concerts given throughout the summer in the large Baroque hall. The palace also has some good pictures by Sassetta, Nerrocio di Bartolomeo, Sano di Pietro and other Sienese painters. From Florence it has a lovely *Madonna and Angels* by Botticelli, and a marble tondo of the Virgin and Child attributed to Donatello. Just near here is the Renaissance **Palazzo Piccolomini delle Papesse**, built by the Sienese Pope Pius II for his sisters to live in. It was designed by the architect Bernardo Rossellini who built the tiny city of Pienza and, like many other of Siena's most graceful palaces, is now a bank. And from here it is just a short walk to the cathedral square.

Facing the cathedral are the church and hospital of **Santa Maria della Scala**, named after the cathedral steps. The hospital is one of the oldest in Italy and probably dates back to the early 13th century. It was here that the two Sienese saints, Catherine and Bernardino, nursed the sick and dying, during the worst summer weeks when plague and disease were rife. In the church are two works by Vechietta, and a *Madonna Enthroned* by Taddeo di Bartolo. Attached to the north of the cathedral is the predominantly 18th-century Archbishop's palace.

The **CATHEDRAL** of Siena has long excited a mixed reception, even among the Sienese. It stands in its high irregular square with a façade like an overdecorated wedding cake – a dazzling combination of Romanesque and Gothic; stripes and arches, animals and leaves, statues and mosaics. Amid all this festivity Giovanni Pisano's monumental figures strain forward out of their niches looking strangely morose. Most of the originals are now to be found in the Cathedral Museum. The lower part of the façade was built by Pisano in c.1284 but the upper part, above the cornice, was added later. Many think it an awkward match – too blatantly Gothic to marry successfully with the wide rounded doorways below. The glittering mosaics were added in the 19th century and come from Venice.

The actual date of the commencement of the first cathedral here is not known, although there are records of a church on the site as early as the 10th century. The present building was dedicated to God in 1258, just two years before the consecration of London's Westminster Abbey. But by the beginning of the 14th century, the people of Siena were clamouring for something bigger and grander. They particularly wanted to outdo their old rival, Florence, whose new cathedral was far larger than theirs. In 1339 a vast new edifice was designed by Lando di Pietro. Building began with the whole of the present cathedral as just the transept. The new façade was the huge wall still standing at the side of what is now the museum. Ten years later these extravagant plans were brought to a halt by financial problems, caused largely by the plague of 1348 in which huge numbers died. The plan was abandoned, never to be raised again.

Like the exterior, the inside of the building is covered in horizontal black-and-white stripes, interrupting any Gothic feeling of soaring upwards that the church might otherwise have had. The general effect is rich and decorative, and is emphasised particularly by the lovely inlaid marble **floor**. This must be the most magnificent floor in Europe: 56 panels of various sizes by as many as forty different artists, including Matteo di Giovanni, Nerroccio di Bartolomeo, Pinturicchio and Domenico Beccafumi. They were completed over a period of more than two hundred years (c.1370–1547) and illustrate the Virtues and Allegories, Sibyls and stories from the Bible. They are really worth looking at closely, particularly those in the transept by Beccafumi (the sacrifice of Isaac, and Moses striking water from a rock), and the lovely delicate work attributed to Urbano di Cortona (scenes from the life of Judith).

The fine **pulpit** by Nicola Pisano was begun in 1265, five years after he had finished carving the one in Pisa Baptistery. He was assisted by his son Giovanni and his talented pupil Arnolfo di Cambio. The general opinion seems to be that the Siena pulpit is the greater; the figures are more natural and expressive, they have lost the monumental wooden quality that characterises the earlier work. But the panels, representing the life of Christ and the Last Judgement, are almost too crowded and perhaps the slightly simpler ones at Pisa are more effective. It is ultimately a matter of taste.

In the left aisle is Lorenzo di Mariana's ornate marble entrance carved in

The cathedral of Santa Maria Assunta, Siena

1497, to the **Piccolomini library**. The library was commissioned by Cardinal Francesco Piccolomini Todeschini, Archbishop of Siena, to house the books of his illustrious uncle Pope Pius II born Aeneas Silvius Piccolomini in 1405. At 26 Aeneas became secretary to the Bishop of Fermo at the Council of Basle, and was sent on missions to Germany, England and Scotland. He did not take orders until he was 42 and became Pope at the age of 53. He was a prolific writer, and his *Commentaries* show him more as a Humanist and lover of nature than a devout religious leader. His past had not been altogether blameless and, for an aspiring Pope, he had written some pretty racy stories. His library is covered in bright frescoes by the Sienese painter known as Pinturicchio, begun in 1502. They illustrate excerpts from Piccolomini's life, including a visit to James I of Scotland. The name Pinturrichio means dabbler and his pictures are the subject of much criticism. He is damningly labelled by *The Oxford Companion to Art* as a 'very prolific artist, with a dangerous facility', but I quite like these pictures – they are decorative and rather fantastic with some marvellous details. On the Piccolomini Altar by Bregno (1503) are four statues, attributed to the young Michelangelo, of Sts Peter, Pius, Gregory and Paul.

In the **Chapel of St John**, which has some more, rather charming, Pinturicchios, is Donatello's late statue of a gaunt John the Baptist, with sunken cheeks and a skinny body. There are two other Donatellos in the Cathedral, the gentle bronze portrait for the tomb of Bishop Pecci in the Capella di Sant' Ansano (where there is also a fine tomb of Cardinal Petroni by Tino di Camaino), and a tondo of the Madonna and Child outside, above the Porta del Perdono, to the left of the main doors.

Off the right transept is the **Chigi chapel**, designed by Bernini in 1661 with his flamboyant and rather repellent statues of Saint Jerome and Mary Magdalen. The chapel used to house the famous Madonna del Voto, now in the Museum. In 1260, just before the great battle of Montaperti, (fought against the powerful Florentine Guelphs) Buonaguida, syndic of the city, re-dedicated the town to the Virgin of the picture with these words:

> O Virgin, Glorious Queen of heaven, Mother of the sinful! I, a miserable sinner give and dedicate and vow to Thee this city and land of Siena; and I pray Thee, gracious Mother, be pleased to accept it, for all our weaknesses and many sins. Be not mindful of our wrongdoings but protect us, keep and deliver us, we beseech thee, from the clutches of those treacherous dogs the Florentines and from all who would torment and oppress us and bring us to nothing.

The next day a chill mist fell over the soliders, which they believed was the Virgin's protective cloak, and the battle was won. The Madonna has apparently been called upon since, but never with such resounding success.

Tacked onto the back of the Cathedral, although much lower down, is the **Baptistery of St John**. Its façade is 14th-century Gothic although the top section remains unfinished. The interior was probably designed by Tino di Camaiano and his less famous father, Camaiano di Crescentino. The vaulted ceiling is covered with 15th-century frescoes by Vecchietta, which were substantially repainted in the last century. The scenes from the life of Christ in the apse are by the Bolognese, Michele di Matteo, and the lunette of St Anthony, also mid 15th century, is attributed to Benvenuto di Giovanni.

But the real reason to go into the Baptistery is to see the wonderful early Renaissance **font**, made by some of the greatest artists of the early 15th century. The marble tabernacle and statue of St John are by the Sienese sculptor Jacopo della Quercia. He also made one of the six bronze panels showing the life of the Baptist; his too is the *Annunciation to Zacharias*. Two of the other panels: the *Baptism of Christ* and the *Arrest of St John* are by the Florentine master of bronze relief Lorenzo Ghiberti, done while he was working on his 'Gates of Paradise' for the Baptistry there. Another Florentine, Donatello, designed the powerful panel of Herod's Banquet, where the revellers shrink back in violent disgust as the soldier presents the Baptist's head on a plate. Two of the bronze corner statues are also by Donatello, though in very different mood; the pensive *Faith* are fervently praying *Hope*. The remaining two panels are by the lesser artist, Giovanni di Torino; one shows the birth of John, the other John preaching. He also carved three of the corner statues. The remaining one was by Goro di Ser Nerroccio and carved in 1428.

The **Museo del' Opera del Duomo** has been built into what would have been the right aisle of the new Cathedral. The land was once used as a sculptors' storeyard and workshop and it was here that della Quercia carved the Fonte Gaia for the Campo. The museum now houses paintings, sculptures, and artefacts from the Cathedral. On the ground floor the Hall of Statues contains Giovanni Pisano's tremendous sculptural figures originally located on the outside of the Cathedral. The first thing that strikes one about these is the extraordinary jutting angles of their heads as they lean forward to be seen from far below. The next thing is the intensity with which each of the figures communicates with the others. They all seem to be participating in some monumental discussion, either talking or listening. Mary, sister of Moses, cranes forward intently to hear what is being said while Plato stresses his point with raised hand and a determined look. Despite their crudity, and the damage which they have sustained, no-one can deny their life-force. In the middle of the room is Jacopo della Quercia's high-relief of Cardinal Casini being presented to the Virgin by St Anthony Abbot.

Upstairs is the most precious painting in Siena: the Maestà, by the greatest of Sienese painters, Duccio di Buoninsegna. The picture was finished in 1311, having taken three years to paint. The townspeople were so delighted with it that they carried it round Siena in a huge procession led by the clergy. The festivities lasted three days, and anyone who has been in the town near the time of the Palio will be familiar with just how good the Sienese are at processions and protracted celebrations. In 1771 the front and the back of the pictures were separated and, in 1878, they came to the Museum. By then various parts had been lost, some went to other galleries, (there are some panels in the National) and some seem to have disappeared altogether, including the original frame which was probably magnificent.

The Maestà is displayed in a smallish room with no windows, which is actually rather effective. You can see it very clearly and so closely that not a single detail need be missed. The Virgin, surrounded by angels and saints, faces you as you enter, aloof and majestic, eyes slightly downcast. The writing on the base of her throne means 'Holy Mother of God, grant peace to Siena, grant life to Duccio because he has painted You like this.' On the opposite wall are the scenes from the life of Christ which were on the back of the main picture (and which seem to have got out of sequence) and, on the left wall, are panels from the predella. Another lovely picture in this room is Pietro Lorenzetti's Birth of the Virgin, with St Anne in a wine-coloured dress, lying on a tartan blanket. One of her attendants is holding a Sienese flag.

In the **Sala del Tesoro** on the second floor can be found various artefacts from the Cathedral, including a 13th-century Reliquary for the head of San Galgano and a small crucifix by Giovanni Pisano. This floor also has more Sienese pictures by Lorenzetti, Sodoma, and Beccafumi and others. There is also the original painting from the cathedral, known as the Madonna with the large eyes, to whom the Sienese prayed on the eve of the Battle of Montaperti. She was painted at the beginning of the 13th century, and is one of the earliest surviving paintings of the Sienese school.

When you have had enough of the paintings, climb the steps to the Facciatore, where you will get a fantastic view of the city. Nearby is the striped side of the cathedral with its elegant dome and belltower, and below lies the scallop-shell of the Campo.

The Pinacoteca

Leaving the Piazza del Duomo by the via del Capitano one comes to the little Piazza Postierla and the Via San Pietro. In Via San Pietro is the **PINACOTECA**, the main picture gallery of Siena. It is situated in the late Gothic **Palazzo Buoninsegna**, a fine redbrick palace with triple-mullioned windows, which dates back to the early 15th century. The gallery contains a large well-labelled collection of early Sienese paintings, mostly taken from local churches and depicting typical religious subjects – crucifixions and Madonnas set against gold backdrops. Many of these pictures are magnificent, but one cannot help feeling how much better it would have been to leave the majority of them on their original altars. There, each would seem unique and special; here they crowd together, often seeming little more than variations on the same theme. Much of the liveliest and most individual painting is to be found in the *predelle*, the little paintings at the bottom of the main work, where the artist has traditionally been allowed a much freer hand, both in subject and interpretation. Here there are some extraordinary goings-on, with a charm, and often a humour, that would be out of place in the main work. My favourite is the panel by Francesco di Giorgio Martini (1439–1502) of Susanna in the bath. Susanna, wearing nothing but her halo, stands up coyly, apparently surprised by the two old men lurking behind a nearby bush.

The Pinacoteca is arranged in chronological order, starting at the top (where the light is best). The first rooms show the work of Guido of Siena and other painters of the 13th century. **Rooms III–IV** have paintings by the greatest of Sienese masters, Duccio di Buoninsegna, who painted between 1287 and 1319. In some ways Duccio was to Siena what Giotto was to Florence – both exercised a profound and lasting influence over the art of their city. But where Giotto broke away from tradition towards a new realism, Duccio remained rooted in his early Byzantine training, developing it towards a perfect symbolism. One of the best of his paintings is the damaged *Madonna of the Franciscans*, against an unusual blue patterned background. The infant Christ reaches towards three diminutive Brown Brothers who have arranged themselves in a neat fan of devotion at Mary's feet.

Rooms VII–VIII are dedicated to the Lorenzetti brothers. By Ambrogio, there are two of the earliest known pure Italian landscape paintings, of a castle on the bank of a lake, and the fascinating *Città sul Mare*. Pietro's work includes a splendid *predella* showing episodes from the history of the Carmelite order.

Unless you are a true devotee of Sienese art, the following rooms can be rather too much of a good thing. They are full of paintings by the prolific local painters; Sano di Pietro, Taddeo di Bartolo, the talented Sassetta and the workaholic Giovanni di Paolo. Again the *predelle* often outshine the centrepiece. There is Sano di Pietro's panel showing a gentle St Christopher with a child on his shoulders, who looks apprehensively at the lion hiding in the nearby trees. In another panel are Cosimo and Damian, patron saints of the Medici, fitting the leg of a dead negro on to an extremely ill-looking amputee. Taddeo di Bartolo's works include a charming baptism behind bars of a prisoner. Giovanni di Paolo's vision of Paradise consists of one huge hug-in. In his *predella* of the flight into Egypt the glowing sun coats the sides of the mountains, the peasants and the donkey's rump in what appears to be golden custard. It is interesting to remember that, in Florence, Massaccio's Carmine frescoes with their immense realism and subtle use of light and shade were painted nearly twenty years earlier, in the 1420s. For many years Giovanni di Paolo was virtually ignored as a painter until, at the end of the last century, Bernard Berenson pulled him out of obscurity, calling him the 'El Greco' of the 14th century.

The first floor has later paintings, by Pinturicchio, Beccafumi and Sodoma. Sodoma's *Christ at the Pillar* is generally thought to be one of his best paintings, with Jesus painted, characteristically, as a beautiful young man. Also on this floor is a *Portrait of an Old Man* attributed to Dürer. Sceptics have graffitied 'No!' on the label and various other Dutch artists have been suggested, their names scrawled untidily over the official attribution.

Sant' Agostino, Santa Maria degli Servi, central Siena

From the Palazzo Buonsignori it is a short walk down to the church of **Sant' Agostino** – a rather unexciting, mainly 18th-century, building with some fine pictures. There is a smooth Perugino *Crucifixion*, painted in 1506, also some rather mediocre Sodoma paintings. In the Piccolomini Chapel is a wonderful, but somehow too cheerfully painted, *Massacre of the Innocents* by Matteo di Giovanni. Simone Martini's charming frescoes of the life of St Augustine show the saint swooping down like Superman to save unlucky infants who have fallen from bed or building with near disastrous consequences.

Directly east of Sant' Agostino, though rather a long walk, is another church full of Sienese paintings – the 13th-century **Santa Maria degli Servi**. The building has a particularly lovely Romanesque bell-tower with windows that increase in number as the tower rises. Inside, the Renaissance aisle is attributed to the Sienese architect Baldessare Peruzzi. The pictures include works by Taddeo di Bartolo, Lippo Memmi, Giovanni di Paolo and Duccio's nephew Segna di Buonaventura. There is another *Massacre of the Innocents* by Matteo di Giovanni, fairly similar to the one in Sant' Agostino, with the soldier on the right about to have his eyes scratched out by a determined mother. This side of town seems to specialise in this rather gory subject. In the right transept there is another painting of Herod's slaughtered babes, this time by Pietro Lorenzetti. Also by him are two marvellous frescoes of the dance of Salome, and St John in Patmos. The *Madonna and Child* (known as the Madonna del Bordone) in the second altar on the right is by the early Florentine painter Coppo di Marcovaldo and was given to the city in return for his freedom after the battle of Montaperti in 1261.

Returning to the centre of the town down the Via del Porrione, one reaches the small Renaissance **Loggia del Papa**, built by Antonio Fedherigi, for Pius II in 1462. Next to it is the much restored church of San Martino after whom this *terzo* (literally 'third') of the town is named. Nearby on the Banchi di Sotto is the fine Renaissance **Palazzo Piccolomini**, which the Pope also commissioned, probably from his favourite architect Bernardo Rossellini. It is based on the Florentine ideal of the time with a grand cornice and rusticated stone façade. The building is now the home of the state archives and is open to the public in the mornings. If you are in Siena for any length of time it is worth a visit, if only to see the fascinating *Tavolette di Biccherna*. The *Tavolette* were originally the wooden covers of the town ledgers which were decorated by Sienese artists with illustrations of religious and civic subjects. They include the works of many well-known painters and some of them are absolutely exquisite. There are also thousands of documents relating to the town, some of which date back to the 8th century, including the will of Giovanni Boccaccio, the letters concerning Duccio's Maestà, the great siege of Siena and the early records of the Palio.

The **Banchi di Sotto** is one of the three main streets of Siena and, for the most part, is lined with shops, (the most appealing of which is perhaps the old hat shop) and various bars. At the Croce del Travaglio it meets the other two main roads, the Banchi di Sopra which leads away from the centre, and the Via del Città which continues around the Campo towards the Duomo. At the meeting of the roads is the **Loggia della Mercanzia**, built in 1428 with a 17th-century upper floor. The rather pedestrian statues are by Vecchietta and Federighi. The best thing about the Loggia is that the carved marble benches with their reliefs of Roman heroes and Virtues.

The **Banchi di Sopra** runs up the hill past a few smart shops and some of the finest places in the town. It is the home of the two great feuding families of Siena – the Tolomei and the Salimbeni. In their most famous act of treachery the Salimbeni asked 18 members of the Tolomei family to a reconciliation dinner and proceeded to murder them over the main course. Ironically, the two families now lie side by side in the church of San Francesco. The Tolomei palace, in the square of that name, is a beautiful 13th-century grey stone building, now housing the savings bank of Florence. Siena must have more beautiful banks than any other town in the world. Further up the Banchi Di Sopra is the Salimbeni palace, now the home of the Monte dei Paschi di Siena, the oldest banking house in Italy. The buildings in the Salimbeni square span 300 years. Oldest is the lovely Salimbeni Palace built in the 14th century. To its left is the 15th-century Spannochi palace begun in 1470 by Giuliano da Maiano – a mixture of Florentine and Sienese architecture with a heavy Renaissance cornice and rustication, and mullioned windows. Opposite it is the 16th-century Palazzo Tantucci del Riccio built in 1548.

The Banchi di Sopra runs almost exactly between two of the great churches of the city: San Domenico to the west and the Franciscan basilica of San Francesco to the east. **San Domenico** was begun shortly after the Domenicans arrived in Siena in 1225, a great Gothic barn in red brick with a high open-truss ceiling. In around 1300 the crypt was added and was so large that it became known as the lower church. The building was not finished until the 15th century. This was St Catherine's local church and it was here that she took her vows, joining the Mandellate Order of the Domenicans, an order usually reserved for widows. In the Chapel of St Catherine are some famous frescoes by Sodoma of the life of the saint, often considered to be his best works, though personally I think these paintings compare unfavourably with his work at the convent of Monte Oliveto Maggiore. Catherine's fainting fit in particular strikes me as being sentimental and charmless. In the centre a 15th-century tabernacle by Giovanni di Stefano holds Catherine's wizened head; her body is apparently in Rome.

In the left transept is a lovely lunette of the Epiphany above *St Barbara between two Saints* painted by Matteo di Giovanni in 1479. The simple fresco of St Catherine holding a lily is by one of her disciples, Andrea Vanni, and is thought to be the only true portrait of her. One of the best things about this church is the view from its windows, over the old red town crowned by the humbug-striped cathedral. Below the church is the ancient covered fountain, Fonte Branda, first documented in 1081 but rebuilt with three large arches in 1246. Nearby is the house where St Catherine was born Caterina Benincasa in 1347. Later, in the 15th century, an oratory was built here which now holds various remembrances of her life and five frescoed angels by Sodoma.

Across the town is **San Francesco**, the rival preaching church of the Franciscans. A church was begun here in 1226 just after the death of St Francis, but the present building was not finished until 1475. Another great lean barn, this time with a 19th-century façade, the church is worth visiting mainly for its paintings by the Lorenzetti brothers, who worked between 1320–48. The detached frescoes of the martyrdom of the Franciscans and St Louis before Pope Boniface VII are by Ambrogio and the wonderful *Crucifixion* is by Pietro. Back outside, on the south side of the square, is the Oratory of San Bernardino, built in the 15th century on the ground where the saint habitually prayed. On the upper floor are some excellent 15th-century frescoes by Beccafumi, Girolamo del Pacchia and Sodoma, showing the life of the Virgin and St Francis.

San Francesco is a short distance from the Gothic Porta Ovile, one of the towns many gates. Siena's gates are all different – the Porta Romana, for example, has the only fresco by Sassetta, while the Porta Pispini has a squat tower built in 1326 by Minnucio di Rinaldo. But my favourite is the narrow Porta Camollia bearing the slogan, *Cor magis tibi sena pandit*, which roughly translated means 'wider than this, Siena opens her heart to you'. Arriving or leaving, this feels true. The waiters may be tourist-weary but the town itself, and particularly the great welcoming space of the Campo, seems made to receive strangers. Once you have stayed there its image will remain in your mind, like a generous friend who will always be there to go back to.

Practical Information

Hotels and Restaurants

Palazzo Ravizza Pian dei Mantellini 34 (tel. (0577) 280462). This hotel, housed in a 17th-century villa, has a nice garden with fine views. It also has a good, if solemn, restaurant but in the high season your booking must include at least one main meal a day there.

The *Hotel Garden* Via Custoza 2 (tel. (0577) 47056). Also boasting a good view of Siena, this comfortable hotel has the added luxury (reflected in the price) of a swimming pool.

Pensione Tre Donzelle Via delle Donzelle 5. Of the cheap *pensioni* in the heart of the old town I have found this to be the most convenient and reliable – simple but clean and pleasant with friendly service.

Siena has various good restaurants. Just off the Campo in the Via Pollaioli is the *Osteria Antica* which has a good atmosphere and hearty food (though it becomes overcrowded in the summer). Beside the Town Hall in the narrow Via G. Duprè was another good *casalinga trattoria* which has recently been renovated. In the Campo itself are various bars and restaurants where one pays for the stunning setting – it is definitely worth having a drink there but in general the food is mediocre. In fact the self-service at the bottom of the Campo has as good basic food as anywhere though in a rather charmless setting.

Museums

Museo Civico Palazzo Pubblico: open April–Oct 09.00–18.30; winter 09.00–13.30; Sun and hols 0900–13.00.

Museo dell' Opera del Duomo (to the right of the Duomo): open mid-March –Oct 09.00–19.30; winter 09.00–13.00.

Pinacoteca Nazionale Via San Pietro 29: open summer 08.30–19.00; winter 08.30–14.00; Sun and hols 08.30–13.00; closed Mon.

Palazzo Piccolomini Via Banchi di Sotto: open weekdays 09.30–13.00; Sat 09.00–12.30.

Palazzo Chigi-Saracini Via di Città 89: visits by request.

13. THE PROVINCE OF SIENA

For the sightseer, the province of Siena is the richest in the whole of Tuscany. Along with the well-known attractions of San Gimignano, Montepulciano and Pienza, there are countless little towns and villages of immense beauty and charm in the most glorious of countryside. In these small, unspoilt places, you may come across a ruined Sienese fortress, a 13th-century town hall or an ancient Sienese painting of the Madonna in a little Romanesque *pieve*. Siena province also boasts the three loveliest abbeys in Tuscany: San Galgano, Monte Oliveto Maggiore and Sant' Antimo – all fascinating, and all set in stunningly lovely country.

As in the other regions of Tuscany, the country is varied. There are the sweeping hills of Chianti, the pastureland round San Gimignano and, to the south, the dry ochre hills of what used to be known as the Accona desert, the area beginning with the Crete hills, to the south-east of Siena and rolling down beyond Montalcino to the lovely Val d'Orcia: a landscape that Dickens described as growing ever more 'bare and desolate as any Scottish moor'. Dickens saw it in winter when the wind was howling around the stick-like remains of the vines. In spring much of it is green. But it is in the summer that it takes on its most characteristic hue – the golden brown of Simone Martini's masterpiece in the Siena town hall, with pockets of cultivation and tiny farms. Virginia Woolf, travelling nearly 100 years after Dickens, described the Sienese landscape as

> . . . the most beautiful of views . . . like a line of poetry that makes itself, the shaped hill . . . cultivated every inch; old, wild, perfectly said, once and for all.

San Gimignano

Perhaps the best place to begin this chapter is with the popular little hill-town whose history epitomises the fate of most of the small Tuscan townships – San Gimignano delle Belle Torre – rising like an ancient Manhattan from the green hills. The town was probably founded on the site of an Etruscan settlement but its first mention in the annals of history is as a Roman village called Silvia. One possible explanation for the name is that the town was surrounded by woodland (Latin *silva*). In the early Middle Ages the town changed its name in honour of the sainted Bishop of Modena, Geminianus, who freed the townspeople from marauding barbarians. Towards the end of the Middle Ages the town grew rapidly in prosperity. It was on the main pilgrimage route to Rome and, as a result became a main stopping place for the Knights of Malta and the Templars. At that time the Piazza della Cisterna was called the Taverna Square because of its large number of inns and hostelries.

Throughout this period San Gimignano had been administered by the Bishops of Volterra but in 1199 the town elected its own Podestà and from then on tried to govern itself. This, however, proved to be no easy matter: the wealthy families of the town fought bitterly for supremacy. As in most of Tuscany the division was mainly between the Papal Guelphs and the Ghibelline supporters of the German Imperialists and the Holy Roman Empire. The two most powerful families in the town, the Guelph Ardinghelli and the Ghibelline Salvucci, were constantly at loggerheads. In 1246 the Ardinghelli burnt to the ground all the Salvucci towers, an outrage which of course initiated massive and terrifying reprisals. The medieval tower houses had become a symbol of power throughout Tuscany; the taller the better, both in terms of prestige and security. At that time towers went up and came down again with alarming rapidity. San Gimignano's skyline must literally have changed from month to month as the feuding and fighting continued. In 1311 the Podestà decreed that no tower should be taller than 178 feet (60m) (the height of his palace). The Salvucci immediately retaliated and built twin towers, side by side, and so it went on.

While the squabbles were beginning to affect the town's internal prosperity there were also problems with the rest of Tuscany. San Gimignano made the mistake of joining with Guelph Florence against the Sienese in the disastrous battle of Montaperti in 1240 when they were soundly thrashed. They then changed sides, becoming Ghibelline, just in time to be severely beaten by Florence at Colle in 1269. Worse still, in 1308 they became involved in a bloody war with Volterra, when vast tracts of their land were laid to waste. After these defeats and still more internal strife, the last straw for the battered little city was the plague of 1348. In desperation Florence was asked to take over for three years. Immediately the three years were up the Ardinghelli and Salvucci were at it again, and the citizens of San Gimignano went back to Florence to offer their permanent allegiance in return for stability. The government of Florence pondered awhile on accepting such a liability but finally voted in favour of the proposition by a majority of one. San Gimignano was never independent again. But although there was now some stability, its former prosperity was never recovered and over the centuries it became something of a ghost town. This decline accounts for its present unspoilt appearance: nothing new was built to destroy the architectural harmony of the Middle Ages.

The best way to enter San Gimignano is to leave your car outside the city walls and walk through the solid mass of the 13th-century **Porta San Giovanni**,

San Gimignano delle belle torre – Piazza della Cisterna

the noblest of the town gates. Most of the great stone and brick wall also dates back to this time. In the Via San Giovanni one starts to get the feel of the place. It was on this road that pilgrims and travellers used to enter the town, trudging up the hill to find places to sleep for the night. Like the rest of San Gimignano the road is still lined with 13th-century houses, though many of them have fallen prey to the booming tourist industry and have become gift shops, *enoteche* or ice cream parlours. On the right-hand side is the small 14th-century Pisan façade of the old convent of San Francesco, which was suppressed and mainly destroyed in 1782. At the top of the road is the big arch which formed part of the Becci family palace, leading into the Piazza della Cisterna, one of the town's main squares.

San Gimignano has two main squares leading off each other. The first, the charming, irregularly shaped **Piazza della Cisterna**, named after the fine 13th-century well in the middle, has been paved in herring-bone brick. Most of the towers and palaces that surround it date from the 14th century when the square was enlarged. Perhaps the loveliest palace is the **Palazzo Tortoli** at No.7, built by the Cetti family from Siena in their home style. San Gimignano had a policy of allowing strangers who had behaved well in the town for a certain length of time to build houses, which accounts for the variation in building styles around the town. Next to the Becci arch, the Ardinghelli palace has only the truncated remains of its original high towers which were decapitated when the family were exiled.

From the Piazza della Cisterna we enter the erroneously named **Piazza Duomo** (San Gimignano never had a bishop or cathedral). Here civic and ecclesiastic power resided side by side, surrounded by more towers and palaces of the most powerful families. The twin travertine towers belonged to the warring Ghibellines, the Salvucci. The old town hall, the **Palazzo Vecchio del Podestà**, (which has an open portico containing the remains of a fresco by Sodoma) was superseded by the grander building on the left of the church.

Presiding over the square, at the top of a wide flight of steps where flocks of tourists sit to change the film in their cameras, is the collegiate church of **Santa Maria Assunta**. The church was built in the 12th century, but in the mid 15th century it was given a new look by the brothers Giuliano and Benedetto da Maiano, who enlarged the building into the shape of a Greek cross, adding some fine chapels. In the plain stone façade are two separate doors for men and women.

The Romanesque interior is particularly notable for its splendid collection of 14th-century religious frescoes. On the entrance wall are various saints by Benozzo Gozzoli. On either side of St Sebastian is a painted wooden Annunciation by the 'Sweet-style' sculptor Jacopo della Quercia.

On the wall of the left aisle Bartolo di Fredi painted a series of pictures depicting scenes from the Old Testament. The sad tale of Adam and Eve in the lunettes at the top is particularly charming. Opposite in the right aisle are marvellous paintings of New Testament scenes by Barna di Siena. According to Vasari, Barna tumbled from the scaffolding and was killed before finishing this work, and it had to be completed by his nephew Giovanni d'Asciano. In the high walls of the central nave are Taddeo di Bartolo's frescoes: *The Last Judgement* (in the middle), *Paradiso* and *Inferno*. *Paradise* has been badly damaged but one can make out angel musicians playing sedately over the good humble citizens. The *Inferno* was obviously far more fun to paint – a grisly collection of devils and miscreants undergoing all sorts of extraordinary tortures and atrocities.

At the end of the right aisle is the elegant chapel of Santa Fina, a Renaissance jewel created by Guiliano de Maiano in 1468. The delicately worked altar was carved by his brother Benedetto in Carrara marble and then gilded. The frieze near the top shows scenes from the life of Santa Fina, the favourite local saint of San Gimignano. Santa Fina was born in 1238 and lived a normal happy life until, at the age of ten, she was struck down by a fatal disease. In her humility, she decided to spend the rest of her life lying on a board in penance for crimes she had never committed. She also worked various healing miracles on other sufferers. Five years later she was visited in a vision by St Gregory and nine days after that she joined him in Heaven. On the board where she had lain violets miraculously sprang up filling the little room with a sweet perfume. (It is possible to visit the little saint's simple house in Via degli Innocenti.) Ghirlandaio's frescoes on the walls of the chapel portray various scenes from her short life. In the picture of Santa Fina waiting for death, the three men on the extreme left in red hats are the artist and his two assistants, his brother Davide and brother-in-law Sebastiano Mainardi.

On the external wall of Santa Maria Assunta in the Piazza Pecori is the archway to the **Baptistery of San Giovanni**. Behind an iron gate is the font, above which is a graceful *Annunciation* generally thought to be by Ghirlandaio, though this attribution has been repeatedly queried, some scholars mentioning Sebastiano Mainardi instead. Compare this painting with the Chapel of Santa Fina and see what you think. Whoever the artist, this is a lovely picture, showing a young, studious Mary in prayer behind a cabinet filled with books and an hourglass.

The **Piazza Pecori** was initially the cloister of the church where the chaplains had their dormitory. Behind the well opposite the loggia is the Palazzo della Propositura, an attractive mixture of brick and stone, with mullioned windows. The present cloisters, the Cloisters of Mercy, open up to the side of the sacristy. In the Piazza dei Pecori is the entrance to the small **Museum of Sacred Art**, which has ecclesiastical treasures and one or two works of art from the Collegiata. There is also a small **Etruscan Museum**, housing various finds from the surrounding area.

Back into the Piazza del Duomo, the **Town Hall** (known both as the Palazzo del Pópolo and the Palazzo Nuova del Podestà) is on the left of Santa Maria and contains an excellent collection of Tuscan paintings. It was begun in 1270, probably by Arnolfo di Cambio, architect of the Duomo in Florence, and finished nearly thirty years later. The tower, known as the Torre Grosso, by law the tallest tower in the town, was completed in 1311. The palace has a fine courtyard, similar in design to most grand houses of the day, with a well, dated 1360, and steps up to an open loggia. In the Judge's loggia where justice was publicly administered, are various frescoes on the theme of justice. The sepia-coloured *St Ivo administering to the Poor before the Rich* was painted by Sodoma in 1507. Close by is *Falsehood being trampled underfoot by a Judge*. The *Madonna and Saints* is by Taddeo di Bartolo.

On the first floor of the palace is the main hall, called La Sala di Dante in honour of the day when the poet spoke here, in 1299, giving an impassioned plea for solidarity among the Guelph cities. The exquisite *Maestà* was painted by Lippo Memmi about twenty years later. The donor of the painting, the Podestà Nello Tolomei, is unusually depicted the same size as the saints as he kneels before Mary in his striped gown. For many years the painting was thought to be an inferior copy of the *Maestà* by Simone Martini in the town hall of Siena. But after cleaning it was shown to be at least as well painted as its predecessor and, personally, I find it lovelier. The 13th-century Sienese frescoes of hunting and sport were possibly meant to illustrate the work of another poet, the native Giacomo da Michele, known as Folgòre di San Gimignano because his words were like lightning.

On the second floor the gallery has a good collection of Tuscan paintings. There is a powerful Byzantine crucifix by the 13th-century painter Coppo di Marcovaldo, who was taken prisoner by the Sienese at the battle of Montaperti in 1260. Later works include a Filippino Lippi *Annunciation* in two separate *tondi*, and pictures by Neri di Bicci, Bartolo di Fredi, Benozzo Gozzoli, and Pinturicchio. Also on the second floor is the Podestà's room in the Torre Grosso. Here there is an absolutely charming series of profane frescoes showing a love story, probably painted by Memmo di Filippucio in the 14th century. Some of the scenes are unfortunately in very bad condition and it is barely possible to make out the young couple reading over each other's shoulders or piggy-back riding. But others, like the couple taking their bath together and climbing into bed, are marvellously intact. Leaving the Podestà's room, you may climb the tower to find a fine view of the town.

The Via San Matteo curves northwards, through more ancient dwellings, to the far end of town and the church of **Sant' Agostino**. On the right you pass the **Palazzo Tinacci** with its mixture of Romanesque, Gothic and Renaissance architecture, shown principally in the three different orders of windows. Further along one reaches the little church of **San Pietro** which contains paintings by Barna di Siena.

Just within the town walls is the plain, late 13th-century basilica built by the Augustinian Canons, containing some extremely good pictures. On the left of the entrance is a marvellous Madonna surrounded by saints, which was painted by Pierfrancesco di Fiorentino in 1494. The modest donor of the picture is shown kneeling in the middle, tinier than the Holy Infant. Nearby is the *Cappella di San Bartolo*, painstakingly carved by Benedetto da Maiano over two years in the mid 1490s. The frieze at the base shows scenes from the life of San Bartolo, who worked and died among the lepers of San Gimignano in the sanctuary of Cellole. The panel on the left shows the saint's toe dropping off as a result of the disease. The chapel was frescoed by Sebastiano Mainardi, Ghirlandaio's brother-in-law.

In the choir is a marvellous series of frescoes by the 15th-century painter Benozzo Gozzoli, depicting the life of Saint Augustine. Here we see the painter at his best, using all the colour and rich attention to detail of his more famous pictures in the Medici-Riccardi Palace in Florence. On the high altar is a sinewy *Coronation of the Virgin* by Piero di Pollaiuolo, painted in 1483. Other pictures in the church include a *Pietà* by Bartolo di Fredi, a *St Catherine* attributed to Salimbeni, and a *St Nicholas* by Mainardi. Outside are some attractive 15th-century cloisters with a brick well in the middle.

A short walk to the west from San Agostino is the little church of **San Jacopo**, built in the 12th–13th centuries by the Templars. Inside are frescoes of the life of Christ by the early 14th-century painter Memmo di Filippuccio. Following the Via Bigazzino southwards you reach the 13th-century *fonti* under an arcade, where for many years the sheeps' wool which provided a major part of the town's income was washed.

Between San Gimignano and Siena

San Gimignano is surrounded by farms and small vineyards where the crisp white Vernaccia di San Gimignano wine is produced. The country is fertile and green, growing more spectacular towards Volterra. In many of the neighbouring villages are charming small Romanesque churches, usually single-aisled with modest bell-towers. One of the nicest little churches can be found near the site of the old leper colony at **Cellole** some 5km south-west of the town. This little Romanesque building, consecrated in 1237, has a beautiful carved apse and a fine old font. Other Romanesque *pieve* can be found at the villages of Racciano, Casale and Montauto. Near Montauto is the large church of **Santa Maria di Monteoliveto**, near the remains of a convent, with a painting by Mainardi over the Altar.

Some 13km from San Gimignano, south of the grim spreading industrial town of Poggibonsi, is the attractive old town of **COLLE DI VAL D'ELSA**. Colle is divided into two parts: Colle Alta straddled along a high ridge, and Colle Basso, the new town down below. It is easiest to park in the large ugly car park at the bottom of the hill and walk up the steps towards the bridge where Colle Alta begins. Over the ravine is the Mannerist **Palazzo Campana** designed by Giuliano di Baccio d'Agnolo. The great gate, the fortified Porta Nuova, is attributed to Guiliano di Sangallo. On the way up through the medieval town the houses and the small churches are a lovely mixture of stone and brick; some of the grander dwellings have their old painted decorations.

In the small Piazza del Duomo is the early 17th-century **Cathedral** containing a crucifix of Giambologna and a bronze lectern by P. Tacca. The elegant pulpit may be by Giuliano da Maiano. In the adjoining building, the 14th-century **Palazzo Pretorio**, is the small Museo Archeologico. The **Palazzo dei Priori** now houses the Museo Civico, which has paintings by Pierfrancesco Fiorentino, Manetti and others. In the **Palazzo Vescovile** is a small collection of sacred art. Colle was the birthplace of the remarkable Florentine architect Arnolfo di Cambio, who built both the Duomo and the town hall in Florence. The tower-house where he was born is at the end of the Via Castello. Before going down to the new town wander around for a while – the walk around the backs of the houses is charming, although the view has been somewhat spoilt by the development in the valley. There are one or two places to eat here, but don't leave it too late – they tend to close early.

Colle Basso is a busy town, specialising in the manufacture of glass and crystal. Its centre is a bustling market square called the Piazza Arnolfo di Cambio. In a leafy piazza on the Via dei Fossi is the 13th-century church of **Sant' Agostino**, with a lovely Renaissance interior designed by Antonio Sangallo the Elder. It also has some fine pictures, notably a Madonna attributed to Taddeo di Bartolo, a 14th-century Florentine work called the *Madonna di Piano* and a rather charmless *Deposition* by Ridolfo Ghirlandaio.

A few kilometres away, travelling south on the Siena road, one comes across the perfect, astonishingly untouched settlement of **Monteriggioni**. Monteriggioni is a complete walled castello which was probably first built by the Sienese as a northern look-out, a warning post in case of attack from the Florentines. It is recorded that the Sienese fortified it in 1219, but the present walls date from 1260 after Montaperti. It would have been these new walls that Dante saw when he described the little settlement as 'crowned with towers' resembling the ninth circle of Hell, an abyss similarly 'turreted with giants . . . uprearing horrible'. In fact, Monteriggioni is now considered an extremely picturesque, if sleepy, place, with a rather smart restaurant and wine bearing the label of the town. A couple of miles west is the **Abbadia**

Isola, founded in 1001. In the church, begun in the 11th century, is a *Madonna and Child* by Taddeo di Bartolo and a polyptych by Sano di Pietro, over the altar.

South of Siena

In an out-of-the-way spot, a few kilometres off the Siena–Grosseto road (turn left about 20km south of Siena), stands the remote **Abbey of San Galgano.** Born in 1148, Galgano Giudotti gave up life as a fashionable and sociable knight to live as a hermit. In his most famous gesture he ran his sword into a rock as a sign that he would never fight again, transforming his sword into a cross. He died at the age of 33. At the top of the hill near the great ruined church is a small Romanesque temple where the saint was buried. The rotunda was begun in 1182 and consecrated four years later by the Bishop of Volterra. Attached to the north wall is a chapel frescoed by Ambrogio Lorenzetti. Much of his work has completely deteriorated but recent restoration has exposed many of the synopie (preliminary sketches).

At the bottom of the hill is the ruined abbey church begun in 1218 on the typical Cistercian model of a Latin Cross – possibly designed by a certain Curzio from Chiusi. The huge, haunting, now roofless, building is 70m long with three aisles and a square apse. Apparently the abbey flourished until the 14th century, when it fell prey to marauding groups. It was raided twice by the company of the British *condottiere* Sir John Hawkwood (who acheived the supreme honour of being buried in Florence cathedral) and soon after fell into ruin. Standing in the huge empty shell is an awesome experience; watching the long shadows fall through the great Gothic windows with only the sky above. If you have time, after leaving the abbey, take the winding but spectacular road (441) south west across across country into the province of Grosseto, to the beautiful little town of Massa Maríttima.

The road (No.2) south east from Siena to Aquapendente near Lake Bolsena was part of the usual route for travellers heading for the capital, the first staging post after Siena was traditionally the scruffy little town of **Buonconvento,** which became notorious among British travellers for its dirt and dishonest inhabitants. In the more distant past, it was here that Dante's 'Lamb of God', his great hope for the Ghibellines, Emperor Henry VII of Luxembourg, was poisoned by a false friar with a sacramental wafer in 1313. The little town retains a certain charm, with some interesting Sienese pictures in the 15th-century church of SS Pietro and Paolo and a small but rewarding picture gallery. It is immediately before Buonconvento that you turn left off the main road onto the 451 for Monte Oliveto.

One of the loveliest excursions into the southern Sienese is a visit to the great red brick abbey of **Monte Oliveto Maggiore** near Asciano. The abbey, which belongs to the Olivetan Order (a branch of the Benedictines), was begun in 1387, some 35 years after the death of its founder, the Blessed Bernardo Tolomei. Bernardo was born in 1272 and lived the first part of his life in luxury in Siena, before retiring to the wilderness with two friends to pray and start a religious foundation. When the plague of 1348 struck he sent his brothers out in pairs to help the afflicted. Many of them died and finally he too caught the disease and perished. After his death the sadly depleted community began to build a monastery on the site Bernardo had chosen as his retreat.

The Abbey's entrance is through a sturdy gate decorated with a bright glazed terracotta Madonna of the della Robbia school. Through an avenue of cypresses, past the 16th-century ornamental fishpond, one enters the abbey itself. Its principal treasure is to be found on the walls of the Chiostri Grandi, the main cloisters. Here are 35 frescoes depicting scenes from the life of the Blessed Bernardo painted by two masters of the Renaissance, Luca Signorelli and Antonio Bazzi, commonly known as Sodoma. The story begins at the second corner to the left of the entrance and follows the version told by Saint Gregory. Of the paintings, the middle nine are by Signorelli, and those at the beginning and end by Sodoma. It is not known why Signorelli, whose scenes were painted 25 years earlier than the others, began by depicting the middle episodes of Bernardo's life or why he left without finishing.

More is known about Sodoma, whom Vasari describes with a mixture of admiration and disdain, as an eccentric whose second nickname *il Mattaccio* (the Madman) is hardly more flattering than the first. Apparently his house was a menagerie filled with

> badgers, squirrels, apes, cat-a-mountains, dwarf-asses, horses and barbs to run races, magpies, dwarf chickens, tortoises, Indian doves, and other animals of a similar kind – whatever he could get into his hands . . .

Sodoma's love of animals comes across humorously in these pictures where dog, storks and monkeys run freely through the narrative. The works have a lively charm quite different to the more sedate and, to many eyes, lovelier, pictures by Signorelli. Predictably, Sodoma was not popular with the Abbot, who felt, among other things, that he was 'using more readiness of hand than care or thought'. Sodoma's reply to these complaints was that his 'pencil danced only in harmony with the sound of coins', and insisted on being paid more, whereupon his work dramatically improved. Even so he still had to make some changes at the end – like clothing his dancing girls, whom he had deliberately painted naked to embarrass the monks. If you look at the third picture in the sequence, Sodoma himself looks slyly back at you, with his beloved badgers at his feet.

In the Abbey's Baroque church are some fine inlaid intarsia choir stalls made by Fra Giovanni from Verona, who made the stalls in Siena Cathedral. There is also a library of ancient books, and an old pharmacy. In the chapter-house is a 14th-century Sienese Madonna, and there are more frescoes in the refectory.

Near the abbey (8km to the north) is the small town of **Asciano**, still partly walled, and situated in the midst of the characteristically rolling chalky Sienese hills known as Le Crete. In the main square is the Romanesque collegiate church of Sant' Agata and, nearby, a museum of Sacred Art with a good collection of Sienese pictures. Look out particularly for the young Matteo di Giovanni's polyptych, Ambrogio Lorenzetti's *St Michael and the Dragon*, and a *Virgin* by Barna di Siena. On the Corso Matteotti, which is lined with fine old houses, is an Etruscan Museum containing finds from the local necropolis of Poggiopinci, about 7km east of Asciano.

The lovely old town of **Montalcino** lies in spectacular countryside, 25 miles south of Siena (9km to the east of the No.2 road through Buonconvento). In the summer the sweeping hills bleach to a pale ochre, dotted with farms built of the same coloured stone. Nearer the towns the hills are lower, with smaller fields and vineyards advertising the local pride and joy – the rich red Brunello di Montalcino, one of the best and most expensive of all Italian wines. The town itself perches high on a hill between the river valleys of the Ombrone and Asso and has wide views of the surrounding countryside.

Montalcino existed as a settlement in Etruscan and Roman times, later becoming a free *commune*, and as such was a perpetual bone of contention between Siena and Florence. After the battle of Montaperti in 1260, it belonged to Siena who built the massive fortress at the top of the town which is now mainly used for selling wine. But historically, the little town's main claim to fame was as the last bastion of the Sienese republic when Siena was invaded by Charles V in 1555 and her people fled south. The Sienese noblemen and the Montalcini held out for two years before surrendering to the Spanish forces. Two years later in 1559 Montalcino became part of the Grand Duchy of Tuscany under Cosimo I.

Today it is a charming place, justly renowned for the courtesy of its inhabitants and with a reputation for the prettiest girls in the country. It has three delightful squares, the most important being the Piazza del Popolo where the Palazzo Communale has a tall tower and an open portico. The Romanesque church of Sant' Agostino contains some 15th-century Sienese frescoes. Next door is the Museo di Arte Sacra, housed in an old convent. Less striking but equally pleasant is the leafy Piazza Cavour, with a small hotel and unpretentious bar where the locals sit out. The former hospital of Santa Maria is frescoed by Tamgni. Nearby in the Museo Civico are various Sienese paintings, mostly 13th–15th century and some interesting wooden figures. In the Piazza Garibaldi you will find the Sienese church of San Egidio, built in 1325.

Ten kilometres south-east of Montalcino, in a beautiful setting near the village of Castelnuovo dell' Abate, is the marvellous Benedictine abbey of **Sant' Antimo**. The abbey first appears in the annals in 812 and is thought to have been founded by Charlemagne. The church, which is all that remains, dates from the 12th century although the south chapel is thought to be considerably older, perhaps Carolingan. The interior is simple but lovely, with galleried aisles and columns with richly carved capitals. Small pillars follow the line of the rounded apse. The combination of alabaster with travertine gives a luminosity to the whole effect. There is also a giant, rather crude, wooden crucifix with a strange profile and some badly faded frescoes in the sacristy.

Back on the Aquapendente No.2 road, the pleasant town of **San Quirico d'Orcia** has known better days. In the 13th century it was important enough to be the seat of an Imperial Vicar under the Germanic Emperors. In 1256 it fell to Siena, at that stage in the ascendant, and henceforth followed the pattern of most of its neighbours. Its collegiate church, San Quirico e Giulitta, was badly bombed in the Second World War but is still very much worth a visit. Among other things that survived the blast, is a fine series of doors. Those on the west side of the church date back to the 11th century. The south doors – carved by a follower of the great Giovanni Pisano – are still lovelier, with a porch supported by two strong-men, standing on the backs of lions. Inside is a good 15th-century triptych by the Sienese painter Sano di Pietro and some exquisite choir stalls by Antonio Barili, dating from around 1500.

Taking the Montepulciano road (No.146) east out of San Quirico through ravishing countryside, one comes to the perfect miniature Renaissance city of **PIENZA**, the birthplace of the extraordinary Pope, Pius II. Pius was born Anea Silvio Piccolomini in 1405, the son of the impoverished lord of Corsignano. After a life of travel and adventure, he joined the church at the age of forty and within a few years became Pope. One of his first actions was splendidly to rebuild his home village into a suitable birthplace for a Pope, renaming it Pienza in honour of his newly acquired Papal name. For the task he chose the Florentine architect Bernardo Gamberelli, known as Rossellino, who had trained with the great theorist and architect Leon Battista Alberti in Florence. Pius – who was a great, if selective, diarist – tells the rest of the story in his own words:

> The Pope had received many insinuations against the architect: that he had cheated; that he had blundered in the construction; that he had spent more than 50,000 ducats when the estimate had been 18,000. The law of Ephesians, according to Vitruvius, would have obliged him to make up the difference. He was a Florentine named Bernardo, hateful to the Sienese from his mere nationality. In his absence every one abused him. Pius, when he had inspected the work and examined everything, sent for the man. When he arrived, after a few days in some apprehension since he knew that many charges had been brought against him, Pius said, 'You did well, Bernardo, in lying to us about the expense involved in the work. If you had told the truth you could never have induced us to spend so much money and neither this splendid palace nor this church, the finest in all Italy, would now be standing. Your deceit has built these glorious structures which are praised by all except those who are consumed with envy. We thank you and think you deserve especial honour among all the architects of our time.' And he ordered full pay to be given him and in addition a present of 100 ducats and a scarlet robe. He bestowed on his son the grace he asked and charged him with new commissions. Bernardo, when he heard the Pope's words, burst into tears of joy.

Rossellino's **Cathedral**, dedicated to the Virgin, is an elegant classical building built between 1459–62. On the pediment is Pius's emblem, combining the family crest with the keys of Saint Peter. The interior is rather unusual for a Tuscan church, being based on the German *hallkirchen* that the Pope particularly admired, with nave and aisles of the same height. Owing to its position on the extreme edge of the hill the apse subsided dangerously and has been extensively underbuilt. At the completion of the building some of the Pope's favourite artists, including Giovanni di Paolo, Matteo di Giovanni, Sano di Pietro and Vecchietta, were called in to paint altarpieces for the chapels leading off the transept. There are also some fine Gothic canon's stalls and a font by Rossellino.

Tucked away to the left of the Cathedral in the **Canon's House** is the Cathedral Museum. The museum contains, among other ecclesiastical items, two fabulously worked 14th-century copes, the most majestic of which was presented to Pius II by Thomas Palaeologus of the Morea. The cope, which was made in England, is embroidered with saints and scenes from the life of the Virgin.

Beside the Canon's house is the **Palazzo Vescovile**, originally a Gothic building which the Pope gave to Roderigo Borgia, later Pope Alexander VI, who substantially rebuilt it.

Opposite is the magnificent **Palazzo Piccolomini**, designed by Rossellino, and showing the influence of Alberti in its similarities to the Rucellai palace in Florence that Alberti and Rossellino worked on together. The palace has an arcaded courtyard, three floors of loggias, and hanging gardens at the back. But Rossellino, presumably in a delirium of artistic creativity, forgot to include a kitchen in his design, so this had to be added later, presumably at still more expense. It is possible to visit the state rooms which house a small collection of portraits, weapons and Majolica pottery. In front of the palace in the piazza is a lovely well, also designed by Rossellino. Across the Corso Rossellino is the **Palazzo Ammannati**, built for Giacomo Ammannati of Pavia, a friend of Pius. Next to it is the town hall built in 1463 with an airy loggia. The little 12th-century **Pieve di Santi Vito e Modesto**, where Pius was christened, lies 1km outside the Porta al Ciglio. Apart from its architectural splendour Pienza's other claim to fame lies in its *pecorino*, delicious local sheeps' cheese flavoured with herbs. On the first Sunday of September a cheese fair is held here known as the *Fiera di Cacio*. For fans of the painter Sodoma, there is another treat a few miles to the north in the monastery of **Sant' Anna in Caprena**, where the refectory was frescoed by the artist in the early 16th century.

The fascinating hill town of Montepulciano lies directly east of Pienza along another spectacular stretch of the No.146 road. If you have time, take a short detour south of the road to the walled village of **Monticchiello** perched on a hill and still dominated by its romantic ruined castello. In the *pieve di SS Leonardo e Christóforo* is a *Madonna and Child* by the great early Sienese painter Pietro Lorenzetti, who probably died in the disastrous plague of 1348.

MONTEPULCIANO is another very ancient town, possibly founded by the most famous Etruscan Lucomo, Lars Porsena of Chamars (Chiusi). Later it became a strong fortress dominating the pass between the Val di Chiana and the Val d'Asso which was an important medieval trade route. As such it was obviously valuable to the local superpowers, and played the usual role of ping-pong ball between Florence, Siena and Umbria. The ruined fortress was built by the Sienese after the battle of Montaperti. But, like Pienza, much of Montepulciano's beauty comes not from the Middle Ages but from the Renaissance, albeit some sixty or so years after Pienza's construction. Strangely, these elegant palaces and churches sit comfortably side by side with the old town which is, as Henry James described it, 'perched and brown and queer and crooked, and noble withal.' And, on a summer's day, incredibly hot and dusty.

Before entering the southern gates of the town, put your head round the door of the 14th-century church of **Sant' Agnese** (named after the town's patron saint), where there is a fine Sienese *Madonna* and some 17th-century frescoes of saints in the cloisters. Passing through the solid mass of the Porta al Prato one begins the climb, past numerous Renaissance palaces, towards the Piazza Grande. At No.99 Via Gracciano is the **Palazzo Avignonesi** designed by Giacomo Barozzi, called La Vignola, with a good Renaissance façade. Almost opposite, at No.32, is the **Tarugi palace**, also designed by La Vignola, and at No.28 is the **Palazzo Cocconi** by Antonio da Sangallo the elder (1445–1534). The Renaissance church of **Sant' Agostino** has a good façade by Michelozzo, who also carved the lovely relief above the door. Inside is a painting of the Madonna and Child surrounded by Sts John the Baptist and Augustine, by Giovanni di Paolo and a 15th-century wooden crucifix.

At the turning to the right where Via Gracciano turns into Voltaia, you have a choice. The Via Voltaia passes Sangallo's **Palazzo Cervini**, built in the 1520s for Cardinal Marcello Cervini who later became one of Montepulciano's two Popes. It eventually becomes Via di Poliziano, named after the Renaissance poet and humanist whom Lorenzo il Magnifico employed to teach his children. The other option is to turn right and then into the Via di Poggiolo for the Piazza Grande. In the Via Ricci is the **Museo Civico**, situated in the 14th-century Palazzo Neri Orselli. Among other items, the museum contains two terracotta altarpieces by Andrea della Robbia and Tuscan paintings from the Middle Ages to the Renaissance.

Arriving at the superb irregularly-shaped **Piazza Grande**, one feels that the steep walk was definitely worthwhile. The rough-hewn **Cathedral** with its unfinished façade was built by the little-known architect Ippolito Scatza and finished in 1630. The campanile is a relic of the earlier parish church, demolished to make room for the cathedral when the bishop moved his seat from Chiusi to Montepulciano.

Inside on the high altar is the masterpiece of the Sienese painter Taddeo di Bartolo (c.1362–1425) – a marvellously decorative triptych of the Assumption of the Virgin surrounded by saints. On one of the pillars can be found a charming *Madonna and Child* by Sano di Pietro, with Christ in a pink and

Montepulciano – 'perched and brown'

gold robe squeezing the breath out of a goldfinch with a small chubby hand.
The cathedral also contains some interesting sculptures – particularly
Michelozzo's dismantled tomb of Bartolomeo Aragazzi who died in 1431. In
the 17th century the tomb was taken apart for some reason, and it is now in
fragments around the building. Particularly fine is the portrait of the old man
himself, lying with arms crossed, and an intelligent if weary face.

Emerge from the shade of the cathedral to look at the other buildings of
the square. To one side of the cathedral is the **Palazzo Contucci**, another
work of the senior Sangallo, built for Cardinal Giovanni Maria del Monte,
later Julius III, Montepulciano's second Pope. Inside are some 17th-century
frescoes by Andrea Pozzo. Opposite is the massive fortress-like **Palazzo Communale**, reminiscent of the town hall of Florence with its sturdy battlements.

It was begun at the end of the 14th century but given its present appearance in 1425 by Michelozzo. It is possible to climb the tower, from the top of which are wide views of the surrounding country.

Opposite the cathedral are two more palaces, the 14th-century Palazzo della Pretura and the magnificent solid shape of the **Palazzo Tarugi**. The Palazzo Tarugi is another magnificent Renaissance building, also probably the work of Sangallo, although some have attributed it to La Vignola. The palace is built in the pale honey-coloured travertine of the area with a solidly built arcade running around the base. Above the front door is a small extra window for checking the identity of visitors before opening the door – a pretty sound idea in those days. The generous corner loggia on the second floor must have been a lovely place to catch the evening sun, before it was filled in. Next to the palace is a well, built in 1520. The columns supporting the plinth are probably Etruscan, the two lions are Marzocchi, the symbol of Florentine power. Between them is the Palle, the shield bearing the six balls of the Medici.

Leaving the square in a southerly direction, past the bogus 19th-century fortress, one reaches the little church of Santa Maria dei Servi just outside the city walls. The church's Baroque interior was designed by Andrea Pozzo towards the end of the 17th century.

Just outside Montepulciano is a real Renaissance gem – Antonio Sangallo the Elder's church of the *Madonna di San Biágio*. It was begun in 1518 on the plan of a Greek Cross, one of the relatively few centrally-planned churches that ever came into being in Tuscany. Initially it was designed with two free-standing *campanili* although only one of these was ever built. Both its lovely setting, at the end of a cypress avenue, and its stunning architectural regularity in exquisite glowing pale honey-coloured travertine, make it an essential stopping point. Nearby is the **Canonry of San Biagio**, also built by Sangallo. Of the Madonna of San Biagio herself little is known; according to the renowned travel writer Augustus Hare one of her many feats was to bring a 'herd of cattle to their knees by the attractive manner in which she winked her eyes.'

A few miles south of Montepulciano (still on the No.146 road) is the spa town of **Chianciano Terme**. Chianciano relies on three main springs, Aqua Sillene, Aqua Santa and the Sorgente Sant' Elena, which between them are said to cure a variety of ills, from liver and stomach complaints to nervous disorders. It is probable that the springs were in use as early as the Etruscan period, since there is evidence of a settlement here then. Later the baths became popular with the Romans, who left various objects here for posterity. In the Middle Ages the town was seen as a valuable possession, fought over by neighbouring powers in both Tuscany and Umbria. But it was only at the beginning of this century that any large-scale development took place. After the Second World War spa bathing became rather less popular, although apparently it has become fashionable again recently and Italians are once more flocking to take the waters.

South east of Chianciano is the ancient town of **Chiusi**, formerly Chamars (Roman – *Clusium*), one of the Etruscan League of 12 city-states or lucomonies, and territory of the most famous of Etruscan warrior kings, the Lucomo, Lars Porsena. At the height of his power Porsena even dared to march on Rome to avenge his ally Tarquinius Superbus, as the much quoted poem by Macaulay tells us:

> *Lars Porsena of Clusium,*
> *By the Nine Gods he swore*
> *That the great house of Tarquin*
> *Should suffer wrong no more.*

An unconquerable romanticism seems to colour even the most turgid historian's view of the Etruscans – a feeling of a perfect time, lost for good with the Romans. This is D. H. Lawrence's impression:

> . . . in those days, on a fine evening like this, the men would come in naked, darkly ruddy coloured from the sun and wind, with strong, insouciant bodies: and the women would drift in, wearing the loose becoming smock of blue or white linen; and somebody surely, would be singing, because the Etruscans had a passion for music and an inner carelessness the modern Italians have lost. The peasants would enter the clear, clean sacred space inside the gates, and salute the gay-coloured little temple as they passed along the street that rose uphill towards the arx, between rows of low houses with gay coloured fronts painted or hung with bright terracottas. One can almost hear them still, calling, shouting, piping, singing, driving in the mixed flocks of sheep and goats, that go so silently, and leading the slow, white, ghostlike oxen with the yokes still on their necks.
>
> And surely, in those days, young nobles would come splashing in on horseback, riding with naked limbs on an almost naked horse, carrying probably a spear, and cantering ostentatiously through the throng of red-brown, full-limbed, smooth-skinned peasants. A Lucomo, even, sitting very noble in his chariot driven by an erect charioteer, might be driving in at sundown, halting before the temple to perform the brief ritual of entry into the city. And the crowding populace would wait; for the Lucomo of the old days, glowing ruddy in flesh, his beard stiffly trimmed in the Oriental style, the torque of gold round his neck, and the mantle or wrap bordered with scarlet falling in full folds, leaving the breast bare, he was divine, sitting on the chair in his chariot in the stillness of power. The people drew strength even from looking at him.

Chiusi is not quite as thrilling as it once was. The plain below is now rather built up and there is a big railway terminal in the once lovely valley. Up at the top of the hill the old town is quite pleasant and has one of the best Etruscan museums in the province, housed in a bogus antique temple. For those interested in the far-off days of ancient Etruria, the collection of sarcophagi, ash urns and pottery gives a fascinating picture of the Etruscan way of life and, particularly, death. Opposite the museum is the 13th-century

195

Cathedral, San Secondario, much restored in the 19th century, built on the site of a 7th-century church. Under the campanile is a Roman cistern hewn out of the rocky ground. The nave is defined by 18 differing Roman columns pilfered from local sites. In the chapter house of the Cathedral are several finely illustrated choir books from the Sienese Abbey of Monte Oliveto Maggiore. All around Chiusi the countryside is littered with the tombs of ancient Etruria. Perhaps the most interesting lie to the north and east of the town. On the road to the Lago di Chiusi is the early 5th-century BC **Tomba della Scímmia** (Tomb of the Monkey) named after one of the paintings on the wall of the tomb. Also on this road, known as the Via delle Tombe Etrusche, is the **Tomba della Pellegrina** containing some old Sarcophagi, and the **Tomba della Granduca** with more burial urns. To the east is another 5th-century tomb, the **Tomba Bonci Casuccini**, which has fascinating paintings of Etruscan sport and the original stone door still intact, and nearby the 1st-century BC **Tomba delle Tassinaie**.

A few kilometres south-east of Chiusi are two relatively undiscovered but extremely attractive towns: Sarteano, and lovelier still, Cetona. **Cetona** lies on the side of Monte Cetona which rises to a height of 1148m. The sleepy medieval town sits in the shadow of its ruined castello, built by the Sienese in 1458. Like many of the border towns, Cetona constantly changed hands between the powers of Tuscany and Umbria until in 1560 it became part of Cosimo I's Grand Duchy. In the little 14th-century Collegiata is a painting attributed to the Sienese painter Pinturricchio. Behind the town are some pre-historic caves which can be visited via the tourist information office (if it is open, which it rarely is). A few kilometres away is **Sarteano**, also charming, with its own 15th-century castello. Inside its two main churches are paintings by various lesser known Tuscan artists, including the painter Giacomo di Mino.

Right in the south of the province is the little town of **Radicófani**, dominated by a bleak ruined Rocca on the top of a lonely hill. The castle was originally the property of the monks of nearby San Salvatore, but became important to the Sienese as the last outpost of their territory. Like Buonconvento, Radoco-fani was a usual stopping-place on the Rome road, and was, if anything even more unpopular. Travelling in the 19th century, Charles Dickens was given the creeps by the whole experience:

> . . . there is a windy, creaking, wormy, rustling, door-opening, foot-on-staircase-falling character about this Radicófani hotel such as I never saw anywhere else. The town, such as it is, hangs on a hillside above the house, and in front of it. The inhabitants are all beggars; and as soon as they see a carriage coming, they swoop down upon it, like so many birds of prey.

At one time the three churches of the town were filled with terracottas of the della Robbias but many have since been removed. In the little church of San Pietro, however, there can still be found a graceful pure-white St Catherine of the school.

To the south-west of Radicófani, at 882m, on the eastern slopes of Monte Amiata, is the resort of **Abbadia San Salvatore**, named after one of the oldest religious houses in Tuscany. The Abbey was founded as early as 743 by the Lombard ruler, Racchis. Initially Benedictine, it was passed on to the Camaldolese order of northern Tuscany (see Casentino, p.155) and finally to the Cistercians. All that is left now is the 11th-century church, which has been repeatedly restored. Under it is the fine original crypt with groined vaulting which was originally divided into 12 or 13 aisles by finely carved columns.

The town itself is now a thriving resort with ski-ing in the winter (and an industrial zone). It is also increasingly popular in the summer with Italians who prefer the cool mountain air to the sweltering, overcrowded beaches. But the small medieval centre is still there, with its history of domination by the powerful counts of Santa Fiora, until finally in 1347 the Sienese took hold. The narrow streets and small churches have remained much as they were, protected from today's threat – the developer – by solid Sienese walls.

Practical Information

Hotels and Restaurants

SAN GIMIGNANO   The most famous hotel here is the old *La Cisterna* Piazza della Cisterna 23, 53037 San Gimignano (tel. (0577) 940328), splendidly situated in the heart of the town with a restaurant which has lovely views over the hills.

Rather more modest is the *Bel Soggiorno* Via San Giovanni 91, 53037 San Gimignano (tel. (0577) 940375), also 13th-century, with fine views and, many say, better food than its grander rivals.

A few km outside the town in **Pescille** is a restored farmhouse inn, *Hotel Pescille* (tel. (0577) 940186) which boasts a swimming pool and pleasant terraces for a cool evening drink.

COLLE VAL D'ELSA   The *Villa Belvedere* Colle Val d'Elsa , 53034 (tel. (0577) 920966), is a comfortable, pleasant establishment housed in a late 18th-century villa.

The *Hotel Arnolfo* at Piazza Santa Caterina 2 (tel. (0577) 920549) has an excellent restaurant serving an upmarket version of traditional local dishes. There are two good restaurants near Siena itself – the stylish, if rather over-priced, *Il Pozzo* (tel. (0577) 304127) in the tiny main square at Monteriggioni, and *Il Vecchio Maniero* in the Via Stretta (tel. (0577) 314340) in the old village of Sovicille some 13km west of Siena.

MONTEPULCIANO   Centrally located in the middle of town is the pleasing hotel, *La Terrazza* Via Pie' al Sasso, Via di Voltaia nel Corso 84, 53045 Montepulciano (tel. (0578) 757440). Another good choice is *Il Marzocco* in the Piazza Savonarola 53045 Montepulciano (tel. (0578) 77262), which has a good restaurant.

MONTALCINO   There are several interesting restaurants and bars throughout the town, two of the most popular being *Il Giglio* and the more serious *Cucina di Edgardo*, both in the Via San Salone. A few km out of town on the Grosseto road one finds the picturesquely situated *Ristorante Poggio Antico* which also has good food and wine.

SINALUNGA   The *Locanda del Amorosa* (tel. (0577 679497) is an increasingly popular hotel/restaurant right in the east of the province, created out of a cluster of farm buildings, with excellent food served in the old cowshed.

Museums

SAN GIMIGNANO
Palazzo della Podesta   Piazza del Duomo: open summer 09.30–12.30 and 15.30–18.30; winter 10.00–13.00 and 14.30–17.30; closed Mon.
Palazzo del Popolo   Piazza del Duomo: open summer 09.30–12.30 and 15.30–18.30; winter 10.00–13.00 and 14.30–17.30; closed Mon.

COLLE DI VAL D'ELSA
Antiquarium Etrusco   Palazzo Pretorio: open Sat and Sun 10.00–13.00 and 15.30–17.30 or 19.00 (summer weekdays 16.00–19.00); closed Mon.
Museo d'Arte Sacra   Palazzo Vescovile, open Sun 16.00–18.00.
Museo Civico   Palazzo dei Priori, open as Antiquarium, *see above*.

MONTALCINO
Museo Civico e Diocesano   Via dei Ricasoli 2: open winter 10.00–13.00 and 15.00–17.00, summer 10.00–13.00 and 15.30–19.00, closed Mon.

ABBEY OF MONTE OLIVETO MAGGIORE   Open daily 09.30–12.30 and 15.00–17.30.

PIENZA
Palazzo Piccolomini   Piazza Pio II: open daily 10.00–12.30 and 15.00–sunset, closed Mon.
Museo della Cattedrale   Casa dei Canonici: open winter 10.00–13.00 and 14.00–16.00, summer 10.00–13.00 and 15.00–17.00, closed Tues.

MONTEPULCIANO
Museo Civico   Palazzo Neri-Orsini, Via Ricci 1: open April–Sept 09.00–13.00 and 16.00–19.00 (closed Mon and Tues), winter 09.00–13.00, closed Mon.

CHIUSI
Museo Nazionale Etrusco   Piazza del Duomo: open summer 09.00–19.40 (Sun and hols 09.00–12.40), winter 09.00–13.40 (Sun and hols 09.00–12.30).

14. GROSSETO AND THE TUSCAN MAREMMA

The province of Grosseto is one of the least known and most fascinating in Tuscany. Much of the countryside is dramatic and beautiful, with wide hills dotted with increasingly prosperous farms, growing corn and other crops, vines and olives. At the top of the highest hills perch winding medieval villages where, for the moment, few tourists lurk. The children run in and out of doorways calling, and outside the tiny bars old men sit on wooden chairs. Further into the heart of the province, the villages are increasingly small and remote, with names that evoke the tougher, wilder life of southern Italy, an altogether bleaker style than we expect to find in gentle, civilised Tuscany – names like Impostino, Fornace, and l'Abbandonato.

The Grossetan Maremma has never been a favourite haunt of travellers and tourists. From the Middle Ages to the Second World War it was scrupulously avoided by all who could pass by on a different route. Nobody stopped to look at the lovely cathedral at Massa Maríttima or stayed to wander the hills or sample the garlicky Maremman snails and the crisp white wine of Pitigliano. As early as the 13th century the area had been given a bad press by Tuscany's greatest son, Dante Alighieri. Dante tells the story of La Pia, beautiful daughter of the Sienese family of Tolomei, whose husband locked her up in a Maremman castle, finally killing her so that he could take another wife. It could be argued that her death was not the fault of the Maremma, but her haunting words 'Siena mi fè, disfecemi Maremma' (Siena made me, the Maremma destroyed me), have become a testament to the area and its power of destruction. The Maremma's overwhelming and crippling problem lay in the undrained marshes of Scarlino and Raspolino, and the vicious malarial mosquitoes rising in their millions from the swamps. In 1610 the painter Caravaggio died of malaria at Porto Ercole, just one of the many thousands who perished. Even at the beginning of this century, the comments of English guidebooks were not exactly encouraging for the casual visitor:

No doubt it is an infected land: there are no villages anywhere in sight, and such tenements as there are – railway stations and the like – have gauze over their windows. The mosquito's bite, they say now, is death.

Grosseto and environs

Grosseto itself, the capital town of the province, has been, to say the least, unlucky. First mentioned by name in the 9th century as a small river settlement, it took over as a bishop's seat after the decline of nearby Roselle, in 1134. Like all the towns in Tuscany it was involved in constant battles with its neighbours. After prolonged and bitter fighting it finally fell in the late Middle Ages to Siena, which, in turn, fell to the Medici Grand Dukes in 1559. But by far the most vicious of Grosseto's enemies were the ever-encroaching swamps and their inhabitants, the *anopheles* mosquitoes. Despite attempts by Cosimo I and subsequent Medici Grand Dukes to drain the area and free the people of this scourge, by 1745 the population had dropped to a mere 212 struggling families. It was not until the advent of the Dukes of Lorraine that the draining really started to become effective. Credit for the final permanent defeat of the swamps must go to Mussolini in the first half of this century. By the late 1930s Grosseto was back on its feet, with a rising population and a spate of new buildings for accommodation, industry and agriculture. But there was yet another blow about to fall in the shape of the Second World War, when the city suffered massive destruction in the air raids. Since then however a rigorous programme of rebuilding, plus various recent agricultural and industrial initiatives have meant that Grosseto is at last becoming a prosperous and thriving modern town, with a growing population of around 80,000.

Driving over the flat Grossetan Maremma you see the city rise up, gloomy in its modernity, with drab flats and warehouses, and extraordinary modern churches. But inside the new metropolis there is still part of the fine old walled town remaining. The huge walls themselves are very impressive, built in a monumental hexagon by Grand Duke Cosimo di Medici in 1574. In 1835 Leopold II turned them into shady gardens with avenues of eucalyptus, and they are now a pleasant public park. Inside the walls is the old main square, dominated by the **Cathedral of San Lorenzo** and the Palazzo della Provincia. The cathedral was begun in the 13th century but has been much restored – the pink-and-white striped marble façade was added, not unsympathetically, in the 19th century. The symbols of the Evangelists above the pilasters are original, as is part of the right flank of the building, but much of the rest of it has been redone. Inside is a 15th-century font, and in the left nave there is a fine altar by Antonio di Ghino (1474). The altar houses a panel of the Assumption by the Sienese painter Matteo di Giovanni.

On the right of the cathedral is the **Palazzo della Provincia**, rebuilt rather unconvincingly in the 19th century in Gothic style. One of the very few 19th-century guidebooks to bother with Grosseto at all has this to say about it:

It [Grosseto] has lost the picturesque. It has rebuilt its Palazzo Communale in the most modern antique. I hardly remember a villa on the Riviera as its parallel. Harsh red brick, pointed to death with white plaster; thin, exaggerated battlements which could not withstand a boy's catapault – but enough. The Cathedral is no better . . .

The critic is too harsh – the whole effect of the square is actually quite attractive, with arcaded buildings and uncrowded cafés.

Grosseto also has some fine Sienese paintings. Behind the bare façade of the little 13th-century church of **San Francesco** in Piazza Indipendenza is a *Crucifixion* attributed to the young Duccio, and the remains of some interesting 14th-century frescoes. And in the pretty cloisters of the convent next door is an old well – probably 16th-century. The **Museum of Art** is situated above the Archaeological Museum in Piazza Baccanini. The **Archaeological Museum** has a good collection of material from local sites, particularly the nearby ancient city of Roselle. In the picture gallery are pictures by the early Sienese painters, Guido da Siena, Segna di Bonaventura and Sano di Pietro. There is also one of Sassetta's best paintings – the lovely *Madonna of the Cherries*, with the greedy infant lifting the fruit to his mouth.

Grosseto is also worth visiting for its food, which is strongly flavoured and distinctive – seafood and game. But the best restaurant of the province, perhaps in the whole of Tuscany, is situated in the village of **Istia d'Ombrone** about 8km up the river (on the No.322 road). Istia is a little Maremman township with a fine gate and some attractively dilapidated houses. In the small church are a couple of interesting Sienese pictures. But the real reason to go to Istia is for the amazing restaurant Il Terzo Cerchio, named after the third circle of Hell, where Dante discovered the fate of gluttons. Here you may try all the specialities of the Maremma at one sitting, served with friendly courtesy and washed down with some good unlabelled wine from Scansano. For a set price you may try as many courses as you can cope with – they recommend that you taste all of them. The food is local and very good, but you really do have to be a glutton to do it justice, though if you are remotely greedy, this is one not to miss. Next door, for the more abstemious, is a good pizzeria with an outside terrace, run by another branch of the same family. A few kilometres south-east of Istia, down a track off the Pancole road (No.322), is the 16th-century Maremman castle of **Sergardi di Montepo**.

Away from the plains, the hills of Grosseto are spectacular and alluring. To the north of the province are the high medieval villages of Montepescali, Batignano (with a restaurant with a fine view), Campagnatico, tiny Montorsaio, Scarlino, Roccastrada, Belvedere and Prata. The list is almost endless and while initially they may appear rather similar, you will find that each place has something special about it, a tiny Romanesque church, an antique well in the square, or a sturdy Medici portal. Many of these towns grew up on sites which have been populated since the Bronze Age (12th–11th century BC), but it was only during the Middle Ages that the rough huts were replaced by stone-and-tile dwellings and the present defensive walls began to enclose the whole hilltops.

Massa Maríttima

North of Grosseto lies one of the loveliest places in the whole of Tuscany – the little cathedral town of **MASSA MARÍTTIMA**. Situated on the high slopes of the Colle Metallifere (the Iron-Ore Hills), the town has been a mining centre since Etruscan times, flourishing under the Romans who found huge quantities of copper and silver. In the 8th century AD, Bishop Cerbone of Populonia fled to Massa to escape the malaria which was decimating the coastal areas, and established himself here. The town remained the seat of a bishop until the 13th century, when the grossly extravagant Bishop Alberto had to pawn the little city back to the townsfolk in an effort to pay off his debts. During much of the Middle Ages Massa was the main town of the province, but the lucrative mines made the town a valuable target and Massa was constantly being fought over by the major powers in Tuscany. At one point, Pisa controlled the upper town, while Siena ruled the lower. In 1335 the whole town finally fell under the domination of Siena, whose chaotic and quarrelsome regime, combined with the dreadful increase of the killer malaria, virtually destroyed it. In 1428 the population of the once busy town had dropped to 400. The mines were closed and Massa began to resemble a ghost town. A Tuscan saying of the time ran 'Va a Massa, guardala e passa' ('he who goes to Massa, looks at it and passes by').

This dire situation lasted for hundred of years, until the 18th century when the Dukes of Lorraine intervened. Even their attempt to save the little city was not a success at first. Deciding that the main problem lay in the town's ever falling population, Charles III imported 600 Germans, setting up each family with a house, land and a team of oxen. Even less able than the Italians to withstand malaria, the Germans started dying within months of their arrival, and soon there were literally none left. But this disaster helped to highlight what was really the only solution – the draining of the marshes – which was begun in earnest at about this time. By 1839 the population was back up to nearly 3000 and the mines were operating again on an increasing scale.

It is rare, even in Tuscany, to find a place as lovely as Massa's **Piazza Garibaldi**. Small and rather irregular, the square is dominated by the cathedral, set at a gentle angle almost opposite some exceptionally elegant civic buildings. The **Cathedral** is 13th-century, a gentle mixture of Romanesque and Gothic, standing gracefully at the top of a fine flight of steps. The carvings above the main door show the life of San Cerbone, to whom the building is dedicated. The cathedral is built of pale stone that reflects the changing light of day with a gentle luminosity; sometimes eerily silver; sometimes warm honey. By comparison, the giant cathedrals of Siena, Grosseto and Florence seem tawdry and grandiose.

In the beautiful, tranquil interior is a fine font, carved from one block of stone by the migrant sculptor, Giroldo da Como, in 1287. It was here that San Bernardino of Siena was baptised in 1380. Bernardo Albizzecchi was born in Massa but he moved to Siena when he was orphaned at five years old, and never lived in his native town again. In the right transept is a wonder-

The cathedral at Massa Maríttima

ful Sienese painting, *Madonna alle Grazie* dated 1316 but of uncertain attribution. Many believe it to be the work of Duccio, or his nephew Segna di
Buonaventura; others give the credit to Simone Martini. In the underground
crypt, which is not always open, is the shrine of San Cerbone covered with
eight reliefs showing the saint's life, carved in the 14th century by the Sienese
Goro di Gregorio.

Almost opposite the cathedral, to the west, is the grey travertine **Palazzo
Pretorio**, seat of the city's governors. The numerous coats-of-arms are those
of the ruling families between 1426 and 1633. Beside it is the fine 13th-century
tower house of the counts of Biserno. Next to that is the large Palazzo Comunale, which was made by combining three smaller palaces of different dates.
The **Palazzo Communale** houses the marvellous Simone Martini *Maestà*, a
particularly affectionate Madonna and Child. The saint standing in the background with some geese is St Cerbone. Also in the square are a couple of
pleasant bars, one used predominantly by tourists and the other by locals. As
yet Massa is not very touristy, perhaps partly due to its rather out-of-the-way
situation; but a few visitors, mainly Germans, now wander its narrow streets.
The narrowest of these are to the west of the town, where the alleys become
tunnels and lead off to the old mines. There is only one place to stay in the
old town, the very simple and cheap Hotel Cris. Because of its small size,
you need to book your room in advance in the summer.

The upper town is also worth exploring and enjoys a wide view over the
Maremma down to the sea. It has a mysterious feel about it – dominated by

the vast Sienese fortifications, which are linked to those built by the Massetani by a huge arch. Near the mineral museum is the 14th-century church of **San Agostino**. In the main square, Piazza Matteotti, is the **Museo Archeologico**, where there are some interesting Sienese paintings, as well as various local archaeological remains. On 20 May and the second Sunday in August the Massetani stage the *Balestae di Girofalco*, a crossbow competition in medieval dress, between the different areas of the town.

Etruscan sites in the Maremma

For the historically minded, the hills and plains of the Grosseto region are the places to search for ancient Etruria. Driving through the countryside one constantly notices small yellow signs pointing down roads that are often little more than tracks, with the words *Necropoli Etrusche*. Here, often three-quarters buried under sweet-smelling bushes and prickly undergrowth, are the ancient tombs of Etruscans, some extremely complete, others in disrepair and hard to make out. The tombs vary remarkably in shape and size. There are great chamber tombs for multiple burial, some of which date back as far as the 9th century BC, such as those on the coast at Populónia. Later tombs show the remains of coherent design. The early 3rd-century BC tomb at Sovana, near Pitigliano, is built in the style of a temple. Other necropoli can be found all over the region, near the southern towns of Magliano and Manciano, and the villages of Sovana, Marsiliana, Saturnia and Vetulonia.

Vetulonia, situated in lovely countryside in the hills 22km north of Grosseto, is historically one of the most important sites in Tuscany. It was briefly a town of great wealth and importance, one of the Etruscan League of Twelve. It depended on local mineral resources from the nearby hills, the Colline Metalli-fere, and apparently traded in gold and silver. Three kilometres outside the village to the north-east are some ancient chamber tombs like large bee-hives, mainly dating from the 7th century BC. The finest of these are the tombs of Pietrera and Diavolino, named after a statue resembling a devil that was found there. Many other treasures were discovered, including gold jewellery, bronze and some fine ceramic pots. As with nearly all the necropoli, most of the loot went to the archaeological museums of Florence and Grosseto. In the 6th century BC the apparently thriving city of Vetulonia suddenly and rather mys-teriously began to lose power. Archaeologists have suggested that this was related both to the growing success of the iron works at nearby Populónia, and to the rise in importance of the hitherto small town of Rusellae (now Roselle).

Roselle, about 6km north of Grosseto on the Siena road, is one of the most extensively excavated sites in Tuscany. Like Vetulonia it had been virtually an island in the days before the Grosseto lagoon had turned into marshland, over which there is a wide view. Although the great walls are Etruscan (6th-century BC), most of the town is the work of the Romans, whose domination began after a fierce battle in the early 3rd century BC. The excavations have exposed a straight main street with several buildings and a public square. There are also some fine mosaics and decorative brickwork. One of the main buildings was made to house the body of citizens known as the *Augustales*, whose sole function was to organise the town's worship of Emperor Augustus, who had turned the town into a colony. Rusellae's decline began around the 2nd century BC but, despite this, the colony remained the seat of the diocese until 1138 when Grosseto took over.

The coastal areas are also rich in archaeological finds. To the north is **Populónia**, once a powerful port, in the gulf of Baratti. Don't be put off visiting it by its proximity to the great rusty steel-works of Piombino. The town itself is in a lovely position, looking out towards the Ligurian Sea and northwards along sandy beaches. The fact that much of this coastline is dangerous for swimming, particularly for children, with a steeply shelving beach and a strong undertow, keeps it pleasantly free from tourism. Populónia's small beach is streaked with grey sand from the days when the whole area was covered in a huge and ancient slag heap. When the area was cleared the tombs were found remarkably intact, protected by the layers of waste from the iron works. Etruscan Populónia was initially the port and smelting works for the mineral-rich island of Elba, which did not have enough trees to keep iron furnaces burning. Some of Populónia's most impressive tombs date back as far as the 9th century BC; others, like the Tomb of the Bronze Statuette, are from the 6th–5th centuries BC. In the 4th century BC the city was still flourishing, despite attacks from the Syracusans. At this time Populonia even minted its own coins, with a Gorgon's head on them. In 205BC the town supplied iron for Scipio's campaign in Africa, but it is probable that soon after, at the hands of the Romans, it began to decline. The Roman historian Strabo, who was born c.63BC, mentions that when he visited Populónia it was deserted except for a few lonely metalworkers.

Standing on the hill above the tombs is the medieval *rocca* and, further round, the village with a small Etruscan museum. In the bay is a small marina of fishing and pleasure boats and a couple of homely fish restaurants.

The Maremman coast and hinterland

Further along the coast, past the dismal industrial port of Piombino, (where some years ago a stray shark recently caused a 'Jaws' style sensation) and the dreary town of Follónica, is the smart modern resort of **Punta Ala**. Here, for a price, one can swim and waterski, play golf and tennis or even polo on the headland opposite Elba. About 18km further south, with more charm and cheaper restaurants, is the busy fishing village-cum-resort of **Castiglione della Pescaia**, dominated by a 15th-century Spanish fortress and massive walls. The medieval town, nestling under the formidable *rocca*, is pretty but has an aura of having been done up for the tourists. In the lively harbour, fishing boats and pleasure crafts are moored side by side. There are plenty of fish restaurants of varying standards to be found. Perhaps the best is Da Romolo in the Via della Libertà, but, like many resorts, the standards rise and fall with each new season. There are various beaches on both sides of the town. The beaches to the south are sandy and are backed by the famous Pineta del Tombolo, a long stretch of pine forests running south to Marina di Grosseto.

Thirty years ago the long sandy beaches of the Tuscan Maremma were nearly deserted. Now, unfortunately, this is no longer the case. **Marina di Grosseto** and neighbouring **Principina al Mare** have become victims of the most charmless kind of tourist development possible, with concrete cafés and ugly houses. Their only redeeming feature is that they are small and easily avoided. Rather better, though still crowded, is the **Marina di Albarese**, reached by driving through the edge of the **Maremma National Park**. The park is open to the public on Wednesdays and at weekends; here the white Maremma oxen can be seen wandering through the rough vegetation. Once through the pine woods and sand-dunes, the beach is a narrow strip of greyish sand, with good views of Monte Argentario and the small islands known as the Formiche di Grosseto. The beach is free and there is no resort, just a car park (where overnight stops in camper-vans are discouraged) and a refreshment stall.

At the other end of the Maremma National Park is the small habour of **Talamone**, another picturesque medieval fishing-village-cum-resort. Legend has it that in the distant past, Jason moored his ship here after stealing the Golden Fleece; the village is supposedly named after an Argonaut named Telamon. In 225BC it was also the site of a fierce battle between the Romans and the Gauls; a mass grave of horses and men, probably dating back to this time, was found nearby at Campo Regio. In 1303 the Sienese bought the little village, intending to expand it as their major port, but never got round to doing much about it. Now there is a modern marina and various rather touristy restaurants with mediocre food. A better bet is Da Dono, a restuarant three or four km to the north east.

One of the best places in Tuscany for a typical Mediterranean seaside holiday is still the rocky promontory of **MONTE ARGENTARIO**, some 32km south of Grosseto. Originally an island, Monte Argentario became joined to the mainland through the gradual silting up of the sea into sand banks. The area is mainly wooded with some cultivation and at its highest point, the summit of Monte Telegráfo, reaches some 635m above sea level. For many years the wealthier Romans have been coming here for week-ends and summer holidays, and the ports are popular with Mediterranean yachtsmen. Despite this Monte Argentario retains plenty of charm, especially out of the main tourist season. The rocky western coast is still fairly unspoilt but in other parts holiday apartments and bungalows have sprung up between the trees, intermingling with the older, and infinitely more charming, holiday villas of the Romans.

The small dusty town of **Orbetello** lies on the middle road on to the promontory. The two outer roads are lined with beaches, many of which are now

Porto Ércole

attached to camp sites, but which tend to clear towards evening. From 1557 Orbetello was the capital of the Spanish garrison states which were established along the coast. The town gate still bears the arms of Philip III. The small Duomo has a Gothic façade and contains two things of interest – a pre-Romanesque altar in one of the side chapels and a rather peculiar fresco of Pius XII. Turning right on arriving in Monte Argentario, you come to the busy port of **Santo Stefano**, where the boats leave for Giglio and Giannutri (see chapter on Elba and the Tuscan Archipelago). Porto Santo Stefano was badly bombed in the Second World War and has been substantially rebuilt. However, it is still quite an attractive place with houses painted in the traditional ochres and reds of the Italian coast, a lively fish market on the quay and good seafood restaurants.

On the other side of the promontory lies the little holiday town of **Porto Ércole**, another fishing village that has traditionally been popular with the discerning English. Porto Ércole is dominated by three forts, the late Renaissance Forte Filippo, the abandoned hexagonal Forte Stella, and the Rocca Spagnola (Spanish Fort). The Rocca Spagnola is situated on a hill dominating the harbour. Within its walls are some charming houses and a magnificent view across the little town and harbour. Porto Ércole also has some good seafood restaurants round the harbour. Have a look at each one before you choose; my favourite is the little one with tables outside (whose name I cannot remember), directly across the harbour from the Rocco Spagnola.

Just south of Monte Argentario is another good place to visit – the ancient

Roman town of **Cosa**, situated on the top of a hill near **Ansedonia** with its small beach and restaurant. The excavations at Cosa have brought to light a town which was founded in 273BC, probably on the site of an earlier Etruscan settlement. The whole area is surrounded by ancient walls and towers enclosing the remains of the town with a basilica, two temples and a walled acropolis. The whole area within the walls is overgrown and charming, with olive trees and sweet-smelling bushes among the ruins – a pleasant, if scratchy, place for a picnic. Nearby, past a few rather dull modern villas, is the newly excavated Roman Villa, Settefinestre. Along the coast is the Tagliata Etrusca (Etruscan Cut), which is actually a Roman device, built to drain the marshes and preserve the nearby Lago di Burano (now a bird sanctuary). The device, which is simply a vast channel hewn into the rock, also prevented the little harbour from silting up. Over 2000 years later it is still effective.

Leaving the coast and heading inland, one comes to the fascinating walled towns of Capálbio, Manciano and Magliano. The fortified town of **Capálbio**, 17km from Monte Argentário, near a large hunting reserve, is situated on a hill with wide views over the plain, it was founded in the 12th century and, like many other Marremman towns, soon fell under the domination of Siena. The small town centre is still paved with flagstones in the medieval manner. In the 12th-century church there are some medieval frescoes and in the nearby Oratorio della Providenza is a Pinturicchio Madonna (probably early 16th-century).

Magliano (midway between Capálbio and Grosseto), another walled medieval town, was initially the main port for all the local communities. In the central square is the church of San Giovanni with a Renaissance façade, containing a 14th-century Sienese fresco of Saint Sebastian. The Renaissance Palazzo dei Priori is covered with 15th-century coats of arms. The medieval Palazzo Aldobrandeschi, with its fine mullioned windows, belonged to the powerful family of the same name from nearby Sovana. Near the town are the ruins of the 13th-century church of San Bruzio which was probably never completed. There is also an ancient olive tree known as the Oliva della Strega (the Witch Olive), supposedly worshipped by the last pagans. **Manciano**, 20km from the coast on the No.74 road, is another sleepy old town with a fountain in the main square. A short but lovely drive (6km north-west) takes you to the pretty, well-kept village of **Montemerano** with its charming Piazzetta di Castello.

The most spectacular town in southern Tuscany is undoubtedly **Pitigliano**, built along a sheer escarpment of rock above the meeting of three ravines. Of Etruscan origin, Pitigliano became the seat of the great Orsini family in 1292. Their fortified palace was begun in the 14th century but expanded in the 16th. In the cathedral square, on a grey travertine pillar, perches a bear (*orso*), the symbol of the family. The cathedral itself was originally medieval, but it was greatly altered in the 18th century, and now has a Baroque façade. Inside are paintings by the 18th-century artist Francesco Zuccarelli. The town itself is a fascinating place to wander through, with narrow streets and dramatic views across the ravines. Under the town, cut into the tufa rock, are countless caves,

Pitigliano

some of which were ancient tombs. Now they are used to store the white Pitigliano wine which can be bought cheaply throughout the town.

Nearby are two small towns, **Sorano**, (built, like Pitigliano, on a rock) and **Sovana**, near a famous Etruscan cemetery. The remote village of Sovana (8km from Pitigliano on a twisty mountain road) is particularly interesting and has a fine medieval main street, with a 13th-century town hall at one end and a lovely Romanesque cathedral at the other. In the little church of Santa Maria is an unusual pre-Romanesque *ciborium*, probably dating from the 9th century.

Twenty or so kilometres to the east of Pitigliano, over the Tuscan border, is the large **Lago di Bolsena**, where hot and weary sightseers can cool off in the clear, surprisingly clean waters. In the summer many Italians still go to the northern lakes for their vacation, but recently the mountains have become popular again with holiday makers. And of course there is now ski-ing in the winter. As a result, modern resorts have sprung up around medieval towns like 680m **Arcidosso** (55km east of Grosseto) and **Santa Fiora** (8km south of Arcidosso), on the western slopes of Monte Amiata. Monte Amiata peaks at 1738m, on the border of Grosseto and Siena. The drive up is twisty and tiring but at the top the view is stupendous. The whole of southern Tuscany is laid out before you, in a vast uneven patchwork of ochres and greens that rise and fall into the far distance.

Practical Information

Hotels and Restaurants

MONTE ARGENTARIO *Il Pellicano* Cala di Santi, 58018 (tel. (0564) 833801). Very expensive, but in a fine situation and retaining some of the glamour and style on which its high international reputation is based.

A more modest alternative in **Porto Ércole** is the nice hotel *Don Pedro* Via Panoramica 23, 58018 Porto Ércole (tel. (0564) 833914). Both Porto Ércole and **Porto Santo Stefano** have various good fish restaurants among the best are *il Gambero Rosso* on the Lungomare at Porto Ércole and the homely *Fontanina di San Pietro* on the harbour at Porto Santo Stefano.

The two little resorts of **Talamone** and **Castiglione della Pescaia** generally offer rather disappointing accommodation, though perhaps the best options are the *Capo d'Uomo* (tel. (0564) 887077) in a lovely position on the Talamone point or the simple, cheap *Gli Archi* in the old town of Castiglione at Via Montebello 28 (tel. (0564) 933083). Of the many rather touristy fish restaurants here perhaps *Da Romolo* is the best.

PUNTA ALA Perhaps the best hotel in this smart modern resort is the *Alleluia* one of the few older buildings in the complex.

MASSA MARÍTTIMA Incredibly cheap and simple is the *Hotel Cris* (tel. (0556) 90 23 05), the only hotel in the old part of town.

GROSSETO Outside the town is one of the best restaurants in the whole of Tuscany, the wonderful *Terzo Cerchio* situated in the small village of Istia d'Ombrone.

Museums

GROSSETO
Museo Archeologico e d'Arte della Maremma Piazza Beccarini 3: open 09.00–13.00 and 16.00–19.30; Sun 09.00–13.00; closed Wed.

MASSA MARÍTTIMA
Museo/Palazzo del Podestà Open 10.00–12.30 and 15.30–19.00; closed Mon.

PORT ÉRCOLE
Rocca Spagnola Open 10.00–13.00 and 15.30–sunset.

ROSELLE Ruins, hours unrestricted.

ANSEDONIA
Ruins of Cosa Open daily.

CAPALBIO
Lago di Burano Admission by special permission only (tel. (0564) 898829).

ALBERESE
Parco Nazionale della Maremma Open Wed, weekends and hols only; access is by bus from the Park Information Office (tel. (0564) 407098).

15. ELBA AND THE TUSCAN ARCHIPELAGO

The little group known as the Tuscan Archipelago is made up of seven small islands, well known to Mediterranean seafarers since almost the beginning of time. They are: Gorgona; Capraia; Elba; Pianosa and, still moving southwards, Montecristo; Giglio and tiny Giannutri. Elba, by far the biggest, is also the most interesting, with a varied landscape and a periodically fascinating history.

Elba

Elba lies some 9km off Piombino in the Tyrrhenian Sea. About 28km long and 18km wide, the island has a winter population of around 30,000. In the summer, of course, this rises dramatically with the onslaught of the tourist season when Italians, Germans, Swiss, and British (plus a few Americans from the giant cruise ships) descend for their holidays. They come for swimming, sunbathing, underwater fishing and seafood – Elba offers all these things in abundance. So, if at all possible, try to visit the island in the lower seasons (from Easter to late June and September to October) when the weather is still usually warm enough for swimming but there are far fewer people. Then Elba can be a good place to spend a few seaside days, particularly after a week's concentrated slog in Florence. If there is little to see in the way of masterpieces, there are other, less highbrow, compensations. The coastline is generally picturesque (and relatively unspoilt when compared to the mainland) with small fishing villages, beaches, rocky bays and a surprisingly clear blue sea. In general the character of Elba is very different to that of the rest of Tuscany. Perhaps this is partly because of its very separate history, which, like that of many small islands, is dominated by invasions and piracy. Perhaps also the island's remarkable geological structure has given the Elbans an independent source of wealth and pride which they have been understandably reluctant to share.

The main source of this wealth lies in the massive amounts of iron ore along the east of the island which have been extensively mined since the time of the Etruscans, forming much of the basis of their power, and of which Virgil commented, 'Insula inexhaustis chalybum generosa metallis.' But iron ore is not by any means the whole story and many other precious minerals and rocks can be found here. The British estimate up to 150 different kinds; the Italians say there are around 1000. Among the most commonly found now are pyrites (fool's gold), black-and-purple haematite, sparkling marcasite and various types of quartz.

For non-geologists one of the best things about Elba is the plant life. Much of the land is covered with the aromatic but extremely scratchy Mediterranean scrub known as macchia, here distinguished by being of the less usual Cystus variety, where a small species of rock rose adds its scent to the traditional wafts of sage, rosemary and thyme. The Cystus resin is thought to be the base of biblical myrrh. In the spring and, to a lesser extent, in autumn the wild flowers run riot and the ground is speckled with irises, anemones, orchids, helebores, periwinkles and countless others. If you are interested in botany remember to take a flower book. There is also a splendid variety of mediterranean trees – deciduous forests and sweet chestnut woods. The old trees, vines, olives, carobs and planes live alongside the more recent imports of oranges, lemons, eucalyptus and mimosa. As in other parts of Italy, owing to hunting restrictions, the birds are beginning very gradually to creep back into their old haunts. It is possible to hear nightingales in some of the woods to the east and, apparently, to see the Sardinian warbler with a flash of white in its tail.

The history of Elba appears to be dominated far less by its natives than its visitors. Jason is supposed to have moved his great ship into Porto Argos (now Porto Ferraio) after stealing the Golden Fleece. St Paul is said to have preached to the Elbans. Later came Cosimo, first of the Medici Grand Dukes, following a string of pirates. And, most famous of all, Napoleon, whose name more than any other is inextricably linked to the island where he in fact spent less than ten months.

As early as the 6th century BC iron ore was being mined and, initially, smelted on the island. When wood for the furnaces started to run out the ore was taken to the Etruscan settlement of Populonia on the mainland. Later it went to the slightly nearer port of Piombino where the great rust-stricken ironworks still dominate the landscape. The Romans, who called the island Ilva, meaning iron, also exploited Elba's numerous other resources. The giant columns of the Pantheon come from the quarries at Seccheto. But as centuries passed Elba became increasingly prey to the growing number of seagoing marauders: Lombards, Saracens, and a seemingly endless stream of pirates. In the 11th century the pope gave the island to Pisa, then at the height of its power, which revived the flagging quarries: Elban stone was used for some of the city's loveliest buildings – San Michele in Borgo and San Francesco. Remains of the Pisan fortifications are still visible round the island, most impressively in the fortress of **Volterraio** perched high on a rock by Rio nell'

Elba. In 1399, after a series of changes, Elba came under the rule of the Appiani family of Piombino who, unable to protect the island from intruders, eventually found themselves under the domination of Spain. The 16th century was blighted by the worst piracy Elba had ever suffered. The Turkish pirate Admiral Khair-ed-Din and his brother Arouj (confusingly both known as Barbarossa) ransacked the towns and villages, taking all the booty they could lay their hands on, including thousands of slaves. A few years later, in 1550, the great pirate Dragut executed a terrifying ten-day raid. He took 900 Elbans for slavery and systematically laid waste many of the villages. Two years later he was back causing still more destruction.

A more positive force was Cosimo de' Medici, first Grand Duke of Tuscany. He was given the island in 1546 by the Holy Roman Emperor Charles V in return for unpaid loans. After various altercations Cosimo found himself effectively in charge only of Porto Ferraio, which he quickly and modestly renamed Cosmopoli. He then set about fortifying the town, hoping to make it a suitable base for his newly established chivalrous order, the Knights of Santo Stefano. The sturdy new Forte Falcone, on a rock above the town, and the star-shaped Forte Stella, along with the substantial walls were fairly successful in keeping marauders at bay from the little town while the rest of the island suffered ever more acutely. Even the Medici were helpless against the repeated international squabbles which resulted in a string of different rulers for the island over the following centuries. Then, in 1805, Napoleon Bonaparte, almost at the height of his powers, assigned Elba and Piombino to his sister Eliza Baciocchi.

We now enter the shortest but most illustrious period of the island's history – the nine and a half months between May 1814 and February 1815, when the Emperor, after an enforced abdication, was exiled to Elba as his only kingdom. There have been over 2000 books written about Napoleon and probably hundreds of those are about his time on Elba. Generally they give the impression of a giant forced to sit in a child's playpen – the proportions are all wrong. Nobody can have felt this more than the man himself. On his arrival he commented, 'Ah, mon île est bien petite.' Despite the propaganda, the Elbans were also somewhat sceptical about the new plan working out. But Colonel Campbell, one of the four allied commissioners appointed to escort Napoleon, noted that on Elba

> . . . dislike of the French Government and Napoleon was outweighed by the hope and belief in the advantages that Napoleon's presence would afford them.

And there were some real advantages gained. Napoleon was never lazy; on his first morning he rose at four for a six-hour inspection before breakfast. From then on he was constantly planning and scheming about improvements. He found, for instance, that existing sanitation was minimal and set about changing it. He took over the modest Palazzetto dei Mulini at the top of Portoferraio and immediately began renovating it. But this was not enough and soon he had acquired the Villa San Martino as a country residence, followed by various other temporary abodes, in an attempt to assuage his boredom. He also decided that he must have a fleet, a national guard and a military academy, and made extensive plans to these ends. In August Madame Mère arrived, and in November his favourite sister Pauline, whose constant sociability made yet more demands on his rapidly dwindling funds. To bolster his finances he began to impose extremely unpopular taxes on the people of the island. But, notwithstanding this, by the end of the year Napoleon was nearly broke and increasingly restless. He wanted to see his wife and son, who had shown no intention of joining him in Elba; more importantly, he saw in the international situation a chance to regain his old power. On Sunday 26 February, after much secret preparation, Napoleon and a small army set sail for France. 'Tonight's ball,' said his sister Pauline, 'has been cancelled by History.' And so Elba returned to the Grand Duchy of Tuscany. But the three golden bees that Napoleon chose as his symbol, along with many of the improvements that he started, still bear testimony to his brief reign. On his departure he told the people, 'I leave you peace, I leave you prosperity. I leave you a clean fair city, I leave you my roads and trees, for which your children at least will thank me.'

Like their predecessors, most of today's visitors come to Elba by boat, either from Livorno or, more frequently, Piombino. There are two main lines running from the mainland: Toremar and the smaller Navarma agency. In the high seasons boats depart almost hourly, but it is advisable to book if you are taking a car across. The crossing from Livorno takes around three hours, from Piombino little over an hour. There are also hydrofoils which are slightly quicker, but rather more expensive and much less fun. Most of the boats go to Portoferraio but they are also fairly frequent to Cavo, Rio Marino and Porto Azzurro. For those who wish to fly there is a small airport with daily flights from Pisa and Florence in the summer.

Portoferraio consists of two parts: the old town, and the new port where the ferries and other big boats dock. Embarking in the modern harbour is somewhat disappointing. There are modern shops selling beachwear, a big ugly hotel, pizzerias and travel agencies. The old town is hidden behind the massive rock of the Falcone. Only the natural scenery remains impressive. But five minutes' brisk walk round the Punta del Gallo takes you straight into the old port of Darsena, which, apart from a few new buildings on the front, has remained surprisingly untouched. Through the sturdy portals, the small houses rise in ochres and pinks up the steep incline to the Medici forts. Looking at the words of one of the first English travellers to write about the area, one feels that little has changed. Richard Colt Hoare was in Elba at the beginning of the 19th century.

> . . . In regard to situation, neatness, and construction, it surpassed the expectations I had conceived of what was to be seen in the island. It is commanded by two lofty forts, Il Falcone and La Stella . . . From these two forts, particularly from the first, the eye is gratified with the finest views of the port, adjacent coast, and country. The approach to the harbour and its entrance are picturesque. The houses are built on the

The gardens of the Palazzetto dei Mulini, Portoferraio

declivity of a hill, forming a species of amphitheatre; and the harbour is shut up with a chain, which opens to admit vessels. The interior of the town is neat: it contains the only inn on the island . . .

The town is still dominated by Cosimo's ambitious fortifications and the old hotel, L'Ape d'Elbana, where, in Napoleon's time, the town officials would meet for lunch, is still doing trade in the pleasant main square. The hotel is named after the gold bees 'which will one day sting again', that Napoleon chose for his Elban flag. Also in the Piazza della Repubblica is the town hall, the fruit market, and nowadays, numerous small restaurants. Nearby is the little 17th-century church of the **Misericordia**, where the Emperor's bronze death mask is on display. Every year on 5 May a Mass is offered here for his soul. The church also houses a painted *Madonna* by the Tuscan sculptor Tino di Camaiano.

Near the top of the hill is the charming pink **Palazzetto dei Mulini**: Napoleon's official residence, named after the two windmills that once stood nearby. The Emperor's house is decidedly modest. The ground floor includes a study, the *Grand Salon* with murals by R. Morghen, and the remains of Napoleon's library. His books range from Cervantes to Voltaire and Fanny Burney. Nothing is left in the bathroom where he often spent the whole afternoon, either planning, or trying to calm his frequently agitated nerves. Upstairs is the apartment of his sister, Pauline Borghese, which had initially been added in the hopes that his wife and child would soon be joining him. Although most of the furniture has been replaced and few of his possessions remain, the little palace is well worth visiting, if only to see the pretty Italianate garden with the blue bay of Portoferraio behind it.

A trip can also be made to Napoleon's other main house on the island – the summer villa of **San Martino** – a few kilometres west of Portoferraio. (The same ticket can be used for both the Mulini and San Martino but it is worth checking opening times as they can vary.) This originally small residence was later bought by Napoleon's nephew by marriage, Prince Anatole Demidoff, who proceeded to erect a large Neo-classical building to house a museum in honour of his uncle. The museum now contains various (mainly 19th-century) Italian paintings, including some of Elba and a few statues. Canova's fine statue of Galatea is thought to be modelled on Pauline Borghese. Behind the museum is the villa itself, bought by the Emperor with proceeds from the sale of Pauline's diamonds, and furnished with pieces pirated from the ship of his brother-in-law, Prince Borghese. But little remains of the original contents: only the frescoed walls testify to the little villa's illustrious past. The best of these are in the main reception room, commemorating Napoleon's Egyptian campaign, in his words, 'the most beautiful time of my life'. Also on the wall, protected by glass from the grubby paws of many tourists, are the rather touching words, *'Ubicumque felix Napoleo'* – wherever he is, Napoleon is happy. The words are scrawled in the emperor's own hand but, for all that, they are not altogether convincing. The ceiling of the Council chamber was also decorated on an idea of his – two doves, (supposedly symbolising Napoleon and his wife, Marie Louise) joined by a ribbon, are flying apart. As the distance between them grows greater, the knot tightens. Yet more wishful thinking.

Back on the spectacular coast road going west, you go past the beaches of Biodola and the gulf of Procchio where Princess Pauline apparently swam naked. Soon after you come to the attractive little fishing village of **Marciana Marina**. The harbour is now rather dominated by a large modern pier near the old Pisan watchtower, where fishing boats and small trawlers drop anchor. Despite the usual cafés and pleasure boats the towns to the west of Elba are, in general, less spoilt and have retained their original character more successfully than the villages to the south and east. From Marciana Marina, looking inland, you can see high up the two inland settlements of Marciana Alta and Poggio. In the 18th century, when the Barbary pirates were rampant, most of the Elban fishermen would have had a small house down in the port and a bolt-hole in the upper town for whenever pirate sails were spied on the horizon. The road up to the villages climbs steeply through the chestnut woods on the slopes of **Monte Capanne**, the island's highest peak at over 1000m. It is possible to go right to the top by road or, for the more adventurous, to take the cable-car which leaves from the small medieval town of **Marciana Alta** half-way up the hill. Marciana Alta was the seat of the ruling Appiani family, who built the 15th-century stronghold. In the charming leafy square is an old table made out of a sundial. There is a tiny archaeological museum and a few bars situated on the Via delle Coste which has a fine view down to the sea.

Poggio, Roman Podium, lies a couple of kilometres to the east of Marciana Alta, near the mineral spring known as the Fonte di Napoleone from the time when the Emperor's bladder complaint was apparently eased by the diuretic qualities of the water. Poggio is another maze of steep steps and narrow streets made bright by pots of geraniums and other flowers. For centuries the people of the two villages were at loggerheads, but now the ancient squabbles have at last subsided and Marciana and Poggio once again live sleepily side by side. On nearby **Monte Giove** is yet another Napoleonic site – the place where he was reputed to have hidden his Polish mistress Marie Walewska and her son when she visited Elba in secret. The visit ended abruptly after only 48 hours, when the couple thought that they had been found out. Near their hiding-place is the little sanctuary of La Madonna del Monte, which houses a 15th-century picture of the Virgin painted on a granite slab, much venerated by the Elbans; and down on the coast is the so-called **Sedia di Napoleone** – a rock where the Emperor would sit with tears in his eyes, straining to catch a glimpse over the horizon of his native Corsica. It is almost impossible to escape Napoleon on Elba: every part of the island has its own myth to add to the great legend.

Following the coast road one reaches **Seccheto**, now a small resort but formerly the main granite-quarrying area on the island. The granite was generally taken to be cut on the slopes of Monte Capanne, where remains of the cutting can still be found among the cystus bushes. One pillar left there was quarried by the Pisans for their cathedral and still bears their inscription. On the south coast is **Marina di Campo**, famous for the long beaches which have made it one of Elba's largest modern resorts. Originally it was the port for the villages of San Piero and Sant' Ilario in Campo, mainly used for the shipping of wine. It was also used at another time as the sailing point for the nearby island of Pianosa, where the Elbans tried briefly to grow wheat in an attempt to be more independent of the mainland. It is still the departure point for Pianosa and the tiny island of **Montecristo**, which is now a gaol.

A few kilometres inland, some 230m above sea level, are the twin medieval villages of **San Piero** and **Sant' Ilario**. Both townships were fortified by the Pisan Governors in the 12th century although only San Piero's Appiani fortress remains. Equally, both were disastrously sacked by the pirate Dragut in 1553. In San Piero's main square is the Romanesque church of San Niccolò, built on the site of a Roman temple dedicated to Glaucous, the protector of sea-farers. Inside are some fine capitols and the remains of some 15th-century Spanish frescoes of St Peter, fisherman of souls, and the human target, St Sebastian.

The Golfo della Lacona and the larger Golfo Stella are divided by a thin tongue of land called the Capo Stella. Golfo Stella, the larger bay, has many sandy beaches and is as a result touristy, with modern hotels, bars and the usual pizzerias. High above the coast, in a lovely position, sits **Capoliveri**, an old town, also fairly popular with visitors. Despite its name, derived from

The village of Poggio

Caput Liberum (free hill) the town was initially a sort of open prison-cum-refuge. The Romans, and later the Pisan authorities, sent debtors and other miscreants to the little town, where they were able to live normally, but unable to leave. In 1814 the citizens of Capoliveri incurred Napoleon's wrath by being the only people on the island that refused to pay his extortionate new taxes. Resistance to the tax collectors became so aggressive that the Emperor threatened to install a garrison of his guard permanently to keep the rebels in line. But incidents like this worked against Napoleon and soon his British Escort, Colonel Campbell, was noting that, 'Napoleon appears to become more unpopular on the island every day . . . every act seems guided by avarice and personal interest . . . the inhabitants perceive that none of his schemes tend to ameliorate their situation.' Round the edge of the town grow the vines from which most of the island's Moscato wine is produced. Just to the south is Monte Calamita, a mountain so full of lodestone that it diverts the compasses of passing ships.

Porto Azzuro (formerly Porto Longone) on the east coast is another typical Mediterranean port. In the 16th century it was taken over by the Spanish and in 1603 Philip III had the massive fortress built on the hill above the town. At the beginning of the 19th century the Forte Longone became a prison and it has remained one ever since. The town was unwillingly lumped together with the gaol whose name it shared, so in 1947 it decided to change its name to Porto Azzuro. Across the bay from the Forte Longone is another Spanish edifice, the 17th-century Forte Foccardo, now used as a lighthouse.

Back on the sea road, following the coast northwards, one reaches Rio Marina, which used to be the island's main iron-ore loading port. And high above it is the erstwhile important mining town of **Rio nell' Elba**. As early as the Etruscan age, Rio was the island's mining capital, but now only the red oxide-stained mountains indicate the area's former prosperity. In the 18th century the population of Rio Alta was over 5000. Now it is less than a thousand. Because of its pleasant location by the sea, Rio Marina has fared rather better, benefiting from the advent of the tourist trade. It is possible (and very interesting) to visit the great mines of Rio and there is also a small mineral museum in Rio Marina which is open throughout the summer. If you walk to Spiazzi there is a good view of the little islets of Cerboli and Palmaiola. Following the coast past Capo Ortano you will find some good swimming places with small coves and rocky bays. On the northern tip of the island is the modern resort of **Cavo**, set in an otherwise unspoilt region near more good beaches. In the village of **Magazzini** on the road back towards Portoferraio is the restored Romanesque church of **San Giovanni delle Trane**, which reflects the Pisan style with blank arches and an interesting apse.

A few kilometres inland, in a fabulous situation, is the Spanish sanctuary of the **Madonna di Monserrato**. The 17th-century church was built by the Spanish governor Pons y León to house a copy of a painting of the Madonna from a church near Barcelona. And perhaps the best place to end a tour of Elba is above the small church at the top of Monte Castello. The pizzerias and the beach umbrellas are out of sight and out of mind, and the view is much as it has been for centuries, spectacular and intensely seductive: a gorgeous panorama of tree-clad hills and bright blue sea.

Gorgona, Pianosa and Capraia

The three most northerly of the islands of the Tuscan Archipelago are all in use as prison colonies. Tiny remote **Gorgona** and **Pianosa**, just south of Elba, can presently be visited only with a special permit from the prisons administration at the Ministry of Justice. Gorgona, 35km from Livorno, is just a partially cultivated rock housing a prison. Since Etruscan times, it has usually been the home of religious orders and recluses dwelling in constant fear of piracy and invasion. Today there are a few free inhabitants who glean a rather meagre living, mainly by salting anchovies. Pianosa, a flat, fertile island covering about 10 sq km, has been a penal colony since Roman times, when the Emperor Augustus exiled his nephew, Postumus Marcus Julius Agrippus, there for life. The present penal farm was established in 1635 and the prison building was erected in 1865.

The largest and most accessible of the prison islands is **Capraia**, named after the wild goats that used to roam over its terrain. Here, also, is a long history of pirates, monastic orders, and recluses. Although it is possible to reach the island – ferries go from Livorno and Elba – tourism has been somewhat hampered by yet another penal settlement. But there are now some hotels and the small typical town (also called Capraia) is quite pleasant to visit. And, like most of the other islands, there are some good walks to be had through the *macchia* along the rugged coastline.

Montecristo, Giglio and Giannutri

By far the most remote and mysterious of the Tuscan islands, some 65 kilometres from the coast, with no regular boat service, is **Montecristo**. Montecristo is surrounded by legend. In the 5th century Bishop Mamiliano of Palermo spotted the island after escaping by boat from prison in his native city. Far from being put off by its remote situation, he decided that it was the only place that he could be at peace and, after killing the resident fearsome dragon, remained there in perfect seclusion for the rest of his life. Later, optimistic friars erected a monastery in his name, only to depart with record speed when the sails of the mighty pirate Dragut appeared on the horizon. The other great legend revolves around the buried treasure which some other monks, fleeing from the inevitable pirate invasions, were supposed to have hidden on the island. Although attempts were made by many to find the treasure (searchers included the Appiani, ruling family of Piombino, Cosimo I and the Knights of Santo Stefano) the loot remained undiscovered. Only Dumas's great fictional character, the Count of Monte Cristo, ever found it,

221

Giglio Porto

and spent it in exacting a bitter revenge on his enemies. In the 19th century an incurable English romantic bought the island with hugely ambitious plans to develop and cultivate it. His plans failed dismally; in a few years he was bankrupt and he too departed. Now the island's remoteness has been put to good use and it has become a nature reserve, the home of wild goats and lonely migrating birds. Lonelier still is the reserve keeper, the island's sole inhabitant.

A much more sociable place is the holiday island of **Giglio**, an hour's boat ride from Porto Santo Stefano on Monte Argentario. Like some of the other islands, Giglio is in fact the top of a submerged granite mountain. But, as well as the inevitable *macchia*, the island also produces crops and the inhabitants make their own wine, including the topaz-coloured Ansonaco which the Romans reputedly adored. It was the Romans who established the large granite quarries that were the island's main industry until quite recently. After the Roman era Giglio's history followed the pattern of the other islands, dominated by recluses and pirates. Throughout the late Middle Ages Giglio frequently changed hands, passing between Perugia, Pisa and Siena. In 1446 it passed to Spain, which held it for 13 years before selling it to the Sienese pope, Pius II. One hundred years later it was finally bought by Eleanor of Toledo, Cosimo I's wife, and henceforth it was part of Tuscany.

Recently Giglio has become a popular resort. In summer the boats from the mainland are crowded with holiday-makers clutching their towels, suntan oil and snorkels. It is best to arrive as early as possible in the morning when there are fishermen waiting to take tourists to the less accessible and better beaches where the coarse sand has the consistency of Demerara sugar. It is unnecessary to take a car over unless you are staying for more than a few days. The small towns are linked by buses that judder and swing hair-raisingly round the narrow mountain roads.

Giglio Porto is a jolly little place, not much more than a semi-circle of painted houses, some shops and bars and a small marina. A few miles up the hill is the island's other main village, Giglio Castello, surrounded by defensive walls with cylindrical turrets. In the restored 14th-century church is a 16th-century crucifix attributed to Gianbologna. In easy walking distance is a small fortress with a rather interesting 14th-century door. An extremely twisty road leads down to the island's busiest beach resort, Campese, situated near a pyrites mine. At various points around the coast there is good deep-sea fishing and scuba diving. You can find out about the best areas locally by asking at the information office in Giglio Porto.

If you enjoy island-hopping, try to get to the tiny island of **Giannutri**, roughly 9km south of Porto Èrcole. Giannutri, only about 3 sq km in size, is made up of a series of small hills. The largest is Capel' Rosso which is about 90m in height. The Romans named the island Dianum because its sickle shape reminded them of the moon Goddess Diana. On Giannutri there are some remains of a 1st-century villa belonging to the powerful Enobarbus family with the remains of murals and mosaics. The well-preserved granite columns with ornate capitals would have been quarried in Giglio. Recently a tourist complex has been built on the island for those who enjoy scuba diving and other marine activities, so refreshments are now available.

In my view, the islands of the Tuscan Archipelago taken as a group, are a better bet than the mainland for those who simply want a seaside holiday. Their landscapes and coastlines are generally rugged and on the whole they have remained quite picturesque. The walking is often good, if hot, but it is worth picking up a really good map that shows paths and tracks. The small ports and villages are also still charming with abundant seafood and good local wines. While it would be untrue to say that the beaches have remained unspoilt, many of smaller, less accessible ones have, for the moment anyway, avoided the desperate overcrowding and dismal architecture of parts of the mainland. Most people do not think of Tuscany, with its profusion of wonderful art and architecture, in terms of solely a seaside holiday but the islands, particularly Elba, are perfect for a few days' seaside relaxation before or after the strenuous business of 'culture'.

Practical Information

Hotels and Restaurants

PORTOFERRAIO   For those who are not after the beach life there are two simple hotels with a certain run-down charm in the attractive old town: the extremely cheap *Ape d'Elbana* (tel. 92245) Via C. de Medici 2, which overlooks the charming main square; and the rather smarter *Touring* in the narrow Via Roma (13) (tel. 915851). Outside the town is the luxurious *Hermitage* hotel in a fine position overlooking the sea at La Biodola, 57037 Portoferraio (tel. (0565) 500219/211116). Portoferraio has many fish restaurants along the harbour and in the main square but a good choice is the little *La Barca*, a few minutes' walk up towards the *rocca*.

There are various beach hotels and holiday villages dotted around the island. Among the most popular is the comfortable *Lo Scirocco* Fetovaia Casa 19, 57034 Campo nell' Elba (tel. (0565) 987060) with a good beach.

Museums

PORTOFERRAIO
Palazzina Napoleonica dei Mulini Open summer 09.00–17.00; winter 09.00–13.30; closed Mon.
Villa Napoleonica di San Martino Open as dei Mulini (the same ticket is valid for both sites).

RIO MARINA
Museo Minerale Open (summer only) weekdays 09.00–12.00 and 15.00–18.00; Sun 09.00–12.00.

BIBLIOGRAPHY

Austin, R. S. and Harrison, Ada, *Some Tuscan Cities* (A. and C. Black, London, 1924).

Avery, Charles, *Florentine Renaissance Sculpture* (John Murray, London, 1970).

Bartlett, Vernon, *A Book About Elba* (Jonathan Cape, London, 1964).

Bentley, James, *A Guide to Tuscany* (Penguin Books, London, 1988).

Berenson, Bernard, *Rumour and Reflection* (Constable and Co., Simon and Schuster, out of print).

Berenson, Bernard, *Sunset and Twilight* (Erich Linder, out of print).

Borsook, Eve, *The Companion Guide to Florence* (Collins, London, 1973).

Christophe, Robert, *Napoleon on Elba* (Macdonald, London, 1964).

Clark, Kenneth, *Civilisation* (John Murray, London, 1969).

Clarke, Oz, *Sainsbury's Book of Wine* (published for Sainsbury's, London, 1987).

Colt-Hoare, Sir Richard, *A Classical Tour through Italy and Sicily* (J. Mawman, London, 1819).

Cooper, James Fenimore, *Excursions in Italy* (Paris, 1838).

Dante Alighieri (trans. C. H. Sissons), *The Divine Comedy* (Carcanet Press, 1980).

Del Fiorentino, Dante, *Immortal Bohemian* (Prentice Hall).

Dickens, Charles, *Pictures from Italy* (Andre Deutsch, London, 1973).

Douglas, Norman, *Alone* (Chapman and Hall, 1921).

Du Colombier, Pierre, *Sienna and Siennese Art* (Nicholas Kaye, London, 1957).

Forster, E. M., *A Room with a View* (Penguin, London).

Hale, R. (ed), *The Literary Works of Macchiavelli* (Oxford University Press, 1961).

Hamilton, Olive, *Paradise of Exiles* (Andre Deutsch, London, 1974).

Hamilton, Olive, *The Divine Country* (Andre Deutsch, London, 1982).

Hare, A. J. C., *Cities of Northern Italy* (George Allen, London, 1896).

Hewlett, Maurice, *On the Road in Tuscany* (Macmillan and Co., London, 1904).

Hibbert, Christopher, *The Rise and fall of the House of Medici* (Penguin, London, 1979).

Holme, Timothy, *Vile Florentines* (Cassell Ltd, London, 1980).

Hutton, Edward, *Siena and Southern Tuscany* (Methuen and Co. Ltd, London, 1910).

Hutton, Edward, *Florence and Northern Tuscany* (Methuen and Co., London, 1914).

Jennings, Elizabeth (trans.), *The Sonnets of Michelangelo* (Carcanet Press, 1988).

Lawrence, D. H., *Etruscan Places* (Olive Press, 1986).

Lyall, Archibald, *The Companion Guide to Tuscany* (Collins, London, 1973).

Mackenzie-Grieve, Avril, *Aspects of Elba* (Jonathan Cape, London, 1964).

Maurel, André, *Little Cities of Italy* (G. P. Puttnam's Sons, London and New York, 1911).

Mayne, E. C. (trans.), *Selected Letters of Dostoevsky* (Peter Owen (London) Ltd).

Meek, Christine, *Lucca 1369–1400* (Oxford University Press, 1978).

Molajoli, Bruno, *Florence* (Thames and Hudson, London, 1972).

Murray, Peter and Linda, *The Art of the Renaissance* (Thames and Hudson, London, 1963).

Murray, Peter and Linda, *The Architecture of the Italian Renaissance* (Thames and Hudson, London, 1963).

Origo, Iris, *The Merchant of Prato* (Penguin, London, 1957).

Piozzi, Mrs, *Glimpses of Italian Society* (London, 1892).

Raison, Laura, *Tuscany, an Anthology* (Cadogan Books, London, 1983).

Ross, Janet, *Florentine Palaces and their stories* (J. M. Dent & Son, London, 1905).

Ross, Janet and Waterfield, Michael, *Leaves from our Tuscan Kitchen* (John Murray, London, 1899).

Rubinstein, H., *The Good Hotel Guide* (Which Books, 1988).

Serpell, Jean and Christopher, *The Traveller's Guide to Elba and the Tuscan Archipelago* (Jonathan Cape, London, 1977).

Spadolini, Giovanni, *Florence: A thousand Years* (Le Monnier, Firenze, 1984).

Thomas, Dylan, *Selected Letters* (J. M. Dent and Son, London, 1965).

Twain, Mark, *The Innocents Abroad* (Chatto and Windus, London, 1897).

Vasari, Giorgio (trans. G. Bull), *Lives of the Artists* (Penguin Classics, London, 1975).

Vettori, Giuseppe, *Toscana – I Canti, Le Fiabe, Le Feste nella Tradizione nella Tradizione Populare* (Lato Side Editore, Roma, 1981).

Whelpton, Eric, *Florence and Tuscany* (Robert Hale Ltd, London, 1965).

Woolf, Virginia, *A Writer's Diary* (Hogarth Press, London, c.1940).

Florence and Tuscany (American Express, Mitchell Beazley).

INDEX